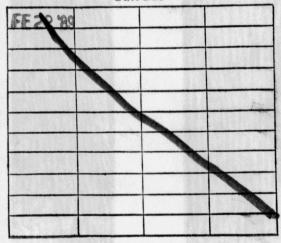

Twayne's United States Authors Series

Sylvia E. Bowman, *Editor*

INDIANA UNIVERSITY

Max Eastman

MAX EASTMAN

By MILTON CANTOR

University of Massachusetts

Twayne Publishers, Inc.   ::   New York

To My Parents

Preface

MAX EASTMAN'S LIFE spans two very different periods in the social and intellectual history of the United States—the vibrantly radical days of pre-World War I; the war itself; and the troubled, virulently anti-Communist years after World War II. Eastman's place in this history, especially in the events of the second and third decades of this century, is assured, owing to the work of his contemporaries and of more recent chroniclers. His reputation rests principally upon his contribution to the *Masses*, his observations of the Russian Revolution, and his associations with its leading firebrands, especially Leon Trotsky. Much of his writing suggests a tendency to glibness, most of it is syncretic rather than original, and a few works are foci of achievement. But nearly all tell us something about the tumultuous days through which their author lived, and are thick with *apercus* on life and thought at home and abroad.

There are some writers, Jean Giraudoux once wrote, whose lives and works run together; Eastman is one of these. Rarely an innovator, the contours of his thought were at most points consonant with the perplexities and epiphanies of his existence. Quite logically, therefore, this existence cannot be ignored. Hence, this study is organized along chronological lines. It relates Eastman's thought to his environment—and traces the development and interrelationships of his ideas about politics, philosophy, literature, and regnant social issues. These ideas hopefully suggest something of the richness and diversity of Eastman's range of interests; hopefully, too, they tell us about the general intellectual background of his times.

Eastman is not a great literary figure, nor one of the giants of American radicalism. His true significance lies in his contributions to social history in the first half of our century and in his typicality. If his age was one of paradoxes, inconsistencies, divergen-

MAX EASTMAN

cies, so is the man; if it is difficult to subsume these years under a single appropriate rubric, so is Eastman a person of parts. He merits our consideration because he was a representative of the discrete radicals of two decades, because he gave encouragement to those serving their literary novitiates and to those who were professional revolutionaries, because he listened to a distant drummer when it came to revolution in our times and to the hard realities that others refused to hear, and because his voice has in it the assonance of radical America.

MILTON CANTOR

University of Massachusetts
Amherst

Contents

Contents

Chronology

1883 Max Eastman born on January 4th; the son of Bertha and Samuel Eastman.

1891– Family moved from a farm on the outskirts of Canan-
1892 daigua, New York, into the town itself, where the father, who was also a minister, turned from farming to a grocery business. Bertha Eastman, being ordained, obtained a parish in West Bloomfield; the family moved to this town.

1894 Family moved to Elmira, New York, where Bertha Eastman became a preacher in the Park Church.

1900– Entered Williams College, traveled about the country, and
1906 entered a Kingston, New York, sanitarium due to psycho-somatic ills.

1907 Moved to New York City where he enrolled in courses leading toward the doctorate. Became John Dewey's assistant, and taught logic and philosophy for four years at Columbia.

1911 Married Ida Rauh.

1912 Elected editor of the *Masses;* guided it until the government closed it down in 1917.

1913 *Enjoyment of Poetry* published.

1918 *Liberator* begins to be published, and Eastman is its editor for three years. Indicted under the Espionage Act; case closed after two trials and two hung juries.

1921– Ends association with *Liberator;* travels to Europe. An
1922 observer at the Genoa conference; then settles in Russia.

1924 He departs from Russia and, after journeying to Paris, publishes *Since Lenin Died,* which created an international furor. He traveled through Europe, but mostly in France and Italy.

1927 Returned to the United States and to New York City.

1932 Went abroad again, to the Near East; visited Trotsky on Prinkipo.

1933   Victor F. Calverton provided another forum, the *Modern Monthly*. Eastman began his association with the journal with his criticism of Sidney Hook, which was enlarged into *The Last Stand of Dialectical Materialism* in 1934.

1934   Publication of the controversial *Artists in Uniform*.

1936   Publication of the highly successful *Enjoyment of Laughter*.

1940   *Stalin's Russia* and *Marxism is it Science*.

1941   Contributor to *Reader's Digest*.

1948   *Enjoyment of Living*, the first volume of his autobiography.

1964   *Love and Revolution*, the second volume of his autobiography.

Max Eastman

CHAPTER *1*

The Shaping Years

FOR two hundred and fifty years before Max Eastman was born, the fortunes of his ancestors were interwoven with New England history. The Eastmans were churchmen, Congregationalists mostly, some being stained by revivalism or by rebelliousness too insolent for orthodoxy. Max Eastman's mother and father were both ministers; indeed, she was "one of the first women ordained in the Congregational church." They both entered divinity school at Oberlin College at a time when the influence of Charles Finney, its former president, still cast a shadow; and both were touched by its residual evangelism.

Born on January 4, 1883, in Canandaigua, New York, Max Eastman was, therefore, the product of twin streams of ministerial piety. His father was pastor of the town's First Congregational Church, and the family lived in the parsonage of this sleepy, upstate town for nearly four years. Then, following an earlier family tradition, Samuel Eastman purchased a nearby farm where, except for occasional ministerial summons, he cultivated his own garden. A frail and sickly man, he played only a shadowy role in Eastman's early years. These years, as they rolled by, were filled with the joy and routine of farm life for the country boy. He developed an appreciation of nature which never deserted him: nature, was always a lodestar, to be returned to in difficult and burdensome times and to be worshiped with pantheistic devotion.

After four years on the Old Farm, his father, unable to endure the physical strains of rural life, turned to the grocery business; and the family moved back to Canandaigua. In the same year, 1891, his mother Bertha Ford was ordained, and took her family to West Bloomfield, New York, a little town near Rochester. Here the family dwelt in the large and comfortable parsonage, lived mainly on Mrs. Eastman's earnings—though her husband con-

tinued to work the Canandaigua grocery, daily commuting there
—and was shaped by her presence.

Bertha Eastman's aspirations suggest those of most American
feminists. She wanted "to be something," a feeling which "never
died in her heart." [1] She had studied Greek and Latin with her
husband; become vice-president of the Woman's Home Mission-
ary Union of New York; taught history and English in a local
ladies' finishing school; and then, in the course of helping her husband write his sermons, discovered that she could do at least as
well. " 'I must be content with the crown of motherhood,' " she
unhappily declared; but she was not. She eschewed the drudgery
of housework and "never sold herself completely into motherhood." But she was as unprepared to assert her sexual freedom as
she was to proclaim publicly her doubts about religion. Inevitably, it seems in retrospect, she turned to a creed of service, one
within the bosom of the church, and became possibly the fore-
most woman minister of that period.

Max Eastman lived in a time when the close-knit community of
an earlier age suffered from fragmentation and decay. The story is
well-known—how urbanization, industrialization, immigration,
and status-resentment groups overpowered those who held local
eminence and contributed to the erosion of the formerly cohesive
local community structure. This community had been inseparably
wedded to the family, which was a miniature society itself. Dissolution of the one, therefore, brought dissolution of the other—at a
time when the question of women's rights assumed a national importance. The male breadwinner, traditionally head of the
household and master—socially and legally—of all he surveyed,
was still enthroned; but his was an increasingly meaningless over-
lordship.

The growing recognition of women and their rights was accompanied, therefore, by a collapse of the old system of paternalism,
catalyzed as it was by collapse of the community and its values.
Walter Lippmann's observations, written to describe a later generation, are appropriate: "we inherit freedom, and have to use it.
The sanctity of property, the patriarchal family, hereditary caste,
the dogma of sin, obedience to authority—the rock of ages in
brief, has been blasted for us." Responding to the chaos in family
life and in society itself, some women cut completely loose from
the family structure and took up the banners of feminism; some

entered into vocational competition with their male counterparts; still others filled the vacuum abdicated by paternal authority. These last, *mutatis mutandis,* more than ever preserved the middle-class cult of the home; they represented cohesion and the unity of private life; they became the moral custodians of family and of society.

Bertha Eastman was archetypal. Her rebellion had manifold aspects. Though buried and inarticulate, a sexual contest was partly involved: if domination were masculine and submission feminine, then she would reject the latter; and she was in "unregenerate revolt . . . against the embraces" of her gentle husband.[2] Her insurgence also took another form: if externally imposed societal codes prevented the full development of a woman's personality and defined her place in customary terms, then she would, like those of her sex who desired self-realization, reject this orthodox definition; and, in her desire "to be something," she was forced paradoxically to lead a man's life. She inadvertently thwarted Samuel Eastman and, in the course of it, stifled those emotions of which women traditionally are surrogates. She filled the role which he vacated, but she did so with guilt and a sense of unworthiness.

Nonetheless, Bertha Eastman thrived in inverse ratio to her husband's neurasthenia and fading vigor. Challenged by the "disaster of his collapse," she recovered her own strength. She assumed breadwinner duties as Samuel Eastman, a failure by ordinary standards, resignedly pursued his vocation as grocery-store accountant. She was both family and community center, with men coming from nearby Rochester and elsewhere " 'to hear good talk,' " as Carl Carmer reminisced; and West Bloomfield knew it was "getting [in her] more brains and eloquence . . . than they could have in a man." [3]

Thus Max Eastman, from the age of six to nine, was the child of a woman who disappeared every weekend to preach and returned to the family on Monday to resume her household command. Her forceful intellect and personality clearly dominated his early years. Her impulse to govern had full play in the parsonage, and her son was clearly and happily "mamma's boy." To some degree, this confession was viable: the son never rejected his mother, deeply loving and admiring her until she died.[4] He inherited her "rapid way of sensing the implications of an idea" as well as her critical posture. Bertha Eastman, it must be recalled, was never loyal to the entire creed of Christianity. She even persuaded her congregation to abandon the doctrines of Trinity and the Virgin Mary—in effect, transforming Congregationalists into Unitarians —and to rest their faith in God and in the example of Jesus; and her doubts increased as she grew older. Her son also inherited her interest in psychology which, as a succeeding chapter shows, caused Bertha Eastman to consult A. A. Brill, then the pioneer analyst in the United States, an experience which helped shape her decision to leave the church. Her son also acquired her taste for activism and her desire to live the full and spontaneous life; and she even served him as an exemplar of the new woman, in whose cause he rendered an important contribution.

But his mother may also have served him unfavorably. Eastman's early years were riddled by a sense of inadequacy. We may conjecture that he early sensed, as he later admitted, that his mother "did not want" him and that his coming was a "momentous catastrophe . . . ," marking "the end of my parents' physical relations." The fact of a woman minister who partly foreswore the domestic ideals and who was somewhat equivocal about motherhood itself, may have had a deleterious effect. Certainly, as he later confessed, his childhood was marked by a growing sense of inferiority. "It was helped along farther," he recalled, by "being clad in a 'cutaway' coat and vest with short pants." [5]

I   *The Influence of Mark Twain*

The Eastmans, in July, 1894, moved to Elmira, a city which left its mark upon young Eastman in two ways. First of all, it offered the company—and the competition—of other children, and thus deepened his sense of insecurity. Feeling not "good enough" to participate in baseball or other sports with his peers, young Eastman turned to his studies—the one competitive area in which he felt able to achieve distinction.[6] He was enrolled in Mercersburg, a private academy, in the fall of 1898; and, studying with relentless perseverance, he compiled a brilliant scholastic record. Reward came with commencement. Upon receiving a full board and tuition scholarship to Williams College, he joined the freshmen class of 1900 in the Berkshires.

Secondly, Elmira was the home of Samuel Clemens. Indeed, his in-laws—the Langdons—lived directly across from the Eastman parsonage; and they were the church's central social and financial pillars. The city's nobility, they were not stuffy and a source of social and ideological constraint upon Sam Clemens, as some Twain scholars have argued; rather, Eastman asserts, they were socially more radical than he was. Indeed, Eastman claims that the new environment was for himself a liberating one. He never forgot Mark Twain, whom he met in his mother's Park Church and who was a "shining figure" in the life of Jo Hancock, Eastman's fictional alter ego. Eastman recalled Twain's "princely grace," the "lion-like head with the grey mane and the terrible sharp-lighted eyes like a hawk." [7] With his "genial audacity and his universal sympathy," Mark Twain left an unforgettable impression on his Elmira neighbor; and his vast reputation, his legendary self-reliant climb from an unschooled printer's apprenticeship to national prominence as a humorist was a lesson to be heeded. [8] Of all writers (Whitman excepted) Twain, to Eastman, symbolized America's "characteristic best trait"; and possibly his gift for humor provided Eastman with his initial impulse toward exploring its sources and expression. [9]

Mark Twain was part of the seamless web of Eastman's past, one forever mingled with the history of his adolescence. If there were no "more glorious destiny" for a boy "than to be somewhere in the vicinity of Mark Twain," it was in the context of life in Elmira, a city that had a special place for Eastman. His defense of the Langdons, specifically of Olivia Langdon—against A. B. Paine's claim that Twain was for her a heretic toward societal conventions and, she suspected, "might even have unorthodox views about religion"—was also a defense of Elmira. Eastman insisted that the Langdons were not closed off from liberality and culture. Unlike the city's *nouveau riche*, they were aristocrats in a traditional sense whose sense of superiority rested upon "intellectual culture and moral elevation." This intellectual élite "cherished great literature; it valued bold and iconoclastic thinking." Upstate New York towns like Elmira, "had much of New England's spirituality, little of its tightmindedness."

II *Williams College and Revolt*

Writing these observations retrospectively, Eastman was perhaps thinking of his four years at that tight little island of learning, Williams College. These years were not notable for scholarly distinction, since he was determined "not to lead" his class, having done so at Mercersburg. He showed, to the contrary, negligence and some scorn for college studies and flirted with athletics. Jo Hancock, his ideal ego figure was "the strongest man in his class," and "would have been a varsity football player, if his eyesight had been as good as his build"; but Eastman could not match the hero of his imagination or his classmates on any athletic field. Jo Hancock, however, also "had poetry in him"; and, Eastman continued: "It is really a gift for feeling the qualities of experience. If you can feel them well, and have a good brain, then you can convey them to other people by means of words. That is poetic imagination. Jo was a poet, but he did not know that. He only knew that he could feel things better and more accurately than his brother. He was more vividly alive than his brother. He wanted everybody to know this—especially his mother." [10]

Once again, in this reference to a woman in Bertha Eastman's mold, Eastman does homage to his mother and obeisance at the shrine of experience. Her insistence upon activism, which thrust her out of the home, and her refusal to live at second hand, was transmitted to her son. Max Eastman always believed that excessive cultivation of the mind at the expense of feeling was a mistake. He always associated overcivilization with a betrayal of man's essential nature.

Eastman's rebellion against middle-class America may be dated from these college years. Partly a revolt against the dominant cultural values, his was in some measure a revolt of youth against those seeking to transmit these older values. But the generational conflict of these years is less important than its resolution. Unlike many radicals at the turn of the century, for example, Eastman displayed no interest in politics. He did, to be sure, speak at a mass meeting in East Greenbush, a town near Albany, where he exhorted voters to reject William Jennings Bryan and support the McKinley ticket; but it was done in the spirit of a freshman prank.

Indeed, Eastman lacked the "ancestral interest in the affairs of peace," defining such affairs in political and economic terms.

Even at the age of twenty-five, living at the peak of the Muck-rake era, he had not read its major tracts. The articles and books of Lincoln Steffens, Charles E. Russell, David Graham Phillips, George Kibbe Turner, Ida Tarbell were unknown to him. "I was not interested in journalism," he confessed. "I was not interested in politics; I was not adequately interested in the moment." Affirming as much a few years later, upon learning of Mark Twain's death, he wrote: "I'm glad Mark Twain belonged to the 'old regime.' I'd stay there gladly if I could be with him. And I hope to God some day this world will get sick of 'society' again, or get the thing settled, so we can go back to the old days of heroes and friends and strength, liberty and hospitality." [11]

"Innocent of political thinking," he was therefore insouciant about it as well. He could assert, with Jo Hancock, that "he grew up a pagan as well as a poet." [12] He, too, was "cut off from the beauty and the significance of the best parts of the Hebrew Bible by being compelled to learn them by heart." The nearest approach he made to religion in these years was a worshipful attitude toward nature. He "grew up in a lake country amid hills and waterfalls no less lovely than those which were the prime movers of Wordsworth's song," but he rejected any comparison. "If I loved a tree, I loved it as a tree," he stated, ". . . I have no wish to imagine a dryad, much less the Hebrew God Jehovah, sitting in some position within or around behind me." [13]

Eastman's viewpoint is not really *that* clearcut, however. His words and protestations notwithstanding, he was closer to a pantheistic appreciation of nature than he cared to admit. The poem most admired in his freshman year was Shelley's "Ode to the West Wind," which left an unforgettable impression and which accompanied him on walks in the Berkshire hills. The first sonnet he memorized was Richard Realf's, which included the following lines:

> . . . every humble hedgerow flower that grows;
> And every little brown bird that doth sing;
> Hath something greater than itself, and bears
> A living Word to every living thing.
> Albeit it holds the Message unawares.

> All shapes and sounds have something which is not
> Of them: A Spirit broods amid the grass;
> Vague outlines of the Everlasting Thought
> Lie in the melting shadows as they pass;
> The touch of an Eternal Presence thrills
> The fringes of the sunset and the hills.[14]

The student friend closest to him was a lover of Realf; of nature; and of those who, like the Berkshire County yeoman, lived close to the soil. The American poet who was possibly closest to him was Sidney Lanier; and Eastman's earliest verse effort—"An awful poem" chanting Mount Greylock's "grandeur" and modelled on "The Song of the Chattahoochee"—was a pagan poem if ever an American wrote one.

Eastman's love of nature did not derive from religion or from a religious experience; indeed, religion was not an "experience," which made it easy for Eastman to get out of it. "I was not genuinely worshipful," he recalled; "prayer played no part in my moral struggle; God was not a fact in my experience but a conclusion in my mind." [15] Eastman's attitude toward religion was fashioned by his times and by his personality. In part, it was shaped by generational conflict; and, in part, it evolved out of the crisis that overtook Protestantism in his day.[16] Their twin impact made institutional religion less than useless for him. But his rejection of it was not traumatic: absent was the "break" accompanying most youthful revolts, the kind of polarized transference that made freethinkers of Robert Ingersoll, Clarence Darrow, and James Harvey Robinson. Eastman's belief in immortality, for example, faded so early that no conflict was ever attached to its rejection. Given this smooth transformation, Eastman was left unbruised, quite capable of contemplative and reasonable judgments. Thus he was able to admire Reverend Thomas Beecher of Elmira's Park Church for his magnanimity, his rejection of sectarianism, and his all-embracing ecumenicalism. But Eastman also admired Mark Hopkins of Williams for the same qualities; and he honored both men for their devotion to science.[17]

Still wavering about deity and church while at Williams, Eastman read Herbert Spencer "and became an agnostic." He even projected a book, "The Agnostic's God," which would dispense with Christian doctrine as the substance of religion. Such thinking was typical of the author of a "Pagan Prayer," a service which he conducted—and in which God was conspicuous by His absence. Emerson's essays "became a kind of scripture," and Eastman's "religion" was little more than an apprehension of divinity in nature.[18]

Mysticism, therefore, was a principle resource of Eastman's early life, and it prepared the way for his later *ad hominen* attacks upon the clergy and the church. But these attacks were, in all probability, rooted in the general Bohemianism of the day, with its broadsides against all middle-class manners and institutions. Perhaps, too, they were more firmly based upon his increasing devotion to science which, he realized, was an ancient enemy of religion. Paradoxical though it was, and Eastman never seemed conscious of the inconsistency, the mystically inclined child of nature supported science in its conflict with religion.[19] He failed to apprehend this contradiction because of his ability to keep applied science and a religion of nature in separate mental niches. Inadvertently publicizing this practice many years later, he stated: "It is a clash [between science and religion] of two contradictory attitudes toward the world. For this very reason it is easy to acquire the trick of keeping both science and religion alive in separate chambers of the same brain; they do not conflict because of the completeness of the separation."

Nature, while not religion, provided certain religious satisfactions for Eastman. For one thing, it was therapy; it was surcease from pain; it was relief from the insupportable burdens and tensions of daily life; and it was a restorative at the vital center of his freshman resolution to "live life." [20] By this pledge, Eastman meant to live fully, directly, spontaneously; to live to the outer limits of his potentialities; to immerse himself in the steam of experience. Nothing less would suffice. Such an aspiration was archetypal, the characteristic gambit of the American intellectual in these years, valuing as he did the richer life of the doer— whether the yeoman farmer or the urban worker.

It was this sense of the sanctity of experience that prompted Eastman to walk and run, ski and write verse in the Berkshire hills, to reach out beyond his books to the world of nature; to seek companionship in Lanier, Wordsworth, Shelley, and Goethe; and to insist upon the primacy of feeling, particularly the one associated with sexual excitement. "Goethe was my hero during that autumn of 1902," Eastman confessed; and the story of his love affair with Frederica Brion in *Dichtung und Wahrheit* specifically interested Eastman. Identifying with Goethe, he also sought romance, and was moved by those sentiments appropriate to college students enamoured of poetry, unconventional behavior, and "a love of nature" that was "so strong and large a part" of him. He found a "slim, swift-moving, dancing, laughing girl." [21]

> Upon that ground [he recalls], given so unequivocally by the chemism of our bodies, we reared a romance for our minds out of our twin worship of the Berkshire Hills, their woods and ferny glens and sweetbriar-rose-infested meadows. Ours was a landscape love, a pastoral, an idyl. Her hazel eyes and color like dark leaves in autumn were harmonious with the mood of my unmystic love of nature. She seemed born to be the mountain nymph or dryad of a poet who could never find these beings in their spirit form.[22]

Eastman never resisted these attempts to plunge into the stream of experience. His mood was not transitory, not merely adolescent posturing; it became an acquired part of his personality, essential to the life and thought of the man.

CHAPTER 2

Pre-War Years, 1904–1912

EASTMAN ARRIVED in New York on January 1, 1907. He had spent part of the post-graduate period trying to cure a mysterious backache, and in the attempt he began to consider the importance of the unconscious as a causative agent in pain. Moving toward Freud's propositions in a pre-Freudian age, he seized upon mental healing and then upon health foods. Meanwhile, he was reading incessantly, having resumed serious studies in his senior year at college. He had, at that time, wrestled with Herbert Spencer, discovered Emerson's "Self-Reliance," refuted St. Anselm's argument proving God's existence, gravitated toward empiricism as the basis for epistemology, and in the "oratorical contest" at graduation eulogized "that stormy and uncertain-hearted martyr," Giordano Bruno—"the prophet of an unfulfilled hope," the "evangelist whose error, boldly spoken, worked in the service of truth."

Eastman had been on probation at Williams, owing to his continuous pranks. He had railed against the fraternity system and attacked college customs, abjuring starched cuffs and collars. He had begun to arraign most social institutions and values, an arraignment that would broaden in scope, take on philosophical depth, and eventually strike against everything associated with the cultural ascendency of the middle class. His attraction to Bruno, therefore, and to Bruno's heresies, his insistence upon "some heresies of my own," were more than an instance of the afflatus of youth; they prefigured an unchanging attitude of mind.[1]

These were years of growth, moral and intellectual. Life was pleasant at Dr. Sahler's New Thought sanitarium in Kingston where, for his back pains, he tried a form of Christian Science which was "a mixture of suggestive therapeutics, psychic phenomena, non-church religion, and . . . sentiments of optimism." [2]

[25]

His room at Sahler's was clean and comfortable, and he inevitably found two attractive employees who helped wile away the leisure hours. Women always attracted him—first his mother, and then a long line of slender, lovely girls. He was, in the end as in the beginning, sensitively alive to feminine beauty and ceaselessly seeking it. Dr. Sahler's held other charms as well: a library in abnormal psychology that he devoured.

I   New York City and John Dewey

Then, in 1907, Eastman went to New York, a young man of twenty-four who had only a vague knowledge of the direction in which he was headed. Sentiment had not hardened into conviction, and he had no clearly formed ideas; he was just a learned young man who had begun to think about things, to ask questions, to feel his way toward some positive positions. His initial reaction to the city reflected all his rural prejudices. He hated cities, dreading their noise, tensity, and cold commotion; and New York, which "was the stiffest purgatory I could put myself through," could not compensate for nature, where he could "'meet the universe.'" [3] Understandably, he escaped to Glenora at every opportunity—to renew his "poetic life-zeal" at the "lakeside utopia."

Without any definite ambition or goal, with only a vague desire to be a writer, Eastman settled near his older, much-admired sister, Crystal, in Greenwich Village. His education now began in earnest. For, after a brief residence there, he moved to Morningside Heights when John Dewey appointed him an instructor in philosophy at Columbia University. This appointment was caused by the timely death of another philosophy teacher and by the skillful advocacy of Eastman's candidacy by Vladimir Simkovitch, a good friend of his sister's. Eastman justified Dewey's faith with his intensive study of logic and the scientific method and with his appreciation of the pleasures of teaching. His mentor was like a father to him—doubtless the sort of father Eastman would have selected had the choice been his. Dewey was always there—to discuss Eastman's work or ideas, to ask his advice about a manuscript, or to ask him to dinner. Indeed, dinner with the Dewey's became a weekly practice. "I would just move in," Eastman recalled, "and become a member of the family. . . . After the dishes were cleared away, Dewey and I would sit and talk together, or, when talk ran out, just sit and think—sometimes for a whole afternoon or evening." [4] Dewey counselled deftly, persuasively, and without a suspicion of egotism. The trust that Eastman placed in his judgment and sure intelligence was natural, considering the close parallelism between their values and formulations. Both men regarded learning as a philosophic adventure; both showed antipathy to metaphysical speculations; both emphasized the athletic, not the spiritual, side of man's nature; both worshiped at a shrine of experience, insisting on the direct perception of life, the spontaneous self.

Understandably, therefore, Eastman wrote of "a native likemindedness," suspecting that "rays of his influence may have helped to mould me long before I heard of him." He fully appreciated his "golden opportunity" as friend and assistant, and responded by swallowing "down Dewey's total mind and attitude." Eastman had been unknowingly seeking a system that combined scientific loyalty to facts and confidence in human values. Dewey's philosophy did just that: it wedded empiricism to humanity. It "gave a biological foundation to my instinctive scepticism," Eastman reported. "If the brain and the mind with it, is primarily an instrument of survival in the life struggle, then no absolute or universal truth is attainable, but this need not stop us from using specific and relative truths in improving life." Almost from his first reflective moments, Eastman had turned away from all absolutes and finalities. Like Dewey, he saw philosophy as an instrument "in improving life," not as an end. Like him, he stood upon the rock of experience—not upon logic or metaphysics or any speculative foray unrelated to man's life. Like him, he endowed man with a role in his future; he took a chance on the heart, on instincts, on feeling; he wished to try new methods. Dewey, to be sure, gave moral judgments the same kind of validity possessed by judgments of facts, to which Eastman objected; but the body of instrumentalism was eagerly grasped. It rested upon individualism, practicality, spontaneity, and hopefulness; it was intuitive and sensationalist-based; it cleared away the fog of theology: Eastman could hardly expect more. [5]

II *Woman's Rights*

Like her mother, Crystal Eastman was a fierce hunter for self-fulfillment. She, too, insisted upon a role outside the home—for herself and for women generally. She and her brother were very close. They "had been baby friends together," and she was his "dearest friend" during his tour of duty in the Berkshires. She shared his zest for "'great experiences'" and "poured magnetic streams of generous love around her all the time, and she loved me with especial warmth. I loved her too," he recalled, "and deeply admired her character." At a later date, he wrote to her: "'You give me a new eagerness . . . to be perfectly honest and open and upright with people'"; and he placed a very high value on her dynamic and absolute sincerity. When he first visited New York, Crystal Eastman was studying law at New York University and, for a living, running a recreation center on weekday evenings. In the autumn of 1908, upon returning from some restorative months of summer at Glenora, the Eastmans decided to room together in the Village. He registered for a doctorate at Columbia, and struggled with philosophy and language requirements; she was writing a book, *Work Accidents and the Law,* and becoming increasingly well-known as an authority on workmen's compensation. Zeal for feminism swept her into the mainstream of social action; and it eventually carried her brother along.[6]

Inspired by his sister, by the Village atmosphere, as well as by the national mood, Eastman organized the Men's League for Woman Suffrage in the spring of 1909. Both Dewey, who was never exclusively an academician, and Bertha Eastman encouraged him, the latter writing: "'I wish you had a life of doing things.'"[7] Thus goaded, Eastman called on Oswald Garrison Villard, who helped him make connections with twelve men of "'civic importance.'" Their number swelled to a hundred after eighteen months of effort. But the League was never more than a newspaper advertisement and Eastman himself, who served as director, treasurer, organizer. In the third capacity, as a suffrage orator, he received his first real taste of political activity.

Eastman, in this manner, began to contribute to the liveliest social movement of his day. As he understood it, the fight for woman suffrage demanded vigor and militancy. He was attracted

to the militant idealist rather than to the "patient persuader" who
sought to further her cause by a quiet educational campaign; and
he had only praise for women like Emmeline Pankhurst in England, who "will stand in history among the heroes of human liberty," and for Mary Wollstonecraft, Susan B. Anthony, Elizabeth
Cady Stanton, and Anna Howard Shaw—who, in their day, would
have used party politics as the means of forcing a constitutional
amendment—had they had enough votes to do it.[8] That is precisely what Alice Paul did in 1918—force an amendment through
the House—and Eastman praised her "and her young army of
militants as one of the three leading radical forces [along with the
Non-Partisan League and the Socialist Party] in American politics
in the near future."[9]

Eastman's attitude toward the suffrage movement is suggested
by this forecast. Such an attitude was formed, not only by the
reform ethos of the age but by Eastman's early environment. By
drawing—often unconsciously—on personal experiences, he could
state with some conviction that "the question of sex equality, the
economic, social, political independence of woman stands by itself, parallel and equal in importance to any other question of the
day."[10] He wrote with an authority borne of personal knowledge
that "there are many women who, on account of their natural disposition, perhaps, or perhaps on account of their social or financial
situation cannot function happily in that sphere [the home]."[11]
Thus, we may conclude, his advocacy of suffrage reform reflected
both his past relations—with his mother and his sister—and his
considered judgment that "the awakening and liberation of
woman is a revolution in the very process of life. It is not an event
in any class or an issue between classes. It is an issue for all humanity."[12]

For Eastman, this issue was his first great one, the cause that
awakened him as a political and social revolutionary. He invoked
the names of Fourier, Marx, Engels, and Saint-Simon; and he attempted to convey the inseparable character of Socialism and "the
freedom of women." Certainly, the cause was pivotal to the entire
reform movement; and he wrote that "the importance of woman
suffrage lies deeper than any special program of reform, or the
platform of any political party." First of all, it had vast social and
economic significance: "I believe that when you have said that 'the
ruin of motherhood and childhood by the merciless exploitation of

the labor of women and children is a crime of capital importance,' you have already said that woman suffrage is a duty of capital importance." Second, it was a stimulus, tending to "wake women up to an active discontent with their situation and [give them] an aggressive self-respecting intention to better it." Third, it provided, by active participation, the necessary knowledge of "the game." Invoking instrumentalist thought, he asserted that it "gives them knowledge-by-experience. It teaches them how to act intelligently in their own behalf." Fourth, citizenship offered a means "of accomplishing things through legislation and government," an argument for suffrage which Eastman found the least convincing.[13]

Fifth and finally, the suffrage issue was intimately related to political democracy which, as Eastman understood it, guaranteed "to every citizen a certain elementary standing in his community." Political democracy endowed each citizen with "a little bit of the personal sacredness of a sovereign"; and, he continued, "it certifies to him that his needs and his wishes shall be of some consequence." Calling up the shades of John Locke, the compact theory of government, and the equally idolized *sui generis* democratic polity, Eastman claimed that woman suffrage appealed "upon the theoretic side, to those fundamental principles of popular government which underlie our constitution, the principles of rule by the majority—that there is *no* majority with a right to rule, until after a single vote is the property of every single citizen." [14]

Eastman thereby wavered between confirmed democracy and incipient Socialism; but, no matter how he viewed woman suffrage, it was a vital issue. He endowed it with practical as well as abstract considerations by declaring that the merit of political candidates be determined by their position on this question. Thus he was equivocal toward Theodore Roosevelt in 1912, observing that the Bull Mooser believed in woman suffrage but that, in a recent editorial, he "five times repeated that the suffrage is 'not important.' There are great and terrible evils," Eastman continued, "high problems which confront women in this country, tragic need of what he calls 'reforms' in their situation; but the suffrage is not important." Considering Roosevelt's traditionalist attitude toward male and female roles, Eastman appears to be reasoning with appropriate logic when he claimed: "Now, his worst enemy would not say that Mr. Roosevelt thinks the suffrage is not important; and so I am forced to conclude that it is women who are not important." [15]

Naturally Eastman condemned such an attitude. He had long been schooled in the viewpoint that women should not "grow up to be, outside the years of motherhood, mere drudges or parlor ornaments." He rejected the prevailing sentiment which held that women "satisfy their ambitions by seeing who can parade the most extreme buffooneries of contemporary fashion on the public highway." He had become too committed to the cause of the "new woman" to maintain such a position; he had known too many restless, striving women; he had read too many manifestoes on sexual freedom. A committed publicist in the cause—political and social —of the emancipated female, he could only deplore those who claimed that "woman's sphere is the home." He scored the antifeminism of the American labor movement and, conversely, praised IWW chieftain William Haywood who told fifteen thousand Paterson silk strikers—when someone suggested that the women in the assembly should be sent home—"send away the men and children, and let the women continue the strike. You will be more likely to win it." [16]

Women must "be as free and happy as men," Eastman insisted; they must be encouraged to be interested and aware human beings and to satisfy their ambitions "only with the highest prizes of adventure and achievement that life offers." It followed that he would celebrate those seeking such a goal, particularly "that small group of women fighting for the rights of their sex in Washington in the last four years." They were fighting for the "fullness of life," he stated; and everything in his environment—the spirit of unorthodoxy and rebellion that endowed the Village with great excitement—confirmed his conviction. [17]

CHAPTER 3

Engagement in Bohemia:
A Tale of Two Passions

"THE FIDDLERS are tuning as it were all over America," wrote old John Butler Yeats in 1912. Indeed they were, particularly in such cultural enclaves as Chicago and New York. This was the "lyric year," when Robinson Jeffers, Joyce Kilmer, Vachel Lindsay, Ezra Pound, Sara Teasdale, Amy Lowell, and a hundred lesser singers published books of verse. *Poetry* was founded by Harriet Monroe in Chicago, and Edna St. Vincent Millay's "Renascence" became emblematic of the age. The Little Theatre movement was already underway. Alfred Stieglitz urged writers and artists to boldness, and Theodore Dreiser had ambitiously plotted three big novels. "Self-fulfillment," "spontaneity," "experimentation," "rebellion," "intuition" were the words on everyone's lips. Sprinkled across the pages of the "new" magazines, the books, the plays, the manifestoes, and the political essays of these ante-bellum years, such words were most familiar to those living in the interstices of American society—Greenwich Village in particular.

The Village was many things to many people.[1] For Eastman, its lure was inseparable from his slow exfoliation; and he eventually regarded it with a fiercely proprietary spirit. He lived there in its heyday—when the Village was more than a neighborhood, when it was a way of life and a state of mind; when, he wrote, it was "a quite unconscious gathering and dwelling place for people . . . who were more interested in joy than respectability. It was the natural abode for those who were seeking in freedom the real value of life." [2]

Its residents, by their powerful example, urged him to have the courage to learn and to know. *Sapere aude!* It was an invitation to criticism, to unorthodoxy, to irreverence toward past dogma, to

scorn for the prevailing "pious moralistic sentimentally-intellectu-
ally verbiage," to embrace the Village's "free-and-easy mode of
life" which, he recalled, was "the mode of life that I hoped when
we got rid of classes and class rule, would be universal." [3] The
Village's residents knew one another, read the same books, shared
the same convictions, joined the same causes. They provided
young Eastman with a rich intellectual and emotional feast.

He was ready for it, eager for good talk and social gaiety. He
enjoyed the company of those who, like Isadora Duncan or John
Reed, were making actual or metaphorical gestures of dissent
from middle-class society. He traveled in circles which included
radicals such as Emma Goldman and Bill Haywood of the Western Federation of Miners; established liberals such as Oswald
Garrison Villard, one of his "refined friends," and George F. Pea-
body; college boys tending toward respectability like Walter
Lippmann; and legends in their lifetime like Alexander Berkman,
who represented revolt *in excelsis*. Some of them, Eastman included, would meet for a drink at the Brevoort Hotel on lower
Fifth Avenue and end their evening at Mabel Dodge Luhan's
nearby apartment.

Unlike John Reed, among others, Eastman was not added to
her collection of admirers, possibly because he attended "Mabel's
only once" as he recalled, on the occasion of her capture of Haywood—"her crowning achievement"—and of the red-bearded future stage designer, Robert Jones. She had, for Eastman, "neither
wit nor beauty, nor is she vivacious, or likely-minded, or entertaining." She nontheless left a marked impression. He never forgot
her peyote party or her "witchlike fascination." As Mary Kitte-
ridge of Eastman's *Venture,* her fictional embodiment was an important character.

I *Accent on Living*

In a sense, Eastman's response was predictable. Mabel Dodge
Luhan was not his kind of woman; she was too competitive and
aggressive. But he shared her romantic insistence upon the natural,
her obsessive fear of being cut off from "life." This obsession
afflicted many of America's intellectuals. They rejected cultivation
of the mind at the expense of the emotion; they "disliked ele-
gance"; they took to heart Malcolm Cowley's advice to "let our-

selves go, abandon wife and job and family, follow our mood wherever it may lead us, and meanwhile be heartened in our driftings by the laughter of the happy and unrepressed Negroes"; they gravitated toward "people who live close to the earth." Learning to them was hostile to life's felt necessities.

Eastman, for instance, holding to a "pagan love of nature," regarded "books as an enemy of life's real joy." With his devotion to Dewey and simultaneous attraction to the contrary Transcendental values of Emerson, Eastman understandably maintained a life-long suspicion of literature. Books, to be sure, were his profession; and most of his friends were writers. Nevertheless, he feared that writers "would raise a veil between me and the downright experience of life whether in sensation or reflection." What he wished above all was to " 'live a wild life,' a life that would 'bring the wolf and lion and panther to the door' "; and he regretted being unable to go to "the upper reaches of the Amazon any more," that he "was too burned with intellect." [4]

Failing to comprehend the internal inconsistencies in his marriage of Bacon and Rousseau, Dewey and Emerson, Eastman impetuously joined the sensationalist mystique to the dual creeds of *realism* and *realpolitik.* "Intellectual people," he later warned, ". . . get to imagining that logical concepts can be strung together in such a form that they will actually somehow *reproduce* reality," a notion to which he took strong exception, since it evaded the experiential: "They are disturbed when you point out, for instance, that the very fact of motion is a little illogical. A body logically 'must be,' you say, at any given moment either in one place or another. . . . An unintellectual, and as you may say, a *natural* person, is not bothered by his observation, because he knows that motion is a fact, and the business of thinking is to deal with facts, and not lay down laws for them." [5]

Sharing Mabel Dodge's aspirations, Eastman followed her only part of the way. He agreed that, far from being "dirty" or censorious, sexual relations outside of marriage were most desirable; they were the ultimate in participatory experience, a mingling of spirits that transcended the sentient. Sex, to Eastman, was a mode of communication, the highest form of love. It was "nearer to Holy Communion than a profane indulgence—a partaking, so to speak, of the blood and body of Nature." The "realist" who, as succeeding chapters demonstrate, claimed dominance for instinctive drives, he could not face up to Dreiser's bio-chemical urges and the sordid implications of Naturalism; and hence he endowed love affairs, especially his own, with a Romantic's coloration and sensibility. Eastman's notions of sex may not have been Mabel Dodge's carnal mysticism, but it was hardly qualitatively different.[6]

Eastman's love of nature remained "strong and large" in his lifetime. He wished, like Emerson and Whitman—the twin literary lodestars in these years—"to revel awhile in the flux of experience." Indicting civilization in Mabel Dodge's manner, he never absolutely renounced it in favor of the cult of primitivism or spiritual regeneration in the desert near Taos. He had opportunity enough as, for example, in the model provided by his beloved classmate, Sid Wood, who turned to a life among the Indians. Like him, Eastman admitted to a very Greek conception of manhood, one approximating Rousseau's "romantic adoration of the noble savage"; but he "decided to stay with the despised Caucasians." He would compromise by occasionally escaping to his boyhood home at Glenora. It became a source of self-renewal, occasioning the recall of his "early delight in the mere fact of being alive." The church bells from the far shore moved him to reverence for Christ and to gratitude for his pagan freedom from Christ. The city was a place where one met people; but, writing with Emersonian hyperbole, he wished "to live in the country and meet the universe" and, understandably, Emerson's essays "became a kind of scripture."[7]

II *Thirst for Earthly Experiences*

Eastman was hardly content with the "pagan prayers" which he conducted, or with a romp in the hills. Searching for sensation, he tried almost anything that might produce it. Thus he was amenable to new taste experiences, such as a raw-food diet—or, while at Williamstown, a prick from a red-hot scarf-pin—in the belief that his "general thirst of life's experience" required fortitude.[8] But Eastman was a hedonist; and, shunning starvation or masochism, he quickly rejected those erotic feelings produced or accompanied by pain. Customarily, his emphasis upon sensation was more conventional. It took a number of forms, and freely mingled with literary views, political postures, a conviction of sexual equality, and an overly simplified view of Freudianism which stressed the libido and which found all repressions to be harmful. Freud, as a subsequent chapter affirms, was a major influence upon Eastman; and he came to Freudian thought, as did many Villagers, out of a desire to eliminate restraints upon personal behavior and to strike a blow against the authority of reason. Eastman's Freudianism viewed in this light became part of an effort to give a new perspective to life.

Van Wyck Brooks, who knew him, believed that Eastman felt "regeneration and revolt were in the air, as of the 'just-before-dawn of a new day.'" [9] This feeling made him representative, and I use the word "representative" to indicate the paradigmatic, not the average. "We were radicals, revolutionaries," Eastman reminisced, "unposing pioneers of what was soon to become a conscious pose called 'Greenwich Village'"; we were "devotees to freedom." Small wonder, therefore, that Villagers like himself were at war with sumptuary legislation or legally-enforced propriety; or that they lived in a state of heightened sensitivity toward the intrusive claims of government. "As for me," he wrote, "I have always felt that this intrusion of the state, or society, or public law, into the sanctities of a private romance is disagreeable." [10]

Such an attitude led inevitably to the advocacy of liberal divorce laws and to a passionate reappraisal of all social and moral restrictions. Marriage, understandably—given Eastman's temperament and romantic ego—"had always seemed utterly unromantic to me, and 'husband' and 'wife' among the most distasteful words in the language." Being "a gypsy lover," one whose "libido is all split up and runs a thousand ways," he categorically rejected the socially imposed restraint of the marriage bond. *Any* state directive would be anathema, and certainly one that undermined that "surge of inspiration" which embodied life and poetry—in effect, one that undermined love itself. To marry Ida Rauh, which he did, was to diminish his "irrational joy in life," to be committed "irrevocably, it seemed . . . , [to] the Folly of Growing Up." Considering himself a "creature of successive claims and passions," a lover who lacked "the exclusiveness of one grand passion," he yielded completely to ego satisfactions. He wanted to be enhanced, to be "lifted up" by love; and he wanted these experiences to be uninterrupted. Prepared to be ruthless and to tolerate the charge that narcissistic catharsis was his goal, Eastman admittedly could "not get my heart, still throbbing and alive, into a pattern of constancy." [11]

Eastman neatly intellectualized his infidelities. It was all part of the "one steady and arrogant and implacable thing in my heart"— "to live my earthly life to the full." It derived, he explained, from his wish to be "a poet and be young and sing," from his insistence upon having courage to take life playfully—as "Rabelais did when, with his dying breath, punning upon the name of the Lord"—from the example of his parents who "woke up every morning full of excitement about doing things"—from which stemmed Eastman's conviction of the necessity of living "life in this world flagrantly and to the full." [12]

III *Hedonism and Social Commitment*

Thus Eastman, much like Jo Hancock or any Byronic hero, struck the Romantic pose; and, like such a hero, his single-minded hedonism occasionally took the shape of social commitment. Eastman, as just noted, believed in sexual equality, spoke at feminist gatherings, and joined in the movement for legalized birth control. He gave considerable thought to this movement that Margaret Sanger had resurrected in 1913. Considering his healthy Darwinian respect for instinctual urges and his tributes to manliness, he understandably rejected the thought of sexual abstinence—except for those "highly sublimated, or not strongly sexed"—and urged contraceptive methods instead. He did so in the *Masses,* countering the objections of critics who found the issue irrelevant to such a Marxist magazine; and he insisted upon the "relation of Birth-Control to the working-class struggle." An unskilled worker is never free, he declared; but one "with a large family of half-starving children *cannot even fight for his freedom";* and, he affirmed, working-class families should be able "to feed and rear the children they want." [13]

So strongly did Eastman support birth control that he committed the *Masses* to a fight against Anthony Comstock who had visited William Sanger and, by a pretext, obtained a copy of "Family Limitation," one of Margaret Sanger's leaflets. Arrested for the distribution of obscene literature, both Sangers were bound over for trial. "So persecute we the prophets," concluded

Eastman; and he led an assault upon the "prurient-prudish super-vision of its [America's] education in hygiene." Incensed at the social hypocrisy surrounding this issue, Eastman charged that "it is a custom of the married in those [upper] classes to receive from their physician illegal information as to the means of controlling conception. But when this opinion is generalized to include all classes, and is acted upon in a generous and forthright campaign of instruction, then it suddenly becomes obscene. It becomes socially abhorrent, morally degenerate, and of criminal intent. . . ." [14]

And he inveighed against Anthony Comstock, the postal author-ities, the secret service—"the whole power of the United States Government"—which, he charged, was conspiring to suppress "the moral, and indeed constitutional right of an individual to speak to his neighbor concerning vital truths." Stridently arguing the question of Margaret Sanger's indictment in a later issue of the *Masses*, Eastman affirmed: "if she goes to Court . . . , we must go too and stand behind her and make her martyrdom—if martyrdom it must be—the means of that very publicity she is fighting to win. There is no more important stand, and no stand that requires more bravery and purity of heart, than this one she is making."

Thus Eastman increasingly responded to social injustice as he conceived it, to the feminist insistence upon a more spontaneous relationship between men and women. For Eastman, more was at stake than opportunity to strike a blow for individual freedom and against state regulation; the Sanger affair was also the occa-sion for an additional affirmation of the open society. Alluding to the larger issue, he stated: "We need not sing the songs nor dance the dances of a future race of children—frank and free and healthy growing in their bodies and their souls—unless we are willing earnestly and openly to consider, and know, and make known to all, the wise control of the physical processes by which those children shall be brought into the world." [15]

IV   *Poet as Romantic Symbol of True Living*

For many, Eastman included, the Poet became a major Ro-mantic symbol. He embraced the religion of life effortlessly, being by nature a social outcast and one dedicated to the experiential. Poetry, as Eastman understood it, could not be written by anyone who spent his life burrowing in complicated literature or who specialized in letters. Poetry, to the contrary, derived from experience and was its embodiment. It could only be "written by persons innocent of the smell of old books." Poets were "lovers of the adventure of life"; and poetry, as Jo Hancock asserted, "has . . . real life in it." Eastman's Romantic hero continued: it "is clothing life in its own form" whereas "prose is clothing life in the form of words. A poet lives—that is the primary thing"—and that was the all-compelling objective for Hancock and for his creator.[16]

Eastman's *Venture* (1927) itself was, above all else, the product of a Romantic imagination. It was an important book, the literary testament to Eastman's pre-war thought. Its pages teem with barely fictionalized characters and incidents: John Reed, Mabel Dodge, Morris Hillquit, Bill Haywood, Archer Huntington, the Paterson strikers, the Village radicals. The central figure, Jo Hancock was, as we have said, an amalgam of Eastman's actual and wish-fulfillment traits, with something of John Reed and Sid Wood added to them. The theme was drawn from Eastman's image of himself at the time—for it described a young man possessed of poetic gifts and a Romantic temperament who was transformed into a militant revolutionary—but it took on generic significance as the story of an entire generation.

Jo Hancock was portrayed as sensitive, athletic, nobly endowed, high-strung youth with "poetry in him." His father had been a minister. He had drifted into New York—after being expelled from college for being a "rebel"—with the aim of becoming a poet. But, coming under the influence of a New Woman, the emancipated Mary Kittredge (Mabel Dodge), he was introduced to Socialism. He met "the greatest authority on Karl Marx in America," one Dr. Moses, a revolutionary theoretician who limited himself to theory. This limitation was rapidly generalized, and made applicable to all Socialists. They talked rather than acted, and they conceived of the class struggle without class hatred. Avoiding violence and "against something called the IWW," they claimed that Christ would not have sanctioned sabotage. Hancock's response was that of the convert to revolutionary activism: "I haven't read the three volumes of *Das Kapital* and I promise you I never will, but I've read histories of the French Revolution and the Paris Commune, and I know you can't conduct a fight about property on the lines of a church social." [17]

It followed that Hancock would be drawn to the man of action, to George Forbes, who was the very antithesis of Dr. Moses (just as Eastman was attracted to Haywood and to Eugene Debs who made a similar observation about a revolution; it is not an invitation to a pink tea party). A robber baron modelled on Archer Huntington, the son of the California railroad magnate, Forbes was earthy, prehensile, intensely vigorous, larger-than-life. There was something of the primordial about him, with his "great gleaming teeth" and the sounds—"like a carnivorous animal"—which he emitted. Forbes was everything his creator admired: he possessed imaginative genius informed by a realistic grasp of events; he confronted the adamantine reality of life with determination and enormous verve; he made a full and satisfying use of his faculties; he perfected his instinctual drives, allowing them to operate untrammelled and unrestrained by societal codes; he celebrated the single and inescapable force which even materialists (defined as those hostile to feeling, Romanticism, spontaneity) recognized as valuable—namely, as life. By "life," Forbes meant struggle—struggle dominated by will. He "sang out in a jubilant chanting voice" the lines of George Chapman:

> Give me a spirit that on life's rough sea
> Loves to have his sails fill'd with a lusty wind
> Even till his sail-yards tremble, his masts crack,
> And his rapt ship run on her side so low
> That she drinks water and her keel ploughs air;
> There is no danger to a man that knows
> What life and death is—there's not any law
> Exceeds his knowledge. [18]

Eastman would have agreed with Justice Holmes who, armed with Darwinian propositions, found that man's destiny on earth was battle. Eastman understood such battle in terms of impulse, life-urge, the ecstasy of power, the conflict of will; and inevitable victory for man was to be attained over all forces—natural and social—that threatened him, providing he develops his instincts to the highest. Such a victory, as Eastman believed, had little to do with "brains," which he minimized. Success in business was the outcome of one kind of battle, and it was a matter of "astuteness, cruelty, daring, practical imagination, pugnacity, energy, self-absorption, 'cheek.'" [19] In the world of the Forbes', much like the world of Dreiser's Cowperwood or Jack London's Wolf Larsen, "brains" counted not at all.

Forbes's forays in the business and financial worlds were inherently dangerous; they were challenges, adventures, accepted for this reason. His responses were conditioned by the hazards involved, whether they be natural or man-made, whether the ventures be "new openings for young men [or the] opening up [of] a *whole* planet." He esteemed those who took risks, who picked up the gauntlet, who bravely accepted and overcame obstacles. Much like Eastman, who admired the "Elizabethan gusto and candor in the strong taste for life," Forbes also looked back to that age—to a time when the national spirit of daring and adventure was at its zenith:[20] "Men were alive in those days you know [Forbes exclaimed]—courage in their guts and brains in their skulls. Even the poets were alive, and poets are a simpering and twiddling sect, for the most part, if you want my opinion. I always think of a poet as a female man piping sweet fog through an oat whistle. But when a poet is alive, those Elizabethans were, he's the livest thing that ever planted a shoe on this earth." [21]

Thus Forbes, in sharp contrast to Dr. Moses, glorified action, will, force. He admired George Washington for declaring, "'government is not reason, it is not eloquence, it is force,' a remark worth all the give-me-liberty-or-give-me-death's in the whole calendar of the expatiating patriots." Forbes knew what he wanted, namely power, and he knew the means to it: "business, pecuniary prospects"; and he would permit nothing to divert him. "Power [was] to be picked up and wielded by the strong," Forbes insisted; and he existed for only one purpose: to accumulate wealth and, consequently, power.[22] He recognized, in an unillusioned way, that this driving ego assertion was untrammeled by moral restraints. Moral codes—and also legal ones—were for the average man; they served as a means to keep the masses orderly; the superior man is permitted the right to make his own rules.

Forbes was surrounded by books: Bacon's essays, Voltaire, Machiavelli's *The Prince*, and two works of Nietzsche: the *Anti-Christ*, and *Beyond Good and Evil*. He recommended Nietzsche to

Jo Hancock—as a philosopher who recognized that truth is a whole, adaptable to the user, and who "talked more reality and less gas than almost anybody else who ever adopted an attitude." [23] Nietzsche realized that morality was simply a veil, hindering man from acting in his best interests; so stated Forbes, who recognized that Nietzschean morality was part of his inner strength—essential to a powerful mind which relished ruthless and cold-blooded analyses.

Forbes was a man of parts as Eastman portrayed him. He possessed both moral idealism and egotistical self-assertiveness, a materialist outlook and an ethics of secular benevolence. A self-proclaimed Nietzschean superman, he sought, as the outcome of his struggle and his will to power, a higher type of individual and a greatly improved social state. Much like Jack London's characters, who reflected his confused and unresolved strains of superman and socialism, Forbes yokes ruthless individual will-to-power with social idealism and social service. Nietzschean thought dominated the ante-bellum literary and radical mind to an extent that continues to be unappreciated. Forbes's main concern, consonant with the teaching of Nietzsche, was to develop "the highest conceivable type of humankind." Hence this Brahmin of business was not interested in power *qua* power, simply to satisfy his Darwinian blood lusts. Forbes had an ideal, one which was postulated on the efforts of men and one which, contrary to all evolutionary dicta, claimed for men a role in shaping their destinies: "To create a race, a real nobility, a species of men, American men, with power, nerve, speed, brain and capacity for pure joy, such as nature never conceived or was capable of producing. . . . What is the whole incredible travail of organic evolution but a clumsy and fumbling effort, admirable only in its persistence, to create something noble out of a stodgy vat of pulp, and what is science for, if not to make something stand up out of it?" [24]

More often than not the atavistic rather than the idealistic dominated George Forbes. Not so with Forbes's disciple, Jo Hancock, why was moved by a warm and boundless human sympathy. Both teacher and pupil, to be sure, shared in common a deep vein of moral idealism and vital lust for life. Hancock insisted, after Forbes helped him to make a start in the coffee business, that he was not in this business but "in the business of living." [25] He was touched by Forbes's definition of *Molodyetz*—which meant "really young . . . , brave, strong, full of life, full of don't care"—

and he wished to live up to its meaning. But Hancock eventually repudiated Forbes and his dream and, true to his creator's pre-war impulses, threw in his lot with the Industrial Workers of the World.

Eastman, we will recall, had been present at Mabel Dodge's when William Haywood, leader of the Industrial Workers of the World, was present and lionized. Obviously, the radical leader made a lasting impression. Hancock had been immediately influenced by the legendary figure who insisted that the working class must be merciless in order to win. Haywood was, for him, very much like Forbes—only "Big Bill" forged Nietzschean power to Socialism, not to industrial and corporate elitism: the means to the Socialist end remained a philosophy of activism; namely, revolutionary syndicalism.

Rejecting Forbes's plans for Hancock, which would have seen him become a captain of industry, Hancock joined the Industrial Workers of the World in Paterson. And in the midst of this city's great strike (one which Eastman also witnessed), in the midst of struggle, Marxism became real to him; it was at last yoked to the real, the instrument by which the "Wobblies" would take power in the name of the working class. Haywood recognized that he, like Forbes, spoke for a minority; and similarly he relied upon an elite; similarly, too, the instrument was power, coupled with a ruthlessly objective assessment of the exigent needs. It was not a question of justice, the protagonists realized, but of the relation of forces. "Both George Forbes and those I.W.W.'s were living reality," Hancock thought. "There was hard light on the earth in both camps." [26]

An "old Russian," an emigre revolutionist, helped Jo Hancock reformulate his position. Now Marxism was something different than it had been in the hands of that "lecturing jabber," Dr. Moses, who had made it into "a vast incomprehensible system of abstract ideas, enabling you to sit back and do nothing." There were the talkers and politicians, and there were the revolutionary engineers, the former being the Mensheviks who compromised away the revolution. But Dr. Moses predicted that the "Marxian engineers—Bolsheviks" would emerge in 1910–1920; and they were "something very different. . . . Our party is ready. Our party understands a whole science of revolution like these IWW only begin to guess about." [27]

Paterson's strike was the catalyst which caused Jo Hancock to rethink his position. It led him to reject the idea of government by a capitalist aristocracy. Others would not be the same as George Forbes—"great-minded, really in love with truth. The general run of men are dirty-mean when they have power." But he was not prepared to offer complete obeisance to the Industrial Workers of the World program. He felt that the "conscious aristocrat"—the supermen—must "understand people and feel at one with them and then try to guide them." His solution was to blend the polar forces, the masses and the elite, into a harmonious working arrangement: "the small minority who will organize the business of society, and yet they will be permitted to do so, not because they own the earth, but because they are friends of the mass." [28]

The "combination of these two programs" was, in effect, the reconciliation of Nietzsche and Marx. Hancock became a strike leader and fell in love with the daughter of one of the strikers. Forbes, meanwhile, supported and organized the mill owners. He admitted, however, that the "Wobblies" "are a sort of aristocrats themselves," to which Hancock replied that they made the best democrats—that they were "a gang of superior fighting men whose power rested on . . . the support and friendship of the masses of the people, the workers." [29]

In this manner, Eastman came to repudiate the cult of irresponsibility. He did, to be sure, dislike "group-consciousness of any kind," and "wanted to live as an individual"; but he had no use for Bohemianism which he construed as personal flamboyance, private rebellion, and suspicion of involvement. Indeed, he had been drawn to the Village because artistic experimentation and radical social thought seemed to converge there. But when Bohemianism began to dominate, when the Village became "conscious of itself . . . as a 'picturesque' thing and . . . began to put on airs," he rejected it. Eastman fought this "provincialism" wherever encountered, for he was repelled by its narcissism and irresponsibility. [30] Detesting the "perpetual puberty of the grey-haired Bacchantes," he nonetheless remained true to some of their ideals—to poetry, to nature, to individualism, to the insistence that "the purpose of life is that it should be lived." But these propositions were qualified to the extent that the asocial poet and Romantic would shortly become the spokesman for left-wing radicalism.

CHAPTER 4

War and Peace:
In the Great Debate

"A FERVENT REBEL—half Nietzschean, half anarchist, believing in free love and a freed proletariat," Ida Rauh would bring Eastman to the marriage vows and to the superman. When she met in 1910 her future lover and husband, she introduced him to the leading Village radicals and to Marx and Nietzsche. From Nietzsche's thought, Eastman plucked only those elements responsive to his own; he ignored, therefore, the Nietzschean proscriptions of progress, utility, reason, and democracy which were symptomatic—for Nietzsche—of society's sickness and approaching doom. Like Nietzsche, Eastman also celebrated the self-fulfilling and self-transcending individual as the source of all health and joy. He also abandoned the restraints of Christian morality, believed God was dead, found modern society to be afflicted, and declared that the strong and beautiful must survive, if necessary, at the expense of the feeble.

I *Superman and Socialism*

Nietzsche's influence seemed particularly relevant to 1914. The outbreak of hostilities was a bewildering event for most Americans and a staggering one for the Socialists.[1] It eroded their hallowed conceptions: it shattered faith in progress which was so essential to Socialist hopes, blasted their belief in human decency and scientific enlightenment. Notwithstanding their insistence upon the "inevitability" of war, they were caught off-guard by the event itself (as they were three years later by America's declaration); and they alternated between hope and despair. They had denounced war, to be sure, and found it the unavoidable result of imperialist rivalry; but their repetitive litany had not been adequate preparation for the great conflict. Nationalism and greed now seemed to govern man and societies.[2] The "primordial instinct of national self-preservation" was in the saddle—so wrote Morris Hillquit, the prominent Socialist Party leader; and, reacting with a sense of shock, he continued: "In common with hosts of others I was dismayed by the sudden collapse of human reason and the ugly sight of the world denuded of its thin veneer of civilization."

Eastman's response was to be expected. Convinced of man's instinctual belligerence, he concluded his essay "What Nietzsche Really Taught" with an approving quote from Nietzsche: war would " 'prepare the way for a yet higher age.' "[3] He rejected the popular assumption that Nietzsche had been responsible for German behavior and, conversely, claimed that Nietzsche hated nationalism and was in fact the "prophet of the 'Unity of Europe.' " The new type of Nietzschean man, Eastman continued, was in direct contrast to "the physiologically botched, the weak, and the degenerate"; indeed, these had to be suppressed in order for the higher man to emerge. But more than suppression of inferior types was required: "the science of eugenics" and "the pagan and heroic virtues" had to be cultivated. Such a combination would give rise to the superman which was, for Eastman as well as Nietzsche, more than an ideal; it was a distinct possibility once the unfit were eliminated.

As Eastman understood it, Nietzschean thought stressed those qualities which ranked highest on his own scale of values; it was optimistic and adventurous; it subscribed readily to the doctrine of progress and insisted that truth was prospective rather than retrospective. It discarded Christian platitudes, which had drenched his own childhood. "He hated such things as the Beatitudes," Eastman wrote of Nietzsche, "because they seemed to him to exalt what is base and weak and ignoble—Blessed are the *meek*, Blessed are the *poor in spirit*, Blessed are they that *mourn*." Nietzschean thought demanded those values which Eastman himself honored—"self-control, intellect, action, discipline." It would reject the "flat morass of mediocrity," as well as the aristocracy of wealth," replacing both with "a genuine aristocracy" of the sort that George Forbes represented.[4]

But such a development could best take place in a society which presented opportunity to talent. Socialism alone offered such an environment, as Nietzsche would have realized; only it was postulated upon equality, which was prerequisite for the "greater ideal—the ideal of a Super-Society." In such a society "all men are free; and those born with heroic and great gifts . . . must inevitably rise to eminence, through their sheer value to mankind." [5]

But Nietzsche was not unqualifiedly endorsed. Eastman criticized him for insisting upon "a general heredity of acquired characteristics," which tended to diminish man's role and nullify "every amateur plan or prediction about the future of man." Rejecting this view—that acquired characteristics may be transmitted—Eastman invoked the canons of biological science. "The nature which a man or any animal inherits," he affirmed, ". . . is transmitted to his offspring unaffected by his personal education, or by any qualities that he may acquire during his life." Discomforted by the implications of an impersonal mechanism, uncontrollable by man, he nonetheless fell into a self-sprung ideological ambush, being forced to conclude "that any 'improvement' which involves an off-hand suppression of *universal hereditary tendencies* will be exceedingly precarious." But Eastman was too romantic to acquiesce in these antihuman implications, and he denied that improvement was non-existent. It could not be transmitted, to be sure; "it will have to depend for its enforcement upon an almost unanimous weight of social tradition, for underneath it, in the neural structure, laid down forever, lie the paths of the old tendency it denies." [6]

Despite his training in scientific methods, Eastman refused to surrender his faith in human will, inquiry, and guidance. He gravitated toward any proposition that would support the doctrine of progress and that would assure to men the possibility of active participation in the drama of their destiny. He eventually made progress contingent upon the contributions of each generation toward its realization, rather than an absolute law of history. He partially defected from and partially refashioned the Darwinian-Nietzschean belief that found man's fate to be determined by mechanical or instinctual powers and not by man himself; and he insisted that man could shape his environment. There was a method of "handling inconvenient instincts [which was] more practical than selective breeding, and more sure and permanent than cultural suppression. That is to alter the environment in such fashion as to offer new objects for these instincts to adhere to."

"Men are incurably rivalrous and pugnacious," but this rivalry and pugnacity can be rechannelled, redistributed, redirected, given "vent in other forms of conflict and display." [7]

Thus Eastman, like Jack London, eagerly joined Nietzsche to Socialism. Refusing to dismiss the Socialist belief in progress, he found man to be "the most plastic and adaptable of animals" and, he continued, one that "truly can be changed by his environment, and even by himself, to a unique degree." Nonetheless, man "inherits . . . 'animal propensities' in the crude sense, a set of emotional drives or impulses . . . [which] cannot be eradicated from the race." Evading the inherent limitations of these admissions, Eastman wedded Socialism and the superman with relative ease. He did so, much like Jack London, by simply ignoring the contrary implications of the two propositions. [8]

II Reactions to World War I

Nietszche's elitist beliefs, to be sure, clashed with socialism's faith in the working class; and the outbreak of World War I exacerbated this clash. The contradiction seemed stark and irreconcilable. Thus human nature, Eastman claimed, was confirmed and "revealed in the Socialist workingmen's support of a nationalistic war." [9] Yet there is his sanguine declaration borne of Socialism that "at least four hundred thousand revolutionary socialists in Germany . . . opposed and *still oppose* their ruler's war." Consequently the working class, he argued, having no property to defend, should logically oppose war. But he rejected the orthodox Socialist explanation of capitalist-inspired struggle, declaring: "People do not go to war for their property. They go to war for their country. . . . The motive to patriotic fighting is not a mere derivative from business interest; it is a native impulse of our constitution. The backbone of the sentiment of patriotism is heredity." [10]

Hence, while war was inevitable, as the Socialists theorized about capitalism, its inevitability was, for Eastman, embedded in the nature of man rather than in the capitalist system itself. He even came to the distinctly non-Socialist conclusion that not all capitalists wanted war. Continuing in the same heretical vein, he flirted with the pseudo-scientific racism popular at that time: "the patriotic and pugnacious tribes survived," he affirmed, and "we are that tribe." Nor did he offer only an oblique rejection of Socialist doctrine pertaining to causation of war. He charged Marxists with "a reckless oversimplification of the truth" when they "explained international wars as wholly due to economic causes." Rejecting such rubrics as "imperialist wars," he urged "the Marxian oversimplification of war's causes" be abandoned and, furthermore, that, when a war has begun, its causes are a secondary consideration.[11]

Patriotism, which Eastman frequently equated with nationalism, was that "most banal of stupid human idol-worships"; yet, he repeatedly asserted, it was "a disposition that lies fixed in the hereditary structure of all civilized races." [12] It was the catalyst, the factor that unleashed man's angry hate; and it was ineradicable. "To argue against it, against these tribal and egoistic instincts, is like arguing against gravitation." [13] Furthermore, to argue against it would be to deny some remarkable emotional satisfaction: that satisfaction derived from "a belligerent self-identification with the group."

Thus patriotism became an insidious curb upon rationality and reasonableness. It combined an irresistible three-fold appeal—to altruism, to infant memories, to the chance to behold ourselves enlarged—out of our selves "and clothed in public splendor." In an almost Jungean explanation, Eastman found that the individual's identification "with the hive" was reinforced by self-love and child-love. By the latter, he declared, "I mean the disposition . . . to return in times of trouble to the affections and passions which swayed them [men] when they were very young"—the disposition to run home to mother, "to father, or sister, or brother, or nurse, or the nursery, or the old homestead, or the home town, or 'my native land,' as the case may be." [14]

Eastman always tended to vacillate on the issue of causation.[15] At times, as we have observed, he added to his "theoretical heresies," thereby setting himself "apart . . . from orthodox socialists," by finding what the war owed to "group psychology in a pugnacious animal." But he inconsistently sought greater balance or party criteria on other occasions. And he even wrote, quite incompatibly for a Darwinian, that the war had "underlying commercial causes." Equally out of character for a votary of Nietzsche, he exhorted: "let us drop the race rant forever. . . . It is not a national trait but a class trait that has given to Germany the position of grandiose aggressor in this inevitable outbreak of commercial war."

At such times he supported the St. Louis Convention of the Socialist Party, with its denunciation of war and of patriotism; and he assailed the "military minority" of Socialists (W. J. Ghent, C. E. Russell, U. Sinclair, J. G. Phelps Stokes, William E. Walling) who defected. He recognized, with a Socialist's awareness, "that moral indignation against any nation as the sole perpetrator of this war, is futile and superficial." He realized, as early as 1914, that England's "perpetuation of a blockade policy against Germany, which openly violated the rules of international law" was a prior offense, and he rejected as superficial England's "alleged reasons" for entering the conflict. Her poets and intellectuals, with their "savage cynicism of the German tribes," were just as responsible for invoking nationalist-belligerent sentiment as "the great cosmopolitan scholars of Christianity" in Germany who proselytized England's "brutal national egoisms." As a result, Eastman charged German leaders with no more than a lack of finesse, an indelicacy of feeling, when they sank the *Lusitania:* "War being essentially a competition in murder, having certain traditional rules that are supposed to regulate the competition, and these rules having been broken by England's starvation policy, Germany announced that in a certain zone they are suspended, and the murder of British will be more general. She expects us, since we have allowed England to break these rules at our expense, to allow her a like privilege." [16]

England, too, he claimed, "has committed 'Lusitania'-sized atrocities"; but she does so in remote places or upon "socially negligible classes of people." Clearly, militarism was not the monopoly of any one nation, nor a trait of any race; instead, it "has the same characters wherever it appears." Finally, advancing a fundamental article of Socialist faith, he reduced it all to this observation: "There is no Christianity, no culture, no civilization. Our whole upper-class polity and pretense of spirituality is built of a leisure that is the loot of predatory competition and the perpetual exploitation and death of the poor." [17]

But Eastman, contrary to his Socialist sense and his conscious judgments, often responded emotionally on the subject of Germany. Her sophomoric national egotism was "even worse than England's suave and hypocritical self-righteousness." France, he declared, had more freedom and "the arts of life more nearly won than any other country of Europe." But Germany, to the contrary, was "a monster, an old-fashioned military autocracy wielding a modern social and industrial efficiency." For her own sake, for the sake of her people, "the Kaiser and his military machine must be whipped back into Prussia and smashed." [18]

Placed beside later statements, this extraordinary—for a social-ist—appeal that "the Kaiser's armies and all his steel engines and feudal military idealism be crumpled back" suggests the tentative and wavering course that Eastman pursued. In September, 1915, less than a year later, he willingly agreed "that the German war party played a larger part" among the causes of war than any other; but, he inquired, "does that commit me to a monomania?" And he rejected America's fixation upon total defeat of Germany. He admitted, in the previous year, that "our heart [is] with in-vaded France"; now, in 1915, he asked, "because France is more advanced in liberty . . . than Germany, do we have to say that France *is* civilization and Germany is barbarism . . . ?" Two years later, a month after America declared war, Eastman was prepared to come full circle. He now worried lest a humiliating defeat "inflame German nationalism as much as a signal victory would." [19]

From whatever perspective it is examined, the Socialist re-sponse to war was varied, fuzzy-headed, and inconsistent in the light of traditional Socialist doctrine. Editors of *The Call*, a Social-ist daily, were among those who saw the war as a Socialist oppor-tunity, one which "leads straight to the social revolution." [20] "There is no cause for despair," Debs counseled in 1915. "The world is awakening and we are approaching the sunrise." And he baldly prophesied: "To end the war prematurely, were that pos-sible, would simply mean another and perhaps even bloodier catastrophe." His plea found echoes at home and abroad.[21] Leonard Boudin inquired, in his regular column in the *New Review*, "Peace—At What Price?"—and vaguely proposed only "a *lasting* peace upon terms that are just and under conditions that will be conducive to the progress of mankind." [22] "Let the war go on," Eastman candidly urged, "for the sake of the German people and of all nations." [23] He did not fear a "devastating war in Europe," believing as he did that "it will hasten" the day of labor's triumph. Cruelly opportunistic, he claimed that the war would eliminate "the ever-waiting army of the unemployed"; and, by making labor scarce, "they will find labor proud." [24]

There was, conversely, a substantial bloc of Socialists, led by Morris Hillquit, who favored an immediate end to the conflict. They believed from the outset "that all governments . . . [were] equally militaristic and reactionary"; they argued the Socialist Party's Peace Program (of May 15, 1915); and they opposed preparedness and conscription.[25] Having come around to an anti-war position by 1917, Eastman scored the drafting of "free citizens" in order to ship "them over a bloody sea to Europe, to be slaughtered in war waging [sic] between other countries than their own." [26] He praised the majority resolution at the St. Louis meeting, which denounced war, and condemned the minority who defected.

Eastman joined those favoring immediate peace in May, 1917. Like them, he denied that he was "an absolute pacifist." Preferring "domestic violence to international violence," he declared, "my reasons for believing that those who love human liberty should oppose *this* war, rather than oppose Germany, are concrete reasons." He was willing to admire murder, he asserted in 1916, but it should be "murders . . . directed to some intelligible gain." Presumably, World War I was not that kind of murder; and, by 1917, he hewed close to the Socialist position: the German state, the "monster," would "go the way of all monsters . . . in the course of its internal development"; but, if he wanted it "to fail of conquest," he also wished England—"an octopus [which] strangles and devours in remote places"—and France to fail.[27]

This position, seemingly so different from the exhortations, "let the war go on" or "smash" Germany, suggests Eastman's sharp departure from earlier views. And an examination of Eastman's attitude toward President Wilson in the 1912–1916 period seems to confirm the marked change of viewpoint after America declared war. Beginning with the Mexican revolution, the *Masses* editorial columns shifted to international affairs as the area of primary concern. Eastman, who first focused on the Mexican upheaval, assured his readers that Wilson did not want war. He praised the chief executive's deft handling of America's involvement with her Latin-American neighbor; Huerta was the villain of the piece. According to Eastman, in his tribute to Wilson, Huerta "had plotted secret hostilities against American citizens in Mexico, in order to provoke intervention by our armies, which would put an end to the revolution, and set him at the head of Mexico in a war with the United States." In what has been characterized as a whitewash by some Socialists, Wilson was portrayed as a man of "unswerving purpose to let the Mexican people govern, or not govern, themselves." [28]

Usually, at this time, the President's foreign-policy decisions were endorsed. The *Masses* of June, 1916, for instance, flatly editorialized: Wilson does not want war. "He has kept us out of war," Eastman declared in August, 1916; "he has attacked the problem of eliminating war, and he has not succumbed to the epidemic of militarism in its extremist forms." This sentiment, shared by many independent progressives and left-wing groups, was also confirmed by Eastman's report of an interview at the White House between Wilson and a group of *Masses* editors. According to this report Wilson, a "graciously democratic aristocrat," handled the group beautifully. Some years later, to be sure, Eastman admitted his mistaking Wilson "for a strong and extraordinarily able politician." But, in 1916, he had been "delightedly surprised" by the President's replies in the course of the interview, and was "irregular enough to say so during his campaign":[29] "I would rather see Woodrow Wilson [Eastman stated, speaking through the Woodrow Wilson Independent League] elected than Charles Hughes, because Wilson aggressively believes not only in keeping out of the war, but in organizing the nations of the world to prevent war."

Continuing in this naïve, un-Socialist vein, he affirmed on another occasion: "Still more he [Wilson] will be re-elected because his party's delegates took the convention away from their stupidly astute leaders, and turned it into a glorious demonstration against war, against maniac nationalism, and against military diplomacy." [30] Eastman, to be sure, voted Socialist in 1916; but he gave voice to sentiments shared by many left-of-center electors who, as the sharp reduction in Socialist ballots from 1912 suggests, turned to Wilson.

Wartime loyalty to the chief executive also resulted from Eastman's own insistence upon an "international federation of the world." As early as six months after the Armistice, he admitted that Wilson's "point of view [was that] of the sentimental moralist, and," he continued, "with all his persuasive diction and stubborn suavity, he is extremely gullible." But the Wilsonian version of the peace settlement was gratefully endorsed, owing to the fact that the vision that dazzled a generation of reformers had also affected Eastman; namely, an international organization which would eliminate "international war from the world." Such an organization, he believed, was "one of the great hopes of civilization." "What we may do there [at the proposed world organization]," he continued, "will be worth more to the struggle against militarism all over the world than even the political revolution in Germany" would be worth.[31]

Such convictions seem, to be sure, strangely out of place in the Darwinian value scheme. But Eastman slipped out of the trap of fatalism by finding hope inherent in the very bellicosity of the human animal: the instinct for self-identification—"this gregarious hunger"—which took the form of patriotism could be made to serve the cause of supra-nationalism. He reasoned as follows:

> Wars will arise between nations so long as the instinct of fighting loyalty is allowed to attach exclusively to nations. And as soon as, and in proportion as, we offer to that instinct larger groups to which it may attach, wars among nations will become less and less likely. We shall eliminate national by international union. That is all we can say. That is all we can do with a trait which is hereditary. We can not ignore it; we cannot mortify it; we cannot preach it away; we cannot pray it away. But we can offer it a different object to cling to.[32]

This unusual set of values for a socialist enabled Eastman to discard the doctrinaire view of causation. His unorthodox position again appears in his readiness to sacrifice the German social revolution if doing so would facilitate the establishment of an international organization. To make his heresy more stark by contrast, there was Eastman's recognition that it would be a "bourgeois" agency, that it was desired by "international capital," and that its success depended in large measure upon Woodrow Wilson—who could be supported for re-election in 1916 for this reason alone.[33]

Eastman's pre-election statements favoring Wilson illustrate more than the ambiguities and cleavages of Socialist thought; they tell us by extension something about the left-of-center spectrum. The entire left-liberal intellectual movement in wartime America was willing, even eager, to engage in this sort of self-deception. It had no answers to the problems of war; it was eager to resist pressures for conformity and regarded such resistance as a holy mandate, while being simultaneously pulled—and not often consciously—toward participation in the great overseas undertaking.

Reflecting all of the contradictions of the left, Eastman argued against preparedness and still clamored for German defeat; he stressed the inherent belligerent impulses that governed man and also proposed their control; he claimed that Wilson, as he later affirmed in the course of admitting his error, was "an extraordinary able politician of progressive capitalism." But he soon regretted such thoughtless assertions as unbecoming a Socialist.

Emphasis upon inherited belligerence was the eternal *cri de coeur*. But anti-militarism, clashing with it, was also at the tap root of Eastman's thought. When he urged an effort to prevent the militarization of "our minds and the minds of our children . . . [which] fill us full of the bigotry of nationalism in peacetime," he was reacting viscerally; for he had a lifelong antagonism to conformity, particularly when it took the form of service to government. "I hated organized fighting," he recalled; "I hated drills, guns, stripes, bars, flags, drums, fifes, bugles, salutes, the whole theme-with-variations of militarism. I could not bear to see this corruption begin to swell in the United States." Urging a frontal assault upon "the panic of patriotism," he proposed that it proceed along three fronts: reorganization of the Socialist international; support for the "bourgeois movements for international federation"; and anti-military propaganda. His proposed rallying-call for the new international would be "United Anti-Militarism and Federation." And this marriage was not one of convenience. It was an organic conception—the only way to thwart man's "instinctive emotional spasm." [34]

From the outset, it followed, the *Masses* lampooned Theodore Roosevelt (as well as Elihu Root and Franklin Roosevelt, then assistant secretary of the navy, as unscrupulous patriots) and his preparedness campaign, charging him with having "the vision and action of a mule with blinders on." [35] Its columns were increasingly consumed by a virulent anti-militarism: it violently opposed the draft, refusing to recognize the "right of government to draft me to war whose purposes I do not believe in." [36] It predicted, with equanimity if not pleasure, Wilson's election "because he has kept us out of war, he has attacked the problem of eliminating war, and he has not succumbed to the epidemic of militarism in its extremist forms." [37] "You ought to prevent the declaration of this war if you possibly can," Eastman told a giant mass meeting in Detroit three days before America declared war, "and if you can't you ought to stay out of it."

When he himself was informed of a Class I draft classification, he wrote to his draft board: "I do not believe in international wars, and I do not recognize the right of a government to conscript the bodies of its citizens for service upon foreign soil. I think it is an abandonment of those principles of human liberty upon which the American republic was founded. In the name of those principles, therefore, I must decline to serve." [38] Fortunately, Eastman was reclassified and did not need to appear before his board. Unlike its editor, the *Masses* was not to escape the heavy hand of the government; the fact that it steadily expanded its anti-war, anti-militarist, anti-administration commentary guaranteed as much.

CHAPTER 5

The *Masses* and the Guns of War

THE PRE-WAR and wartime years were ones of insurgency. A new general conflict had taken shape, led by relatively young men out of the West—out of village and small-town America. For the most part, they were attracted to the task of cultural demolition, laying siege to the dominant social-cultural values, assaulting the provincialism from which they had so recently escaped. Lacking clarity or unity of purpose, they compensated for these deficiencies by élan and youthfulness. They rebelled against their own Spoon Rivers and Gopher Prairies and also, as Van Wyck Brooks has observed, "against the social conditions which the muckrakers had revealed along with the Lawrence strike of 1912.[1]

They flocked to the Socialist locals, which were centers of ideas in a society and an era when ideas were few; and they joined the party itself, which registered nearly a million voters in the 1912 election. They read Van Wyck Brooks's *America's Coming of Age* as *vade mecum,* and took to heart its call to arms, urging writers to rise above America's life-destroying materialism. They descended upon the Provincetown Playhouse to applaud its actors —Maxwell Bodenheim, Floyd Dell, Harry Kemp, Max Eastman— and to admire the dark, brooding genius of Eugene O'Neill. They led an awakening that was all-inclusive: it embraced the anti-industrial instinctualism of Sherwood Anderson and Sandburg's paeans to the machine, the puritanism of Upton Sinclair's Arthur Stirling and the piety of social Christianity. Their awakening "subscribed to the principles of realism in art," declared Granville Hicks; "but its politics tended toward the romantic. It had the seriousness of strong convictions and the gayety of great hopes."[2] It sponsored the little magazines, the *New Republic* and *Seven Arts,* two journals very different from the popular monthly, the *Masses,* which had been established in January, 1911.

I *The* Masses—*Eastman as Editor*

Piet Vlag, the *Masses'* founder, was an excitable Dutchman who ran a cooperative restaurant in the Rand School basement. His "general illustrated magazine" had no assets to speak of: a few thousand mostly unpaid subscriptions, a tiny office on Nassau Street with rent some months in arrears, an editorship not only wholly unsalaried but probably costing the incumbent considerably. The *Masses'* mission was to proselytize the cooperative movement. It carried short stories, articles on Socialism, anti-capitalist cartoons, and advertisements for Karl Marx cigars. A remarkably mild and unsocialist magazine, considering its contributors, it became involved in Socialist Party factionalism in 1912, embraced the moderates' position, and opposed the direct-action Wobbly elements among the party membership. And, consequently, it alienated those Socialists who, like Eastman, were attracted to the members of the Industrial Workers of the World rather than to the "yellow" reformist wing.[3] He had scornfully regarded the magazine as an organ of middle-class Socialism, a sentimental "evangel of humanitarianism and zeal for consumer's cooperatives" which supported legal strikes and condemned Syndicalist violence.

Eastman, to be sure, admired "the sentimental rebels," as he called them, a group which included Hutchins Hapgood, Clarence Darrow, Fremont Older, and Lincoln Steffens. But he considered them anarchistic spirits, by which he meant simply men with "an irresponsible distaste for politics." Consequently, he did not mourn Vlag's *Masses* when it passed from view. The monthly died in August, 1912, owing to a shortage of funds, the usual illness of little magazines. Eastman, who became editor in December, restored it to life.

The list of contributors to the *Masses*, during Eastman's tenure, reads like a roll-call of the cultural-radical community in the United States. William Carlos Williams, Vachel Lindsay, William Rose Benet, Amy Lowell, Babette Deutsch, and Louis Untermeyer were among the poets. The writers included Randolph Bourne, Upton Sinclair, Earnest Poole, John Reed—indeed, nearly every young writer with a rebellious strain. The cartoonists most employed were Boardman Robinson and Robert Minor. Art

Young, who had met Eastman at a Jack London testimonial and who found work for the *Masses* "loosed energies within me of which I had been unaware," was one of the artists; others—including members of the Ashcan school—Arthur Davies, Maurice Stern, George Bellows—sent in drawings for four years; John Sloan, the most uncompromising and the *Masses* art editor; and his savagely independent protégé, Stuart Davis.[4]

These contributing editors, as some of them were, were recalled with mingled scorn and admiration by Eastman; they were a "bunch of utopians" who never discussed such questions as paying the rent; but they were sufficiently in tune with reality to accept Art Young's nominee, Eastman, as editor. In late August, he recalled, they sent a letter "scrawled with a brush on a torn-off scrap of drawing paper," and signed by Charles Winter, Alice Beach Winter, Maurice Becker, Mary Heaton Vorse, Ellis O. Jones, Horatio Winslow, Inez Haynes Gillmore, and Sloan and Untermeyer who drafted it: "You are elected editor of the *Masses*, no pay."

Eastman "managed" the magazine in a literal sense. He was "from an operational point of view—the whole thing," which suited him; for, as Untermeyer recalled, he "had ideas for new departments, schemes for surprises, plans for everyone." Eastman complained, of course; for the chores were more burdensome than anticipated. "None of the 'creative geniuses'" who guided Piet Vlag's magazine, he tartly observed, "ever paid the slightest attention to the business end of it." Hence he was forced to become promotor, entrepreneur, and business executive, as well as editor and writer.[5]

Gradually the magazine acquired character. Its artists and writers contributed without fee to the "'printing [of] what is too naked or true for a money-making press.'" This proclamation, on the masthead, suggested the mood that had been generated. It was one of obvious hostility to and "revolt against commercial journalism," which frequently took the form of publishing "what commercial magazines will not pay for." Eastman, to be specific, shared the Ashcan school's contempt for the "popular" magazines. He had come to his novitiate untutored in artistic fashions, knowing nothing of current trends in painting. But he sensed that a pictorial revolt, a sharp departure from the tradition established by *Life* and by *Puck*, was in the making.[6]

Eastman's own esthetic maturation was shaped by some of the

best names in newspaper cartooning—mostly by John Sloan who, with Bellows, Davis, and Becker, spoke in the language of social realism. They drew the city's crowded streets, Coney Island, markets and saloons, the evils of capitalism, and the plight of the prostitute. Eastman was immensely proud of their contribution, for it expressed the new insurgency with great effectiveness, possibly more so than did the literary contributions; and it was the most provocative and successful aspect of the monthly. It was a product of Eastman's desire to unite art and propaganda or rather, as Louis Untermeyer understood it, to "express propaganda *as* art— an art which combined the free play of the painter and writer with the purpose of the reappraiser." [7] The results frequently were both touching and funny, ranging from Davis's outrageous "green girls" to the famous cover of two pathetically homely, wretchedly dressed girls from Hoboken, with one saying to the other, "Gee, May, think of us bein' on a magazine cover!"

Eastman admitted yielding to the artists' demands for generous space for their drawings. He had the wisdom to confess that the magazine belonged to its contributors. But he and Dell managed the operation in a way that would have appalled some of them. The magazine's editorial board, for instance, usually met once a month, read manuscripts, looked over drawings, and voted. Members of New York's cultural establishment, who often attended, were also encouraged to vote. The meetings were happy and exciting. Genvieve Taggard recalled that "everybody was playing and the editors . . . were playing hardest of all." [8] But this statement should not suggest that affairs always ran smoothly. The artists maintained a continuing quarrel with the writers, and Eastman walked a tightrope between highly volatile groups. "Hell had to break loose," he said, and it did in March, 1916: "Even then [Eastman reminisced] the attack was not against me or against my policy, but against policy as such. It was a quarrel, essentially, between art and propaganda, poetry and practical effort. . . . In more personal terms, it was a war of the Bohemian art-rebels against the socialists who loved art." [9]

Eastman weathered the storm, but the issues remained viable. He continually sought to eliminate the bohemianism and "smart-alecky leftism" which had crept into the magazine. This was a recurrent problem—in part, because of the difficulty of finding reliable criteria that would distinguish between bohemian thought and individual spontaneity, which was an *idée fixe;* in part, because "the practical scientific work of mind or hand that the revolution demands" was, for bohemians, frequently subordinate to "the wish to live a free and real life, and to cherish and communicate its qualities in works of art." Such an impulse, Eastman declared, deserves the respect of every revolutionary but it left him vulnerable to "Greenwich Villagism." The "need to line up fiercely with the ideal" and, as his mother enjoined, to "live out of yourself persistently," helped to transform birth control, feminism, and Bolshevism into mystical syntheses of truth, art, and freedom.

II *Editorial Ambivalence*

The *Masses* was extraordinarily catholic in its tastes; and this very variety tells us something about the fractured visions of its editor. For the ambivalences of earlier years still divided Eastman. No single donation to the radical cause, regardless of its form, was disregarded. But what is significant was the very large place assigned to materials that were not even remotely radical: the jokes without social comment, the lyric of a striking miner longing for spring, the satires of Charles Erskine Scott Wood, the fanciful fiction of Bellow's lithograph depicting children in the park, Untermeyer's "Wind and Flame," and the love poetry of Floyd Dell, of E. E. Cummings, and of Eastman himself.[10]

More than editorial sensitivity to the needs of the creative writer was at stake here; the deep rift between thinker and doer which lay siege to Eastman and to America's cultural community as a whole is evident: "We are distinguished, we literary and artistic people [he later wrote in the *Liberator*], by our ability to realize, to feel and express, the quality of things. We experience vividly the existing facts, and the revolutionary ideal, and the bitterly wonderful long days of the struggle that lies between these two. All the way along we are dealing as experts in experience. . . ."[11]

This ringing emphasis on "feeling" and "experience" worked in Eastman's favor. He quite properly claimed that "this faculty of vivid living—besides the ultimate and absolute value it has in itself—contributes something indispensable to the practical movement. It contributes something that we might call inspiration." The result was certainly inspired; the *Masses* was entertaining, instructive, illuminating. But the word "delightful" seems most appropriate, since it summarizes the magazine's fresh and often beguiling quality. Among other things, the monthly "stood for fun, truth, beauty, realism, freedom." [12] Shaped in his own image, it was lusty and gay, Eastman exulted; and he doubted "if socialism was ever advocated in a more life-affirming spirit." [13]

Eastman even boasted of the monthly's spaciousness, "its freedom from the one-track mental habit of the rabid devotee of a cause." [14] Mabel Dodge remembered the publication as "fearless and young and laughing at everything solemn and conservative." [15] Sherwood Anderson, who wrote "Hands" for it, remembered the "feeling of boldness and joy and life these men managed to get" into the magazine.[16] John Reed affirmed its broad social purposes.[17] In sum, the monthly was unique. It reflected, in its squibs and cartoons, Eastman's belief in the life-giving quality of humor. [18] It could be salty and sceptical, irreverent and innovating; it could also be unabashedly sentimental and unashamedly Romantic, hewing to its editor's guiding ideal "that every individual should be made free to live and grow in his own chosen way." [19]

The "gay laughter" of its editors never entirely disappeared; but the *Masses*, in Eastman's words, gradually "crystallized a cultural event that hung ready in the historic moment." It evolved differently from other verse and humor journals in that it began to champion a political program. To make this program unmistakable and yet to insist upon a non-programmatic spontaneity for the *Masses* became the most challenging task. In a statement that nicely blended the cause of revolution with insistence upon freedom of inquiry as an absolute, Eastman and Reed proclaimed: "A Free Magazine. . . . A revolutionary and not a reform magazine; a magazine with a sense of humor and no respect for the respectable; frank, arrogant, impertinent, searching for the true causes; a magazine directed against rigidity and dogma where it is found . . . , a magazine whose final policy is to do as it pleases and conciliate nobody, not even its readers." [20]

III *Social-Economic Reporting and Reform*

The *Masses*, of course, was drawn primarily to social-economic conditions in the United States. Much of its best reportage was

about New York's sweatshops and slums, life among the immi-
grants, and class war in the textile mills; and the writing had an
uncommon freshness and youthfulness. These qualities, the magazine's style as much as its contents, inevitably made it the conscience of radical America, the mouthpiece for a generation; and
these qualities, rather than its anti-capitalist polemics, made it a
pariah among the respectables everywhere. It outraged "patriotic,
religious and matrimonial, to say nothing of esthetic tastes and
conventions. The state, the church, the press, marriage"; for all
these topics were grist to its mill.[21] Every issue suggests the
sources for hostility. For instance, the July, 1913, number included
articles defending sabotage, the general strike, the indicted Wobblies, Fabianism, *inter alias*. Drawn by Art Young, the cover fea-
tured a billboard announcing a speech by Jesus Christ, "the Workingman of Nazareth" on "the rights of labor"—with the slogan,
"he stirreth up the people."

The *Masses* inevitably became the magazine of labor radicalism.
America's most militant labor leaders numbered among its sup-
porters and contributors: Haywood, Tresca, and Elizabeth Gurley
Flynn who galvanized the Paterson strikers; Giovannitti and Ettor
in jail at Lawrence; Mother Jones and John Lawson who battled
the West Virginia mine owners; Frank Tannenbaum, who led the
unemployed; William Z. Foster and his Chicago Syndicalists.

The Wobblies were the most vulnerable target of patriotic
wrath even prior to 1917–1918, when they were smashed by government repression. Both as underdogs and activists, this group
earned Eastman's affection; but its "sentimental leftism" occasionally discomforted him, possibly because, as Daniel Aaron has suggested, he sensed a touch of it in himself. But as militants, the
Wobblies came closest to his ideal of "revolutionary unionism"; as
direct activists, they evoked his appreciation and sympathy. He
had been pleased when their leader, Bill Haywood, was elevated
to the Socialist's National Executive Committee; and he opposed
the February, 1913, decision to recall him. "My first political
utterance," Eastman declared, "was a defense of the IWW and an
attack on Article VI of the [Socialist] Party constitution under
which he had been expelled." This defense took the form of a
letter to the *Call* on May 29, 1912, in which Eastman advocated
"sabotage and violence" as "excellent tactics in the fight of an oppressed class." He remained aggressively sympathetic toward the

"red" element who defected from the party in substantial numbers after June, 1912; and his heroes were often Syndicalists rather than Socialists.[22]

Eastman's responses were unusually consistent. Since 1912, if not earlier, he had been singularly impressed by the Wobblies, by their vitality and courage. They belonged to "the only genuinely proletarian organization that ever existed in America—one of the few that ever existed anywhere," he thought; and their leader, Bill Haywood, was not of the "blessed-are-the-meek" variety of-Socialist. He and his followers, Eastman believed, embodied "a kind of extreme outpost of the socialist movement." [23] The direction of Eastman's own radicalism was toward party activists, derived as it was from the marriage of Nietzschean thought and an experiential mystique. Consequently, militant class struggle, the fighting workers, the syndicalist faith in individualist acts of sabotage, the charisma and heroism of labor leaders of the Haywood type, and doctrines such as the complete expropriation of the means of production exerted an enormous appeal.

The *Masses'* columns, it followed, supported "every agitator who really intended to overthrow capitalism and inaugurate a working class millenium in the United States. . . ." Eastman himself crossed the river into Paterson; he defended Frank Tannenbaum, then a militant Wobbly organizer who had been arrested for leading a march of the unemployed; he also helped the Rangel-Cline Defense Committee which was seeking funds for "fourteen innocent and penniless men . . . in danger of execution and death for preaching the gospel of industrial democracy in our state of Texas"; he railed against the doctrine of criminal conspiracy, by which such Wobblies as Herman Suhr and Richard ("Blackie") Ford were jailed for life for their part in the Wheatlands Riot, "although nobody in the world knows who fired the fatal shots and nobody testified that either of these men fired a shot." [24] He declared: "This is Justice under the republic as it is meted out to the poorest classes—the nomadic, unskilled laborers that are unorganized, and must be kept unorganized because they are hungry, and the hungry are dangerous when they travel in a pack." [25]

The pages of the *Masses* celebrated the IWW struggles in lumber, oil, construction, and the wheatfields. From its columns, Joseph Freeman recalled, "we learned about the strike in the coal fields of West Virginia which was brutally crushed" and about Wobbly activities in the Northwest where "a real struggle for democracy" had developed.[26] John Reed described the "war" in Paterson, where "all the violence was on one side—that of the mill owners," and Eastman described Wilson's "Prussian procedure" for the magazine's readers: lumbermen, he asserted, were "being persecuted by a military government and strictly for military reasons." But this sin was only one of many against Wilson's name; he failed to act when "the industrial Junkers" who controlled Arizona deported over fifteen hundred Bisbee and Jerome miners; he had "taken the most drastic action [in the Northwest] conceivable under our institutions on the side of and in defense of the notorious plutocrats of that section."

Touring Colorado's striking districts during the memorable warfare in that state's coal fields, Eastman visited the Ludlow scene directly after the "massacre" and walked the violence-stained streets of Trinidad. Events there inspired him to write with the passion of a man who had been seared. Reporting on the "Battle of Ludlow," he condemned "the Rockefeller interests for acts of tyranny, exploitation, and contempt of the labor laws of Colorado." He invested transcendent meaning in "that black orgy of April 20th, when a frail fluttering tent city in the meadow, the dwelling place of 120 women and 273 children was riddled to shreds without a second's warning"; when "flags of truce were shot out of hands"; when "women running in the sunlight to rescue their children were whipped back with the hail of a machine gun"; when "little girls who plunged into a shed for shelter were followed there with forty-eight calibre bullets." This brawl was no local one, Eastman perceived:

The commanding generals are not here, the armies are not here—only the outposts. A temporary skirmish here of that great conflict which is drawing up on two sides the greatest forces of the republic—those same "money interests" that have crushed and abolished organized labor. . . . The strike in Colorado does not pay—in Colorado. It is a deliberately extravagant campaign to kill down the Mine Workers' Union, kill it here and drain and damage it all over the country. And you will neither know nor imagine what happened at Trinidad, until you can see hanging above it the shadows of these national powers contending.[27]

The Colorado articles proved that Eastman was a superb reporter. For example, we have the portrait "of the young Italian mother, Mrs. Petrucci, who survived her babies in that death-hole at Ludlow—sweet, strong, slender-fingered, exquisite Italian Mother-of-God! If there is more fineness or more tenderness in the world than dwells in those now pitifully vague and wandering eyes, I have lived without finding it." Yet he could be firmly unsentimental, as when recording his "true conviction that the purpose to shoot, slaughter, and burn at Ludlow was absolutely deliberate and avowed in the mines and the camps of the militia; that it was an inevitable outcome of the temper of contemptuous race and class-hatred, the righteous indignation of the slave driver, with which these mineowners met the struggle of their men for freedom; and that upon the strikers' side is to be found both more of the gentleness and more of the understanding that are supposed to be fruits of civilization, than upon the mineowners'." [28]

Eastman did not exclusively limit his sympathies to the Wobblies; he unhesitatingly embraced labor's cause at every opportunity. Declaring war *à outrance* against those who attacked the oppressed, he assailed judicially granted injunctions against picketing; he tore apart the prosecution and the chamber of commerce for the "San Francisco Frame-up" of Warren Billings and Tom Mooney; he scored "the godly and respectable of Calumet [Indiana] who hired a gang to beat up the president of the Western Federation of Miners"; he urged the *Masses* readers to "go over to Paterson and fight for the life and liberty of Pat Quinlan . . . who is under a seven-year jail sentence for opening his mouth during a strike." [29] Thus Eastman supported every radical element: Wobblies in Lawrence, anarchists in San Diego, the Indianapolis iron workers, Louisiana's lumbermen, the coal miners of West Virginia—where "United States Steel is out to kill organized labor and organized labor is out to fight for life." [30]

Of Mother Jones, that "saintliest woman," he charged that her eviction from Trinidad at bayonet point transgressed traditional democratic values. It was, he exclaimed, "Violation of liberty, violation of age, of womanhood, of heroism! Violation of constitutional rights! Violation of everything that anybody with a thread of human feeling holds sacred. Violation, uniformed, brass-

buttoned, armed, and sanctioned by us all." [31] This was class justice, he declared; and he expressed a Wobbly-like disbelief in the
possibility of equitable judicial treatment. He urged that legal
inequities be eliminated. "If you want to prove that there is justice
for the poor in this country," he asserted, "don't prosecute a rich
man who happens to be down, but come and do something when
a poor man is being railroaded to jail." [32]

IV *Anti-War Views*

The *Masses* columns also assumed an increasingly anti-war and
anti-military coloration. Its gorge rose against "bloodthirsty ministers"; "War-mongering Christians"; and, as John Reed stated,
"unscrupulous patriots" such as Theodore Roosevelt. Its cartoons
were graphically pacifist—at least as related to the present war:
one cut showed Christ in prison, with greedy profiteers celebrat-
ing the event; another, virgins leaving for inland strongholds to
avoid rape by possible invaders. Eastman elsewhere claimed that
both sides indulged in atrocities, that "every nation in every war
has violated international law," that none had exclusive claim to
the charge of being militaristic, that all have "their stereotyped
egotisms," that there is no such thing as German militarism.

In seeking to explain hostilities, he wavered, as we have seen,
between two contrary causative factors: man's "hereditary instinctive reaction" and socialist-endorsed commercial conflict. Whatever his final choice, and it was not clearcut, he moved toward the
support of those voices who spoke for peace. Hence he attacked
Congress for its failure to stand firm against those who were
propelling the nation toward war. Hence he praised Bob LaFol-
lette—"the one man in the Senate . . . who is not afraid" and
who had affirmed that this nation "favors peace with Germany
upon the terms that Russia has proposed"; and, with growing
fervor, he attacked conscription and America's entry into the conflict.[33]

War, Eastman prophetically declared, "is the destroyer of liberty. And therefore," he continued, "those who are entirely loyal
to the hope of liberty, and to the rights of human life as they may
some day be truly conceived, will refuse to be carried into war
and the warlike passion of nationalism. They will be neutral

whether the government goes to war or not. They will not enlist in the army of the government, and they will not renounce their independence of judgment." [34]

Toward the end of spreading this gospel of neutrality, Eastman "enthusiastically" supported the American Union against Militarism, a pacifist-inspired organization which his sister helped to organize and which included Lilian Wald as chairman and, among others, Oswald Garrison Villard, John Hayne Holmes, and Stephen Wise. Becoming active after America and Germany severed diplomatic relations in February, 1917, it sought to influence the press, lobbied in congress against conscription and against war, and urged President Wilson to avoid "any ignominious eleventh-hour participation in a struggle for mastery which is not our own." [35] Combining their energies, its leaders, Eastman included, met with Bryan, on February 28, 1917, in a vain effort to turn Congress and the chief executive from open participation overseas.

In a very real sense it was paradoxical of Eastman, a champion of the view that man was inherently bellicose, to enlist in an antiwar organization; yet in another sense, as befitting the dissident strains of Romantic thought, it was inevitable. Afer all, the American Union against Militarism included his influential sister; it was Socialist-tinged; it displayed an informed vigilance in libertarian matters; and it had become a highly vocal anti-militarist lobby.

The *Masses*, meanwhile, launched an offensive against the "intellectual class," symbolized by the editors of the *New Republic*, because they helped draw America into war.[36] Charging them with "intellectualized lust," Eastman added that the *New Republic* had a mission; it was "War on Germany and Anglo-American Imperialism—Victory without Peace." [37] These wry comments are significant, for Eastman had levelled his guns at the creative intelligence, personalized most completely in John Dewey who had, after some hesitation, become fully committed to American participation by April, 1917. While not openly attacking Dewey, as did another of his disciples, Randolph Bourne, Eastman had begun to slash at Herbert Croly, Walter Lippmann, Walter Weyl, among others.

Eastman had traveled a good distance with the advanced Progressive leadership. Like Dewey, Steffens, Ben Lindsey, Jane Addams, Norman Thomas, and Amos Pinchot, he had voted for

Wilson in 1916. His desertion of the President was studded with reservations and with vacillating commentary. Like the creative intelligence generally, he was also prepared to believe the best of Wilson. We have, for instance, Eastman's approval of the President's message to Congress (in May, 1918) which seemed pacifist in tone.

Though the *Masses'* anti-war and anti-administration tone sometimes wavered, it was, for the most part, candidly opposed to Wilsonian foreign policy. Its own fate was prefigured with the rising incidence of Socialist publications which were denied the mails by Postmaster General Burleson. The publication must have anticipated serious difficulties; after all, as Art Young recalled, "because of its pitiless reporting . . . , the magazine had earlier been barred from the reading rooms of many libraries, ousted from the subway and elevated news stands in New York, and refused by the large distributing companies of Boston and Philadelphia. . . ." [38] By June, 1917, its editorials and cartoons had become intolerable to administration spokesmen; and it was only a matter of time before the monthly was banned under the Espionage Act. This June issue, though not suppressed, furnishes a good example of the kind of radical and pacifist material that had already been suppressed. It was devoted almost entirely to a tirade against patriotism, conscription, the President, the war. One article argued that "a war must be fought with lies." Wilson, John Reed claimed, had "mock-idealistic pretexts for going to war"; and, he continued, "the masses of America will not enlist, and [therefore] . . . conscription must be used." He categorically stated: "This is Woodrow Wilson's and Wall Street's war." [39]

Eastman, in the lead article, contributed "Advertising Democracy"—in which he claimed: "This is not a war for democracy. It did not originate in a dispute about democracy, and it is unlikely to terminate in a democratic settlement. There is a bare possibility that a victory of the Allies will hasten the fall of the autocracies in Central Europe, but there is a practical certainty that in trimming for such a victory the Allies will throw out most of the essence of their own democracy. We will Prussianize ourselves and we will probably not democratize Prussia." [40]

V   Masses *Banned;* Liberator *Begun*

The administration, Mr. Burleson in particular, gave substance to Eastman's charge that the United States will become Prussianized. The Postmaster General lost all patience with the *Masses* in August 1917 when it appealed for defense funds for the anarchists Alexander Berkman and Emma Goldman, and urged immediate repeal of the Conscription Act. He conferred with Solicitor General Lamar, the Attorney General, and with Judge Advocate General Crowder, and then ordered the New York City Postmaster— T. G. Patten—not to accept this issue for mailing. The September and later issues were also denied second-class mailing privileges, thereby joining other Socialist and radical journals and newspapers banned by an official with almost unlimited power to deal with the stream of supposedly seditious publications. Only two additional numbers of the *Masses* appeared—an October and a November-December issue—and their sale was limited to newsstands. The government had literally killed it.

Four months later, in April, 1918, at a time when the *Liberator* was already in its second issue, the formal death blow was struck —as the editors and former contributors to the August, 1917, issue were indicted under the Espionage Act. The subsequent trial and the second trial, both of which ended with the jurors in hopeless disagreement, have been vividly described elsewhere.[41] Suffice it to say that the government desisted from additional efforts to imprison the accused: the question was academic since the war was to end shortly and since the *Masses* had expired.

Its offspring, though less flamboyant than the parent, was the *Liberator*. It devoted more space to economic and political affairs than the *Masses;* but, writes Daniel Aaron, "it still retained much of the old Bohemian intransigence." It continued to *épater le bourgeois*, which was possibly the most constructive gesture Bohemia could make in the 1920's. Eastman himself recognized the common lineage of the publications when he recalled that "we had pursued together four arrogant aims or ideals: freedom of mind and spirit, unqualified truth-telling, proletarian revolution, and state ownership of the means of production." [42]

Considering the last two objectives, it is understandable that the *Liberator* quite naturally opened its columns to pro-Bolshevik

proselytes and harangues. There would be opposition to this policy from Eastman's assistant editors, but he held the reins even
more tightly than before. His power derived from his control,
with Crystal Eastman, of fifty-one percent of the voting stock.
The *Liberator,* therefore, was unlike the *Masses* in not being co-
operatively owned. Nor was the new monthly consistently Socialist.
Its pages were not the product of a single mind; and even its
single minds were sometimes deeply divided. Shortly after the
second trial, for instance, Eastman published a book of verse
which, he confessed, reflected his " 'own too easy taste of freedom
rather than my sense of the world's struggle towards an age and
universe of it. That struggle has always occupied my thoughts, and
often my energies; and yet I have never identified myself with it,
or found my undivided being there. I have found that rather in
individual experience.' " [43]

The *Liberator*'s comprehensiveness, consequently, was like that
of its parent. It included "bourgeois" poetry, verse more radical in
form than in content, reflecting its contributors. It was torn between poetry and politics or, to alter the polarities, between "experience" and revolutionary ideology, a schizophrenic view that
percolated also into its prose and drawings. Its artists also ranged
the entire spectrum of left-of-center opinion and personal commitment; and the *Liberator* printed, in addition to the drawings
of its art editors, those of George Bellows, Robert Henri, George
Grosz, Jo Davidson, and Pablo Picasso. It published Maxwell Bodenheim, the archetypal Bohemian writer, and, conversely, Mike
Gold's "Toward Proletarian Art," which was an early attempt to
formulate a definition of what would become "the most important
critical term among radical literary groups of the early thirties—
'proletarian literature.' " [44]

The *Liberator,* then, lived up to the great tradition of its predecessor; and it was, as Eastman declared in the opening issue, "distinguished by a complete freedom in art and poetry and fiction
and criticism." [45] But once again he officially shunned the rampant
Bohemianism of the times; he published responsible social criticism and commentary for the most part: Reed on "Red Russia,"
the Wobbly trial in Chicago, the first account of Haywood's conversion to Communism, the Spartacist revolt in Germany, the
Bela Kun regime in Hungary, the Palmer raids in America, the
war aims of Bolshevik Russia. Regarding the last, Eastman, as we

have noted, disappointed many readers by noting the similarity of
Russian aims (immediate peace without annexation or indemni-
ties) to Wilson's, an observation which, after all, could be defended as consistent with the monthly's proclaimed hostility to
"dogma and rigidity of mind."

This flexibility and spaciousness of outlook disappeared early in
1921, when the original editorial board disintegrated. The generation of Eastman and Reed was passing; and younger men, future
Communist ideologues, began to guide the monthly. Under
their direction, as Walter Rideout has observed, the *Liberator's*
"contents showed a steadily decreasing concern with art in any
form." The decade of revolt ended in October, 1924, when the
magazine combined with William Z. Foster's *Labor Herald* and
with *Soviet Russia Pictorial* to form the propaganda organ, *Communist Monthly,* owned by the Communist party and edited
by Earl Browder, the party's future general secretary.

CHAPTER 6

The Bolshevik Cause, 1917–1921

THE *Liberator,* Eastman concluded long after the event, hardly made "a dent on the cultural history of the United States. Few now can imagine what an insular, irrelevant, hole-in-the-corner thing socialism was in the America of those days." [1] Whatever the publication's ultimate significance, this failure was hardly apparent in 1918–1920. For one thing, the magazine's circulation hovered around fifty thousand for some years, which was more than twice that of its predecessor; for another, the new generation of radicals was turning to it rather than to the *New Republic* or to the *Dial.* These radicals, looking for leadership, turned to Eastman, perhaps the best-known literary radical in America, rather than to Walter Lippmann, Kenneth Burke, or Van Wyck Brooks.

Eastman's very presence seemed to generate conflict and exacerbate tender feelings. For example, we have his celebrated quarrel with Brooks and the divisive effect of his support of Wilson in 1916. Eastman had praised the President's treatment of Japan's proposed invasion of Siberia, Wilson's refusal to declare war in order to protect overseas investments, his treatment of conscientious objectors, his congressional messages "that have shocked the Allied imperialists and astonished the world." [2]

Thus Eastman once again flirted with the nationalist-progressive position endorsed by the Dewey-Lippmann-Croly axis, as well as by some of his erstwhile Socialist colleagues who had supported the administration's war program. But, unlike them, he had not been seriously compromised; he had never been deceived into believing that Wilson was leading the nation into a "war to end wars"; he never endorsed the *New Republic*'s "war program for liberals" or Dewey's belief that the war had weakened "the intellectual supports of reactionary conservatism"; he had not engaged in the liberals' self-deception—their insistence that the war

[73]

should be used, in the classic utilitarian tradition, as "an aggressive tool of democracy," as the *New Republic* had stated. He concluded in 1921, clearly referring to such lapses in judgment, "although men's hearts are in the right place, they need guidance to
prevent the lapse into bourgeois romantic sentimentalism." [3]

Eastman's attitude toward Wilson slowly hardened, because of
two developments: the war-time repression, which spilled over
into the post-war period; and the Bolshevik Revolution (and
America's reaction to it) which played an axial role in Eastman's
life. Regarding the former, he felt that, since the war was over,
"no excuse remains for patriotic societies to continue exercising
the powers of policemen, for the Post Office to deny the mailing
privilege to socialist magazines, for cities to pass ordinances pe-
nalizing the display of the red flag, for indiscriminate arrests, jail-
ings and prosecutions against men who wish to bring the United
States forward into her true place in the march of the nations
toward liberty." [4] He demanded the release of "all the political
and industrial prisoners"—Mooney, Debs, Emma Goldman, Alexander Berkman, the Wobblies, and the pacifists. In a number of
ways, Eastman charged, Wilson had actively or tacitly suspended
the Constitution during wartime; by denying the writ of habeas
corpus to "anti-War agitators," by permitting conscientious objectors to be tortured, by depriving the Wobblies of the rights of a
defendant "through a conspiracy between the Post Office and the
Department of Justice," by deporting pro-Bolshevik agitators, by
imprisoning Debs and "hundreds of other social idealists," by
waging a private war against Russia, by conscripting citizens for
war on foreign soil, and by assuming Congress's powers. [5]

Referring to the deportation of Russian aliens and anarchists on
the *S.S. Buford,* the "Soviet Ark," Eastman added to this bill of
particulars, scoring the "deliberate shipping back . . . of a boat-
load of unsubmissive slaves." This event signalled the end "of the
Myth of American Freedom"; it exploded "the romance that
has hypnotized Europe for a hundred years, and that made
Woodrow Wilson's great sanctimonious international swindle
possible." Those opposed to tyranny, he affirmed, were now
turning to Russia, which gave asylum to all who were being
persecuted on account of political or religious convictions. [6] Writing of the post-war round-ups, mob actions, and deportations,
Eastman concluded that "the ruling class of the United States is

more intolerant, more ruthless and brutal, more inconsiderate of the rights of men and of families" than England's or even Germany's.[7]

These illegal and extra-legal measures, however, had been earlier found execrable—at a time when Wilson's efforts to avoid war, to bring peace, to establish the League of Nations evoked praise. Presidential policy toward Bolshevik Russia was the turning point for Eastman. He had markedly shifted by March, 1919, when he constructed an imaginary dialogue between Lenin and Wilson which was prefaced by a sharply critical observation on Wilson's conduct. "His speeches and writings," Eastman acerbically declared, "are always on a plane so far above the ordinary prepossessions of men as to suggest the meditations of a God, and yet his conduct is shrewd and opportunistic in the extreme. The sharpest possible contrast to this unctious and Victorian mode of speech is supplied" in Russia; and then followed the inventive dialogue between the two leaders, in which Wilson's idealistic platitudes were found to be no match for the hard, "deadly candid" facts offered by Lenin, the scientific engineer.[8]

I *Post-War Europe*

Eastman's earlier fervor for the League had diminished sharply by May, 1919, mainly because Wilson's federation would exclude the Soviet Union. For Eastman, therefore, it would merely be an "imperialist alliance of the Five Victorious Allies" and "a conspiracy against the liberties of mankind." Certainly no Socialist could support it. In December, 1918, Eastman categorically charged that the proposed league was a "capitalist International" which would become a "gigantic strikebreaking agency" against socialist revolutions. Five months later, he bitterly and scornfully rejected Wilson's ideal: "Better no movement of the governments whatever [he declared], than this deliberate attempt to settle and establish empire amid the instinctive beginnings of international consciousness."

Equally the target of obloquy was Allied intervention in Bela Kun's Hungary, which was seen as comparable to earlier German actions: "They are raiding and slaughtering the people of Hungary in the same deliberate manner and for the same desperate purpose. Remember with what horror we read only a year ago

that the Germans were 'closing in on Petrograd' . . . in violation
of an armistice. . . . Remember how these Germans were played
up . . . as dishonorable robbers and butchers of men. . . . Do
we have to be instructed that the Allied Governments, too, are
dishonorable robbers and butchers of men?"

Allied intervention in Russia was also condemned in the strongest terms, with Wilson's "disinterested idealism" coming under
fierce attack. Likening the President to Lloyd George, Clemen-
ceau, and the Mikado—all "champions of democracy," Eastman
sarcastically added—he accused the Allies of shipping arms and
soldiers to Admiral Kolchak "to do murder in support of the cor-
rupt and bloody regime of the Czar." In a bellicose speech at Har-
lem Casino in October, 1918, Eastman maintained that it was "un-
lawful for Woodrow Wilson to invade Russia." The Constitution,
he maintained, "nowhere delegates to the executive branch of the
government the right to ship citizens out of the country, and half-
way round the earth, to wage war on a foreign power *without* a
declaration of war by the representatives of the people. . . ."

II *Eastman and Russian Communism*

The intensity of Eastman's commitment to Bolshevism is measured by his willingness to go on tour in the winter of 1919 to plead
for an Allied withdrawal from Russia. He had the characteristic
good fortune to obtain decoded letters from Undersecretary of
State Frank Polk to Secretary of State Robert Lansing, informing
the American delegation at Versailles that Congress was opposed
to Russian intervention. After revealing these letters to "6,000
shouting Reds at Madison Square Garden," as *The New York
Times* reported, Eastman delivered them to Oswald Garrison Villard for publication in the *Nation*. These letters, together with
Lenin's "Last Testament" which he published, did more to popu-
larize Max Eastman than any other single task that he undertook.[9]

Eastman's efforts in behalf of the fledgling Soviet state were entirely consistent and in marked contrast to putative liberals, such
as the *New Republic*'s editors, who found it difficult to understand
the Russian revolution and who offered only perfunctory tributes
to it. For Eastman, the rise of Bolshevism confirmed his radical
optimism, gave greater density to the cherished values of improvi-
sation and experimentation, and also prefigured "the dawn of so-

cial revolution" in Germany.[10] Like the left-wing of the Peoples Council of America, which supported the Petrograd peace proposals, Eastman urged American attendance at the Soviet-sponsored international conference of Socialists in Stockholm. And, unlike many liberals, he was hardly dejected when the more moderate Kerensky government collapsed and the Bolsheviks triumphed. Eastman appeared equally untroubled at the prospect of Russia's withdrawal from the war. Nor did he lament when Brest-Litovsk confirmed liberal anxieties. The treaty that was promulgated there proved a convulsive shock for many liberal journalists who had sought to save Russia for war and for the West. By 1918, however, Eastman had permanently defected from the rush of liberals and quondam Socialists to Communism.

Eastman's was an unqualified defense of the Soviet Union, including denial of any acts of terror attributed to the Bolsheviks. Considering the situation there, and "the comparative seriousness of the crimes being committed, there is a more unscrupulous reign of terror in this country" than in Russia.[11] Besides this mitigating factor, he added, the Bolshevik terror was the direct result of Allied invasion. It was to be understood if not excused when one considers that "in Russia the most just, wise, humane, and democratic government that ever existed was growing into maturity." The United States had no such justification.

III *The Red Scare*

Everything Eastman observed in these years, even developments unconnected with affairs abroad, supported such conclusions. Shortly after the *Masses* second trial, for example, in September, 1918, he went to Cleveland for the *Liberator* to report Debs's trial. Debs and Haywood were Eastman's twin touchstones in the American labor movement; they were the "true revolutionists," as distinct from traditional unionists, such as Samuel Gompers with his "school-ma'am's manner." [12] Eastman, who had met Debs briefly in the *Masses* office, likened that meeting to a "sacrament." His report of the Cleveland trial sharply contrasted the defendant—the "spiritual chief and hero of American socialism"—with Judge D. C. Westenhaver, "a representative of corporate capital"; with the jury, "about seventy-two years old, worth fifty to sixty thousand dollars, retired from business"; and with the prosecutor, Edwin Wertz, jowled and sharp-nosed, "an ungainly, greasy" man with a high whine in his voice.

For Eastman "the religion of socialism" was composed of twin passions: struggle and love. Debs, to be sure, knew how to fight; but "his genius is for love—the ancient real love, the miracle love, that utterly identifies itself with the emotions and the needs and wishes of others. . . . And that is why Debs has so much greater power than many who are more astute and studious of the subtleties of politics and oratory. And that is why Debs was convicted of a crime. . . ." [13] Debs conducted his own defense, Eastman reported, and with "intense magnetic precision"; yet he rested his case on prophecy—upon events that had not occurred. "And he chose well," Eastman stated, "for he *is* a prophet, and there is more than a chance that events will fulfill his utterance, and make him remembered not only as the most beautiful character in contemporary America, but as one of the most wise."

Such trials and convictions, the deepening stain of repression, accelerated Eastman's devolution from part-time advocate of Wilsonism to full-time critic. His speaking tour in the early winter of 1919, undertaken in the midst of the Red Scare, found Eastman at his magnificent best as speaker and radical publicist. In Butte, he addressed striking workers; in Seattle, then in the midst of a general strike, he spoke to "a 'mob' of proletarian thousands in the public square." [14] The *Buford*'s departure on December 21, 1919; the congressional measure of October, 1919, which made anarchists—philosophical or otherwise—deportable; Creel's documents purporting to show that Socialists and Wobblies were pro-German agents; the Palmer raids; Debs's ordeal in Cleveland; the two trials of Eastman himself, and of Charles Ruthenberg and I. E. Ferguson, two Communists who went to prison "for the best years of their lives"—all these events accomplished what the war itself was unable to do. [15] These events provided a liberating shock which left Eastman's energy and imaginative brilliance unimpaired and which gave him a cause—one of the very few in the long trajectory of his life—that he believed unqualifiedly "right." The entire world seemed to be in the throes of incipient or actual revolution. Reports from Germany, Hungary, and elsewhere provided inspirational reading in these immediate post-war years. They offered reassurance about the value of nonconformism under capitalism and the inevitability of an alternate economic order. They convinced him that the Bolsheviks were prophets of a new age.

IV *Other Concerns*

Eastman became more combative, more querulous, more critical than ever. "Withdraw the invading armies" became the battle cry. Permit the Bolshevik state to survive was the plea. The *Liberator*'s column were dotted with odes to Lenin and to Russia. Radical history had clearly altered since the fabled years of the *Masses:* there was the fact of Revolution; and it was something one could not merely watch, one could fight for it. Thus the *Liberator,* while apparently the scion of a famous father—being similar in format, articles, and editorials—was really quite different. There was now a major focal point—the Soviet Union—and it gave sustenance to radical thought.[16] Appearing more often than in the gaily irreverent *Masses* was a note of high moral seriousness that blended into messianism and smacked of the *odium theologicum* that Eastman usually found deplorable.

Eastman may have thought of himself as rigidly scientific, since anything less was to be avoided; but his response to events in Russia was as emotional as it was all-consuming. Moreover, it led him at times to highly expedient solutions. We note, for instance, his willingness to scandalize the anti-war Socialists by proposing that they "join the British Labor Party and the Socialists of France, Italy, and Belgium in endorsing President Wilson's war aims." Loyalty to the cause of Russian socialism rather than to Wilsonian policies prompted him: the St. Louis anti-war program of the Socialist party "bears no relation to a world in which there exists a Soviet Republic in danger of annihilation." [17]

Russia was not the only concern; there was also politics. Eastman compounded a reputation for opportunism in 1920 by endorsing General Leonard Wood, the candidate of "the great American party of Big Business" for the Presidency. Recognizing that Wood was "an ideal" "antediluvian," Eastman nonetheless thought him preferable to Wilson by this time.[18] Developments within the Socialist party were even more fascinating. In 1918, he urged a new program for the party, one which would avoid utopian platitudes and include planks supporting Wilson's Fourteen Points and recognition of the Soviet Union. He duly noted the party's post-war decline, as the old moderate leadership of Hillquit and Berger was left behind by events. But he did so as a spectator only.[19] Eastman remained the speculative radical, avoiding participation in any organizational effort. His concerns were never wholly bound up with the fate of labor or of the Communist movement.

In spite of the heart's pull toward activism, he had urged "united class-conscious voting" rather than dynamite or the "philosophical anarchism" of Steffens and Hapgood. But, words and formulas notwithstanding, his ideal was the Socialist who "loved freedom more than . . . a well-organized economy" or, he might have added, an organized political party. His radicalism was primarily devoted to the "right of the individual in the universe." He never took out membership in the Communist Labor party, though he endorsed it during that party's brief existence. "I behaved," he later confessed, "as though my interest in values that are timeless—like scientific truth and poetry—exempted me from even the momentous battles that were being fought to a finish in the time in which I lived." In all of this, he was being perfectly true to himself—to his insistence upon the "free" and spontaneous life. There was, to be sure, a price to be paid—a feeling of inadequacy and of guilt. His speaking tour of 1917, for instance, was important partly because it offered a "chance to back up all the bold revolutionary things I had been saying in the Masses for the last five years." [20]

But there was another side to Eastman, the non-conforming individualist: that of the Romantic revolutionary who was stirred beyond himself by the Bolshevik experiment, who placed a high value on activism, and who endorsed the Chicago program of the new Communist party because, among other things, it was "a vital, simple and realistic application of the theories of Marx" and because it was "written in a more American idiom . . . , in the language of action." The Russian revolution became activism channelled, directed, triumphant, the one fixed star to which he always returned—partly as relief from the sibling rivalries that confronted him, the dismal burrowing underground of domestic radicalism, the very ugliness of the Red Scare which made the

Soviet Union, by contrast to America, "the most just, wise, humane and democratic government that ever existed." [21]

V *View of Lenin*

Hardly tangential to the *Liberator*'s concern with Russian affairs was its devoted interest in Lenin who, in Eastman's eyes, was "the super statesman"—by which he meant "a man who possesses the exhaustive knowledge of a technical authority in economics, politics and social psychology." He was a master organizer, Eastman declared, a genius of revolutionary engineering. He possessed the heroic virtues, those qualities embodied in George Forbes: militancy, acuity, a seeing-things-straight quality, the power of decision. A leader of rare force, stability, and revolutionary judgment, Lenin was, in short, the superman in politics.[22]

Lenin was "a very great statesman," Eastman persistently affirmed, "the revolutionary general," the "man whose orders are carried out," and "who knows the true relation between facts and ideas in scientific thinking." This last capability was, we are reminded, highly valued by Eastman; and, in mentioning it, he again celebrated the athletic and again indicated his antipathy to speculative thought. Lenin, he emphasized, was "without dogmatic fixations of mind and without those emotional habits which make it so difficult for the man of action to be a philosopher." [23] "Relentless, unsentimental, iron-minded," Lenin was the epitome of the pragmatic thinker. His "ideas were never fixed," Eastman declared.[24]

Lenin divided men of ideas into camps, expelling "without mercy those in whom ideas do not mean action." [25] He confronted all dogmas and turned away from all absolutes; he ignored "a vast clutter of medieval intellectual rubbish"; he cleared away the thicket of metaphysics and historical determinism.[26] As a result, he urged the Russian people "to . . . give all their mind's attention to the definition of the present problems, and all their heart's energies to the kind of action that is demanded now." [27] Moreover, Lenin ignored "this metaphysical conception"—dialectical materialism—"in which he formally believed," and made "practical politics" and contemporary "conditions" the stars to steer by. To be "realistic" as Lenin was, "to think in a concrete situation," and to avoid enslavement to past experience or philosophical immutables meant, for Eastman, to be scientific—to uphold "experience" and to avoid intellectuality; and these qualities, of course, were Eastman's *beau idée*.

Eastman's vignettes of Lenin, therefore, reflected his own prejudices and heroic values. They also suggested the shock of recognition. For Lenin was considered an intellectual comrade of John Dewey, "the first clear teacher of the instrumental character of true thinking." [28] Both shared a "hard-headed idealism" in common. Lenin, "the most pragmatic in his mental operation of anyone who ever attained distinction in the socialist movement . . . reminded me," confessed Eastman, "very startlingly of my teacher in philosophy, John Dewey." [29] He had Dewey's—and Eastman's—willingness to break with the past, reject traditional habits, try new methods, make a future to order. Emphasis was placed by Eastman upon Lenin's elasticity, his "practical intelligence," his insistence upon action. "Less concerned about being philosophic," Russia's leader understood dialectics as "an instrument of temporary struggle." [30] At last, Eastman asserted, "the instrumental theory of knowledge . . . was actively understood." [31]

This view of Lenin as revolutionary superman, as possessed of a "will to power" derived in part from Eastman's undisguised Nietzscheanism. The "fighting mentality" of the Bolsheviki, which America's radicals had to acquire if they were truly to serve the revolution and which Eastman so admired, also was rooted in Nietzsche's thought. Belief in such thought slopped over into other areas; for example, Eastman had a tilt with Bertrand Russell who had once defended the Communists and their methods. Writing in the *Liberator,* of May, 1920, Russell stated: "when I speak of Socialists, I do not mean a milk-and-water system, but a thorough-going, root-and-branch transformation, such as Lenin had attempted." [32] But Russell, after visiting Russia, expressed reservations described in the *Nation:* concentration of power, violation of basic freedoms. Eastman replied in a six-page defense of Lenin and Bolshevism which was drenched in Nietzschean thought. Nietzsche, he declared, would be an antidote for the soft-headed idealists who feared life. He hailed Nietzsche's *The Antichrist* as "a great book; it taught ruthless practicality and had immediacy for the present revolutionary struggle. It was "a book that stands up and will be visible for centuries. And if I were presiding over a course of study in communism. I would begin by asking every member of my class to read it." [33] Had Nietzsche lived, Eastman further declared, he would have realized that his belief in the superman was verified by the "Nietzschean Bolsheviks." He had opposed German Socialists in his day because he believed them soft and decadent; the Bolsheviks would have changed his mind.

Bertrand Russell, Eastman avowed, represented the type whom Nietzsche always opposed; a sentimentalist who inevitably was "'wounded and shocked'" by Bolshevik realism. "He [Russell] presents to us," Eastman continued, "the bourgeois idea that 'kindliness and tolerance are worth all the creeds in the world.'" Scoring Russell for such decadent ideas—which found their "'true world'" in metaphysical speculation, democracy, and the soft ethics of Christianity—Eastman also ridiculed him for being surprised that the Bolsheviks were not Western philosophers. No, he told Russell, they were not social democrats, trade union officials, or Y.M.C.A. workers. They had, on the other hand, created an aristocracy of brains and character which was ruthlessly efficient. "In short they are Nietzeschean *free spirits,* and not Christian saints. Beware of them!" To Eastman, Lenin's description of them "could be almost a quotation" from one of Nietzsche's claims for the "'new mobility.'" They were the revolutionary vanguard; as such, they were realistic and unsentimental fighters who worked sixteen hours a day, lived austerely, and were dedicated to the creation of a new order and a new type of man. These were practices and goals to be copied, stated Eastman, who dismissed Russell as "a humanitarian bourgeois professor"—in sharp contrast to Lenin, who was "dictatorial, calm, incapable of fear, extraordinarily devoid of self-seeking, an embodied theory . . . , an intellectual aristocrat." [34]

CHAPTER 7

The Pilgrimage of a Radical

EASTMAN, writing retrospectively, has denied that he left for Russia in the spirit of a pilgrim; he later asserted that his trip was "in a mood of inquiry." But everything that he had said and done before debarking in early March, 1922, suggests that the trip eastward was in a properly symbolic direction. He had insisted, after all, that the Russians had at last found the answers, that Communism represented a qualitative advance for the human spirit, that "the undistinguished, the workers of Russia," as he wrote in April, 1918, were determined to establish "a republic of free labor." Three years later, all the terrors notwithstanding—and he admitted to "a reign of terror" as early as December, 1918—" 'the Russian Revolution remains the supreme social achievement of mankind.' " [1]

Given the widespread belief that the Soviet Union offered an eternal *hic et nunc*, such sentiments were entirely understandable. Eastman's belief in some sort of paradisiac fulfillment, which occasionally turned him to primitivism and more often to faith in a highly developed social order, seemed on the threshold of realization. Bureaucratization and terror would shortly provide a contretemps to these convictions; but, in 1922, he persisted in regarding the Russian Revolution as the most vital political experiment of his generation; and he understandably wished to observe it.

Eastman went to Russia as an already convinced spectator. The rapturous narratives of John Reed; the repeated setbacks of American radicalism; the compromises, evasions, and fractures among the Socialists; the admirable contrasting conduct of Russia's emissaries at the International Disarmament Conference in Geneva, which he attended; and his growing enchantment with Bolshevism, so markedly dissimilar to domestic forms of radicalism, prefigured his response to Moscow. He arrived there in August, 1922; and everything seemed to confirm his revolutionary idealism. The

Russian capital itself had disappointed him, to be sure, being "much like any other big city." [2] He was disquieted by the practice of tipping: "there was no tipping in my utopia," he admitted, "no such indecent exposure of class relations was tolerable." [3] But generally he looked at Russian life through the tinted glasses of a traveler who saw what he wished to see; and, consequently, he found in the self-created Socialist society what he had been looking for in America—a model for future life.

I *Early Impressions*

Eastman's reports, it followed, were in the optative mood. If he made a mental note of the economic crisis besetting Russia in this period, he certainly did not commit it to paper. There was nothing on the scissors crisis, the credit restrictions, the famine of 1921 which Russia had just experienced, and the unrest among industrial workers—indeed, the near-dissolution of the state itself.[4] Within six months of Eastman's visit there would be all-round economic improvement, but the Bolsheviks had little to celebrate in August, 1922—not with burgeoning unemployment, the influx of hungry peasant labor into Russia's cities, and the increasingly grave plight of the industrial worker. Eastman, however, was determined to find the revolution successful. He "took all the good things" he saw, "and the familiar things as proof that the collectivist experiment was in the main succeeding. Socialism *did* work." [5]

There was, for instance, his observations on the New Economic Policy, which represented a retreat from War Communism after the Kronstadt rising. It revived certain capitalist elements; introduced a new middle class, contemptuously called "NEP-men"; and sought to replace monetary transactions with payment in kind; and, while productive of an economic revival, it was at a cost most revolutionists would lament—the increasing emphasis upon the peasant at the expense of the industrial worker.[6] But Eastman, wholeheartedly accepting this policy, saw none of these things. NEP, he said, "discourages our American enthusiast . . . because he cannot imagine a bunch of politicians announcing that they were going to produce a socialist economy, and then retreating right down the path away from socialism, without that meaning that they were really abandoning the path." [7] This development, which simply shifted the advance toward Socialism to a different starting point, was the "great political miracle of the revolution."

Given these enthusiasms, Eastman naturally looked uncritically at most things Russian. "No one traveling from Western Europe," he insisted in 1922, "could have failed to receive the impression I did of an abrupt step-up in vitality and health." [8] Even his welcome in Russia sustained earlier opinions. A known supporter of the Bolshevik cause and a friend of John Reed, he naturally had a passport into many inner circles. He met George Grosz in Moscow, Big Bill Haywood, James Cannon, William Z. Foster—"an American I then admired, and liked as a political friend"—and Martin Anderson Nexø.[9]

As a known sympathizer of the Bolshevik revolution and as a foreign delegate to the Fourth Congress of the Third International, Eastman had entrée into nearly all Bolshevik circles. He witnessed a meeting of "a revolutionary soviet" in Moscow, and it further confirmed his faith in the dictatorship of the proletariat. Of this soviet, he wrote: "These hard-handed, iron-minded men out of the factories, who have just laid down their tools to come here and say what they want done—how much more noble and more terrible they are than any sovereign the world has seen before. . . ." [10] And he exulted: "Here is reality. Here are the people who live the hard life of man. And their leaders are the best, the simplest, the strongest—that is all. It is an aristocracy, yes—the rule of the best democrats." [11]

Nothing about these early Russian scenes disillusioned him. The Russian Revolution, more than ever, seemed to be a real revolution, a new beginning, a reconstructing and refounding of a political and social organism.[12] The blood and the violence indubitably shed in its name were justified; after all, the Revolution apparently was "going to change things profoundly, almost absolutely, for the better." [13] No doubt that, as he admitted in 1918, "a number of people have been officially put to death for conspiracy to overthrow the Soviet Government and assassinate its leaders." No doubt, too, "a number . . . have been unofficially put to death by mobs of the Russian people for the same crime. . . ." [14] But all was justifiable: Bolshevism was under attack, and "whatever reign of terror exists in Russia today, and whatever extreme measures may have been taken by the Russian government to protect itself against conspiracies" were permissible. Nothing much had altered four years later; and he admittedly remained enveloped "in a rather opaque cloud of optimistic emotion." [15]

The dominant roles which Eastman gave to activism and to science and, conversely, his rejection of intellection and metaphysics were confirmed by these early firsthand impressions. The Bolsheviks would succeed because they alone approached politics as a science, because they were realistic about present conditions and future prospects, because they were ruthless, but "ruthless on principle—in behalf of a superhuman dream," because their leader was a "bold and passionate man of action" if ever there was one.[16]

Eastman had already watched Georgi Chicherin at Genoa and now, observing the Moscow Soviet, he admired the foreign minister's radical wisdom: Chicherin again spoke "crystal clear in wit and logic" in defense of Russian foreign policies. Bukharin, too, delivered an address, one "witty and rich in satire," subtle and inspiring; and so did Trotsky, whose impact on the crowd was remarkable. "He is a born and inevitable leader of men," Eastman observed, in his earliest known firsthand appraisal of him, that of July, 1923: "There is a mature restraint and wisdom in speech, and yet there is a young and flowing boldness." [17] Eventually, Eastman knew nearly all of them; and he then learned not to trust superficial impressions. But now, in the Moscow of 1923, he was carried along on the exultancy of revolutionary emotion that swept nearly all before it; as a result, he rejected the charge of dogmatism levelled against Lenin or, for that matter, the Bolshevik generally.[18] He held out against Floyd Dell's opinion that the Russian leaders were fanatical, and he continued to assert "that the new spirit they had brought into the movement was 'the spirit of Applied Science, and nothing else.'" [19] And he was more than ever convinced that "their course was leading toward a freer world."

Superficial observation in 1923 left the impression that the Bolsheviks were "like a good-natured family," but closer inspection over the next few years ruined this portrait. Eastman saw them, even before the meeting of the Third International had ended, as a group who moved in a highly charged atmosphere, in which quarrels were bitter, debate intense; but he would not yet comprehend that reconciliations were more apparent than real. He could still admire the entire constellation: Vladimir Antonov-Av-

seenko, Leonid Krassin, Nikolai Krylenko, Grigori Zinoviev, Lev
Kamenev, Yevgeni Preobrazhensky, Maxim Litvinov; the poise
and intellegence of Christian Rakovsky; the "clear ringing voice"
of Georgi Chicherin; the small, inconspicuous-looking Marxian
pile-driver, Nikolai Bukharin; Karl Radek, who was his friend;
Leonid Serebriakov, "a stronger-hearted, honester and braver
man I never knew"; N. I. Muralov, "a genial kind-hearted giant"
who was a hero to him and to all Russia; the "slim, gentle, highly
intellectual, delicately organized" Yuri Piatakov. In fact, they all
"looked friendly and congenial." [20] It was hard not to esteem them
or to imagine their internecine warfare. But, even if they were
bitterly at odds and easily intolerant, they were, for Eastman,
lifted into real significance by the fact of their commitment to the
elimination of social and economic injustice in Russia and elsewhere.

II   *First Gusts of the Storm*

Eastman, it is clear, had no idea that Lenin's relations with
Trotsky were clouded by the latter's refusal to serve on the Council of Peoples' Commissars in April, 1922. Nor was he aware that
such a refusal had provided ammunition to Trotsky's growing
number of enemies, such as Stalin who was now the party's general secretary. As a vice premier, Trotsky might have neutralized
Stalin's power and blunted the burgeoning corruption in the party
and in the state; because he did not serve Lenin became understandably impatient. Trotsky's action left Stalin with greater
power than ever and even implied a personal animus toward
Lenin. In September, 1922, the Politburo censured Trotsky for
dereliction of duty, most probably with Lenin's consent, though
the latter continued to hope Trotsky would accept the vice-pre-
miership.

Lenin had been moved to action by the growing bureaucracy—
by the abuses of power which seemed to be proliferating—and by
a quarrel with Trotsky over Stalin's policy toward the Mensheviks
in Georgia, whom the general secretary had on his own initiative
banned. Investigating Stalin's actions, Lenin learned about the
brutality of Stalin and of his subordinate, Grigori Ordjonikidze;
he discovered that the accusations of "deviation" levelled against
certain Georgians was false; he became greatly unnerved by Sta-

lin's abuse of power; and he was impelled to defend the non-Russian nationalists, such as the Georgians and Ukrainians, against "the great Russian chauvinist . . . [the] coarse brutish bully." [21] When Lenin urged, as he eventually would, the removal of Stalin, Lenin could have had no doubt that such advice would establish Trotsky in the saddle.

Eastman was coming to the same conclusions as Lenin. He also saw the Russian Communist party as a disciplined yet inwardly free group of revolutionaries committed to the maintenance of proletarian democracy. He also was becoming increasingly aware that the growing bureaucracy was a corrupting force and that the central committee might fulfill the cynical and time-honored paradigm that the revolution devours its children. When Trotsky and Stalin became locked in the struggle over Lenin's succession, Eastman reluctantly concluded that infanticide was indeed being committed.

But for the moment, in 1922–1923, Eastman found Trotsky overpoweringly impressive. Soon to know the Russian leader intimately and admit to his faults, he would eventually conclude that "the iron core of his character is a selfless and fearless, and to use just the accurate word for it—saintly, devotion to the revolution.[22] Lenin was aware of these qualities, Eastman claimed: "Lenin always believed in Trotsky. He attacked him violently enough, as he invariably attacked people who he believed were making even temporary mistakes. But he never identified him with the Mensheviks. He never broke with him, as he did with Plekhanov, Martov—with all those whom he felt had gone over, whether consciously or unconsciously, to the side of the bourgeosie. He always regarded Trotsky as one of the real leaders of the Russian revolution, and always thought of him as a comrade in arms." [23] Eastman knew that "Trotsky stood head and shoulders above the other Bolsheviks, both in personal force and revolutionary understanding." [24]

Both Lenin and Trotsky were apprehensive about the new bureaucracy. Upon familiarizing himself with the party infrastructure, Eastman also would see its potential malevolence. But he would never grapple with the dilemma between authority and freedom which confronted both Bolshevik leaders; he would readily opt for the latter, his customary safety valve. His reaction to the Revolution was hopeful, spontaneous, joyously affirmative;

but it was also typical in a uniquely personal way: it was not an organic and complete commitment. Eastman rarely responded viscerally to issues and events for he avoided binding emotional ties—of any sort—in the name of individual expression and individual freedom. He sympathized wholeheartedly with the underdog; he almost never displayed empathy. His Russian experiences represented merely another chapter in the enjoyment of living; it lacked any umbilical connection with his emotional life.

There was always a part of Eastman that remained aloof, a core impervious to external experiences; and such a personality has very special limitations: it usually cannot give of itself with any degree of emotional completeness; it cannot fully experience things independent of itself. Positively, such a person remains sufficiently detached to render objective judgments and to appreciate the "other side" of most issues. With Eastman, this emotional reserve was combined with a lust for knowledge, the *libido sciendi* which theological dogmatists had outlawed and branded as intellectual pride and which made all conclusions tentative and open-ended. Thus he was able to admire the Rimsky Korsakovs for their courageous opposition to the revolution; he could write a novel at Sochi while ruminating over his Moscow impressions; he could be as deeply impressed by nude bathing on the Black Sea as he was by the encounter with Trotsky. And this very aloofness eventually enabled him to see the egregious flaws in Bolshevism before any other American observer.

Even Lenin's death in January, 1924, did not move Eastman deeply. He seemed more concerned about the failure of his novel, owing to a neurotic "inner struggle" with loneliness ("nemophobia," as he diagnosed it). Solicitude for his own psyche while in the Caucasus distracted him from revolutionary affairs; and only upon his return to Moscow, where importunate events confronted him, did Eastman turn from personal concerns.

III   *Eastman's Growing Doubts*

Before he left for the trip down the Volga, Eastman had attended the Twelfth Congress of the Russian Communist Party (April 17–25, 1923) which, he wrote, was "an orphan Congress"—the first one from which Lenin was absent—and "everybody was on his good behavior." [25] Since most of its sessions were devoted to sales and production questions, the entire affair was disappointingly colorless. At least Eastman thought so, for he did not perceive those dark and sullen currents that would mount to floodtide in the coming months. There was general agreement that Lenin, had he attended, "would have 'exploded a bombshell against Stalin,' to use his [Lenin's] own expression." [26] He certainly would have blocked Stalin's road to power, Eastman believed, and opposed his reelection as general secretary.

Zinoviev spoke, Eastman recorded, "a rabble-rouser if there ever was one," and he clubbed Leonid Krassin, a Russian businessman who recently returned from a a trade mission to London; and then Radek, whose "blue eyes . . . were not watery, but clearly penetrating," took up the paddle. The only emotional moments occurred when the delegates rose to sing a hymn in memory of those who died for the revolution and when Trotsky first entered the hall. The latter's speech, consonant with the Congress's tone, was devoted to heavy industry; and he concluded that industrial revival was dependent upon a planned economy. "The ovation to him," Eastman recalled, "had been the big moment of the Congress. . . . Stalin had not shown his hand. Whatever their thoughts, they all looked friendly and congenial."

Eastman could not know of Lenin's pleas that Trotsky take up the cause of the Georgia deviationists and bluntly address the Congress, the body that would help the ruling triumvirs to conceal their fallen leader's damning testament. Nor was he aware that Trotsky, magnanimous owing to a feeling of security, would deliver himself to his enemies by agreeing to Stalin's proposal that he limit his role to that of political *rapporteur* of the Central Committee.

Trotsky also failed to reply to Stalin's open attack upon him at the provincial party conference of mid-January, 1924. Overcome by malarial attacks, physical exhaustion, and intimations of approaching defeat, Trotsky listened to medical advice and set out for the warm Black Sea resorts before the conference ended. Now that he had neglected to take the field against his enemies, they opened up on him in earnest. His failure to return in time for Lenin's funeral further strengthened their hand. Eastman came back to Moscow in March, 1924, in time to witness the last phase of the great debate over Trotsky's letter of December 8th.[27] Agitated by Trotsky's moody aloofness, his retreat from active participation in political affairs, Eastman now condemned his failure of nerve and sharply censured him: "He could command men; he could inspire them to action with great oratory; he could expound the grounds and principles of their action; but he could not manage them. He could not *lead* them. Leadership requires tact and adroit personal understanding as well as magnetism. It requires a certain craftiness which Trotsky lacked altogether." [28]

Eastman having cast off his own vexing emotional problems, to the point of devoting his considerable energies to Russian events, must have been profoundly unnerved by Trotsky's indecisiveness. When Eastman noted, with mingled feelings of anxiety and admiration, Trotsky's avoidance of backstage politics, he concluded that the latter really did not want leadership. Such knowledge was frustrating, for Eastman had become aware of Stalin's growing domination of the party apparatus and of the burgeoning bureaucracy which all his opponents loathed. Writing of this domination, Lenin declared: "Comrade Stalin, having become general secretary, has concentrated enormous power in his hands; and I am not sure that he always knows how to use that power with sufficient caution." [29]

These observations were made on December 25, 1922, nine days after Lenin's second stroke and are part of what is known as Lenin's "testament." Placed beside Lenin's memorandum on the national question, written five days later, which attacked Stalin's "hastiness and administrative impulsiveness," and a postscript to the testament dicated on January 4, 1923, they suggest how the stricken leader was brooding on Stalin's rising eminence: "Stalin is too rude, and this fault, entirely supportable in relations among us communists, becomes insupportable in the office of general secretary. Therefore, I propose to the comrades to find a way to remove Stalin from that position." [30] On February 6, 1923, Lenin fiercely attacked Rabkrin (the People's Commissariat of Worker's and Peasant's Inspection), once Stalin's department, owing to its bureaucratic structure, and a month later Lenin broke off "comradely relations" with Stalin because of his rudeness to Krupskaya, Lenin's wife.

Disposition of Lenin's "testament" became a knotty problem for the triumvirs shortly before the thirteenth party congress met in May, 1924. Krupskaya, who presumably knew her husband's will, insisted that it should be read at the congress, a procedure which obviously would have caused an explosion. Zinoviev and Kamenev, who were tartly reminded of their past failures by Lenin, rushed to Stalin's rescue, begging for support and claiming his offenses were not great. Trotsky, however, was the key: if he spoke up, the "testament" would have to be made available to the congress; and Stalin, still loose in the saddle, might have been unhorsed. But Trotsky, as though paralyzed with loathing, remained silent; and Krupskaya's motion was defeated. Then, when the congress convened on May 23rd, the scene of the earlier party conference was repeated; speaker after speaker pronounced anathema upon Trotsky.

Trotsky's failure to do battle in January had been a mortal blow for Lenin. It enabled Stalin to fill the vacuum created by an absence of leadership. On May 23rd, the first day of the congress, Trotsky—talking to Eastman in a small ante-room of the great meeting hall—whispered that Lenin had left a letter bequeathing party leadership to him and warning against inner-party factionalism.[31] Knowledge of this letter caused the most intense anxiety on the part of the triumvirs; and a death-like silence reigned over the hall when Trotsky stepped forward. But Trotsky missed his great opportunity. He sought to be conciliatory which, Eastman remarked, was "a thing for which he had no gift whatever." [32] After his concluding remarks, minor party figures carried the attack on Trotsky, men such as Uglanov, a Moscow party secretary who, Eastman reported, delivered the coup de grâce.

Congress took a break after Uglanov's raw speech; and Eastman, in the intermission, exclaimed to Trotsky: "In God's name, why don't you peel off your coat and roll up your sleeves and sail in and clean them up? Read the testament. Don't let them lock it up. Expose the whole conspiracy. Expose it and attack it head-on. It isn't your fight, it's the fight for the revolution. If you don't make it now, you'll never make it. It's your last chance." [33] But Trotsky did not take his last chance; he chose compromise, in the interest of party unity, and as a result was increasingly isolated. Events marched in locked step toward the climax; but Eastman had departed from Moscow by the time that it came in January, 1925.

IV   *The "Testament"*

Eastman had left Russia right after the congress ended in May, 1924. In Paris six months later, he finished a small book, *Since Lenin Died,* which set forth all the details of "the conspiracy of falsification and slander by which the 'triumvirate' had demoted Trotsky and destroyed his authority." [34] It was the first book to publicize the existence of the document called "Lenin's Testament," and contained those quotations from it which Trotsky had whispered to him. It explained how Lenin had used Trotsky to implement his ideas and had chosen him as the outstanding member of the Central Committee. It offered a detailed narrative of the Stalin-Trotsky struggle, explaining how the former had distorted Trotsky's letter to a party local which alluded to the excessive bureaucratization in the party—"a whole self-sufficient officialdom of appointed secretaries"—and warned of the dangers of an appointment practice which started at the top.

Eastman was not wholly uncritical of Trotsky in his presentation. Trotsky was sharply censured—for passivity and ineptitude; for his failure to acquire Lenin's political skill, "his sly art of handling human beings. And because of that quality in him which Lenin called 'too great self-confidence,' Trotsky never could learn this art. . . . He behaves at times with the blundering presumptuousness of a child." [35] Trotsky's trust and his hybris made him vulnerable as well as his failure as a leader and his inability to "do the practical thing." [36]

In spite of these criticisms, Eastman championed Trotsky's cause and shared many of his views. Such advocacy made the blow of August 8, 1925, which Trotsky gave Eastman even more insupportable. In a telegram published by the *Daily Worker* on that date, Trotsky disavowed *Since Lenin Died;* and he even denied the existence of a "testament" from Lenin's hand. "There is in this little booklet a not inconsiderable number of obviously fallacious and mendacious assertions," he maintained. Eastman's allegation "that the Central Committee has 'hidden away' from the Party a number of important documents written by Lenin in the last period of his life . . . [was] a slander against the Central Committee"; and "all talk about a secreted or infringed 'testament' is so much mischievous invention." [37] " 'No honest worker,' " Trotsky concluded, "'will ever believe the sort of picture drawn by Eastman. It contains its own refutation.'"

A month after this staggering disclaimer came another blow for Eastman; Krupskaya's denial, published in the *Workers Monthly* (ironically, once the *Liberator*).[38] Eastman's book, she said, was "'a collection of petty gossip'"; moreover, its author was ignorant of the task which "'history has imposed upon our party'" and of the Bolshevik attitude toward the working-class. With his "petty bourgeois anarchist leanings," Eastman viewed the proleariat as "merely pawns, waiting to be led by any leader." Moreover, he had invented "various fictions," calling them "testaments," and he had calumniated the Central Committee by alleging that it had deliberately concealed a "testament." Coupled with Krupskaya's repudiation was an abrasive commentary by C. M. Roebuck entitled, "Since Eastman Lied," which also appeared in the *Workers Monthly*. Trotsky's stinging rebuttal of Eastman appeared in *l'Humanité* of July 12th; and Trotsky, upon being accused by the French Communist Party of being temperate and ambiguous in his commentary, replied even more savagely on August 18th.

Redemption came a year later when, on October 16, 1926, *The New York Times* published the entire text of Lenin's "testament." Its publication coincided with the capitulation of Trotsky, Zinoviev, Kamenev, Radeck, and Krupskaya. Eastman, however, had some satisfactions earlier; for *Since Lenin Died* had become a sensation in Russia and was widely read and discussed abroad. As a result, the publication gave its author both notoriety and an international reputation in communist circles. But these satisfactions were limited. Of greater moment was the Trotskyite opposition's "confession" that it had "taken steps" violating "party discipline," that it had pledged "cessation of struggle," and that it now sought "to return to the ranks of the party." [30] The revolution was indeed devouring its children, and the sight of it not only sickened Eastman but transformed him into America's earliest and possibly most effective critic of the Russian experiment as it continued under Stalin.

Marxism and Leninism:
A Minority Report

EASTMAN, as we have observed, thought of Socialism as "an experiment that ought to be tried" rather than as "a philosophy of life, much less a religion." And he had praised the Bolsheviks in 1921 for this reason—for making the experiment, for "the new spirit they have brought into the movement . . . [that] of Applied Science and nothing else." But four years and a Moscow sojourn later produced a distinct dampening of revolutionary zeal and a different response. The party congresses, Trotsky's successive defeats, and Stalin's accession to power verified Eastman's pre-war prediction that "political action . . . [might] be turned into a dogma." [1] A group of Bolshevik leaders were "inculcating, in place of the flexible and concrete realistic thinking of Lenin, a bigoted religious devotion to a supposed abstract canon of Leninism." [2]

Eastman saw Russian events in terms of his customary antinomies—metaphysical speculation versus a scientific attitude; "the adherents of a faith and the participants in an effort"—and there could be only one conclusion with such a yardstick. Thus he began a lifelong feud with the Soviet Union. In so doing, he found himself increasingly isolated, the object of world-wide obloquy, and *persona non grata* in nearly all Socialist and Communist circles.

Eastman's response to Stalinism is inadvertently ironic. It rejected the road to compromise and reconciliation, though such qualities were essentially pragmatic; and it veered toward what Eastman had always feared—ideology. In one sense, an iron law of transference is involved; for Eastman's ideological hardening down the years was in response to the reaction of international Communism to his defection; in another sense, however, his reaction may be interpreted as simply another manifestation of a tough-minded attitude that took nothing on faith. His long-time conviction that there was no "exclusive method," that even "political action ought not to be considered an idol," supported the pragmatist's insistence upon flexibility and expediency. Eastman's response to the question of political action versus direct action is a classic one. Both were correct; both were useful: "adopting a strong, positive attitude toward one, does not involve adopting a negative attitude toward the other." [3] For the Communist, he insisted, no absolute must exist, particularly none that smacked of a church. But such pliability, it should be understood, was not the way of the Communist; instead, it derived from an understanding of "the art of instrumental thinking." Those who have learned this art know "how to hold themselves in doubt, and have foresworn absolutely in all active situations the static love of any idea, the intellectual religion." [4]

Despite Eastman's belief that "political action" was not the sole route to revolutionary power, he had long cherished the romantic's and, in a seemingly strange conjunction, the pragmatist's faith in action. Despite mountains of evidence to the contrary, he had sought to portray Marxism "as a practical science" that "redefines the existing mechanism of society from the standpoint of the *ends* proposed by the utopian socialists." [5] Emphasizing ends, as would any instrumentalist, he criticized Marx for neglecting them. Eastman would never ignore the functions of learning and ratiocination; but he would stress change and flexibility. "By knowledge," he declared, "we do not mean a set of intellectual dogmas which cannot change and to which every new fact must conform whether it wants to or not. . . . We mean experimental knowledge—a free investigation of the developing facts and continuous retesting of the theories which pertain to the ends we have in view." [6]

Hence Eastman dispensed with any idea that claimed exclusiveness; or any idea that was not based on a bed-rock appraisal of social realities. Devoted to the belief that theory and practice were inseparably enmeshed, he nonetheless gravitated toward a creed of action in the belief that "knowledge originally grew out of purposive activities" and that "knowing is itself active." [7] To his credit, he did not step over the border into that irrationality and sentimentality which more often than not derived from the mystique of activism. Indeed, he lashed out at those who, "in love with an ideal . . . , have permitted themselves to idealize the real, to soften and falsify it . . . [and] have no taste for the hard mood of practical action"; he categorically declared that " 'brotherhood' belongs in heaven"; he commended George Bernard Shaw who, like Lenin, was "a man of hard common sense"—in which category Eastman invariably took his place.[8]

Nonetheless, Eastman identified sentimentally with "the genuine rebels of the IWW"; and he enshrined working people in general.[9] Dredging up Romantic concepts, he wrote of wage workers: they were "more natural people who lived by doing something with their hands," an activity always enormously attractive to him. Sharing Eastman's belief in primitivism, in the uncomplicated and the emotionally direct, Jo Hancock "understood their thoughts because he felt their feelings. It was a long journey from one mind to another, but there is that short-cut through the heart, and Jo was familiar with it." [10]

For these reasons, Eastman associated himself with the "social criminals" who "fought in the class struggle"; with Lincoln Steffens, who sought to apply "Christian Socialism"; with Clarence Darrow, "the Christ of failure" and lover of mankind; with Elizabeth Gurley Flynn, who sought an equally ambiguous "liberty and life for the workers"; and with George Bellows and all like him who dedicated their "strength to poetry and truth and liberty." [11]

To these vague goals, Eastman brought an elastic and open-ended attitude. Always tentative in propositions about ideology, he admitted, for instance, that Socialism was not the whole of his moral life. Continuing, he declared: "I have always regarded socialism as an effort to solve a specific problem and *one only* of the engrossing problems that confront our human nature." [12] This insistence upon a flexible, non-ideological approach to ideas must be joined to his deep-seated conviction that the ultimate locus of will and sovereignty was the individual: failure to appreciate the enmeshed character of this duality results in an incomplete understanding of Eastman's approach to both life and thought. His brand of Socialism itself derived from certain instinctive responses to social and economic injustice and from a Romantic's view of the individual. Every person, he never tired of declaring, "should

be made free to live and grow in his own chosen way." Only gradually did he familiarize himself with the theoretical arguments
underlying such claims.[13]

I *Marxist and Marxist Critic*

Eastman always considered himself a Marxist Socialist, whether
writing in 1925 or in the 1930s; yet his character was not such as
to encourage any profound study of Marxist doctrine. His Marxism, like himself, was fluid, simplistic, predictably unorthodox.
Eastman looked at Marxism as he looked at the world about him.
He confronted all dogma; he turned from all absolutes, finalities,
fixed principles. To the philosophy of ultimates, he opposed one of
expediencies; to the mysteries and ambiguities of Hegelian
thought, he countered with evidence of the senses and of reality.

The axial roles played by both pragmatic and scientific thinking, as Eastman understood each, must be recalled against the
backdrop of his growing disenchantment with the Soviet Union.
These conjoined factors rendered his reading of the Russian Revolution and of Marxism more critically scrupulous than it might
have been. For, as has been noted, these factors worked upon
each other: each was both force and product. In choosing to look
at Bolshevism and at Marxism with corrosive objectivity, Eastman
retained his individuality. But he did so at high cost: he became a
lonely man.

Upon returning to America in 1927, Eastman found himself isolated by those who retained their enthusiasm for Socialism and for
Russia. The Communists expelled him from the Workers Party;
and they ostracized him by virtue of a slogan which would become an iron law: no fraternalizing with Trotskyites. "Not a single
friend of mine in the revolutionary intelligentsia or among Socialists or IWW's, or the political left anywhere, took firm sides with
Trotsky in his conflict with the new ruling class." [14] Hence, like his
flawed hero, Trotsky, he stood in splendid isolation, estranged
from left and from right owing to his partiality toward the former
commissar of war. It would be some years before others joined
him in his desolate command post; only after the Great Trials and
the Russo-German pact would any significant group vindicate
Eastman's early opposition and pay it homage. Edmund Wilson,

writing in 1941, declared: "the thing that strikes one today in reviewing the work of the last twenty years [of Eastman's life] is not the softness of his mind but its toughness." [15]

As early as September, 1916, he had begun to criticize Marxism, particularly on the grounds of scientific objectivity.[16] A decade later, ostracized by most of his onetime friends and convinced of a disparity between Marxist theory and Bolshevik practice, he made a serious examination of Marxist thought. And the more obloquy that fell upon him and the more disillusioned he became with the Russian Revolution, the more weaknesses he discovered in its theoretical foundations.

Not that Eastman was ever wholly an apostate. From his first encounter with Marxism, he always found elements that were prescient, compelling, and indubitably correct. The *Communist Manifesto,* he declared in March, 1918, was so "sublimely ordered and intellectual a performance as to . . . raise intelligence and the dissemination of ideas to the highest place in the confidence. Without doubt it is the most momentous event in the history of peoples." Five years earlier, he endorsed a vulgarized understanding of economic determinism—that "every man acts in the economic interest of himself and his family." He modified his acceptance of determinism over a decade later, insisting that it did not deny "the power of ideas to change the course of history." [17]

Hence Eastman never completely repudiated certain of Marx's propositions. He remained convinced that the Marxian theory of history and analysis of capitalism "made indubitable contributions to science." Marx "made discoveries and uncovered points of view that a more mature effort to change the social system will have to cling to": he was the first to realize the major historical role enjoyed by developing techniques of production; he added to our "understanding of business crises and the causes of war." The class struggle, Marxian economics, socialization of land and capital as a means of transforming the instruments of production, the dialectical method were magnificent gifts. Though eventually repudiating dialectics, Eastman continued to find saving graces in it: "In rejecting the naïve notion that the material world is dialectically determined from the lower to the higher, we must retain the wisdom linked up with it—the unremitting awareness of change, and very profound change, in social relations as history proceeds." [18]

II *Marxist Studies*

In his writing on Marxism, particularly before 1940, there was a clamorous insistence upon its scientific base; Eastman simply *had* to believe as much. In March, 1918, for example, he proclaimed his "admiration" for "the fearless faith in scientific intelligence of Karl Marx"; in June, 1924, the scientific foundation of Marxism was affirmed; in 1940, after effectively demolishing Marx's unscientific methodology, he nonetheless declared that Marx "completed the *scientific* task set by his apparently utopian ideas—the task of finding out how the existing systems of wealth production might be changed"; and, in the same year in another study, he wistfully clings to the belief that "there is a great deal of hard sense in the Marxian analysis of capitalism." Eastman, by this time, had made his major contribution to Marxian thought in *Marx, Lenin and the Science of Revolution*, a book marked by literary grace, a clean and adroit style, analytical detachment. Published in 1926, it represented the fruits of over a decade of study and reflected the estrangement that had overtaken him by that time. It also had some very positive features: the class struggle was the "essential feature of modern society"; "the immortal essence of Marx's contribution to the science of history, and to history itself" was his rejection of illusions—religious, moralistic, legal, political, esthetic.[19]

Eastman, above all else, was a complex person. More than the sum of his parts, he was, and is, hard to reduce to formula. Such polarities as idealism and practicality, primitivism and scientific progress were rooted in his thought. By 1926, he had gravitated toward realism, functionalism, and human reason as the tools by which the material world might be explained, and as the only means by which society could be maintained in its openness from generation to generation. The open society in the open world was, more than ever, his goal; and it could be best achieved by utilizing the newly created instruments of science. His single-minded insistence upon the directed intelligence led him—first in *Marx, Lenin and the Science of Revolution* of 1926—to a withering in-

dictment of Marxism. This indictment, which emphasized the utopianism, emotionalism, and metaphysical character of Marxist
doctrine, was broadened and deepened down the years.

In *Marx, Lenin and the Science of Revolution*, Eastman seems
determined to distill the estimable applied-science features of
Marxism from its "wish-fulfillment aspects"; but he was engaged
essentially in the task of demolition. Marxism, he stated, "was a
step from utopian socialism to a socialist religion—a scheme for
convincing the believer that the universe itself is producing a better society." [20] Such convictions set the tone. Eastman, in this tract,
strikes blow after blow against rigidities, fixed principles, and
"Talmudic aphorisms." Marx's writings were "metaphysical," he
claimed, by which he meant that Marx "did not examine this material world, as an artisan examines the materials of his trade, in
order to determine by what means he could make something else
out of it. He examined it as the priest examines the ideal world, in
order to see if he could not find in it, or failing that, transplant
into it, his own creative aspiration." [21]

Eastman agreed with those who called *Das Kapital*, "'the
Workingman's Bible'"; for, assuredly, "It is a book in which the
working class can find not only the 'most adequate expression of its
conditions and its aspirations'—to quote the phrase of Engels—
but also the assurance that these have their due place in a universal scheme of evolution toward something better. . . . with a necessity that is absolute if not divine. . . . They are to be satisfied
on this earth, and not in heaven. The God who is to satisfy them is
not a Loving Father, but a Passionless Process." The mystery
which surrounds him is not emotional, but intellectual.[22] And this
absence of feeling, Eastman felt, was wholly egregious.

There were admittedly good things in *Das Kapital*, including "a
wealth of interesting ideas, and much invaluable empirical material." The study of the rise of English industrialism, he declared,
"ought to be dissected out and published as one of the most significant chapters of human history." The book contained "the material necessary to prove that our system of production for profit,
through the exploitation of labour is inexpedient and uncivilized.
. . . And it also contains the material necessary to prove that
this system is unstable, and will with practical certainty give rise
to imperialistic wars. . . . [and] indirectly it justifies the revolu-

tionary purpose of Marx, and warrants his belief in the practical possibilities of the class struggle." [23]

But *Das Kapital* ultimately and mainly fails because Marx did not comprehend the "art of practical thinking" and because "It is not, except incidentally, an exposition and *empirical* demonstration of that *concrete fact* about the exploitation of labour under capitalism which Marx saw so clearly. It is a flying upward from that concrete fact into the world of unreal abstraction." [24] Such a claim represents the gravamen of Eastman's criticism. Marx, unfortunately for him, was a victim of his birth; as a German, he was predisposed to accept German ideas and, consequently, predisposed to mysticism.

Of German philosophy, "no clear and realistic intelligence can understand it, except as a physician understands the insane"—so declared Eastman in 1917; and again and again thereafter he illustrates this hostility to such philosophy, equating it with religion and/or metaphysical *schema*.[25] Hegel, who dominated German thought in Marx's youth, was the chief villain—"the master wizard," as Marx recognized in *Die Deutsche Ideologie*,[26] Eastman was convinced by the mid-1920's that automatic theological exegesis, to which Marx was prone, had replaced reasoned and critical inquiry in Russia, that dialectics "had become a state religion" which merely gave empirical confirmation to his own theoretical polemics on Marxism, that a "new Soviet scholasticism, with its accompaniment of Mariolatry . . . converted modern Russian scholarly life into a veritable mediaeval wilderness of barren and unreal conceptual disputation." [27]

To further suggest the intensity of Eastman's antagonism to Germanic thought, emphasis upon his definition of "scientific" in the phrase "scientific socialism" is necessary; for Eastman did not turn to the German meaning, which was *Wissenschaft*, but to the English sense of the term. Marx's approach, to the contrary, was "German professorial in the very sense that seems unnatural to us more sceptical and positivistic Anglo-Saxons." From this initial error streamed a variety of Marx's sins. Marxism was utopian, as in its belief in "the automatic 'dying away of the state,'" which was a "dreadful absurdity"; or its assurance of the "indefinite changeability" of human nature; or its "erroneous prediction" of the immiseration of the working class and the decline of the mid-

dle class. Marxism was a romantic and "wish-fulfilling speculation" of the kind Marx himself denounced; Marxism never escaped
from philosophy into science; therefore, it failed to escape from
idealism. It sought to be scientific, "even to out-science the scientists"; but it was "a survival of the intellectual machinery with
which oversoulful people have kept up in the face of science wish-
fulfillment thoughts about the world." It claimed to be "an objective analysis of history and society [but] its pretense to the authority of empirical science is a bluff." It neglected "Mendelian
laws, of genes and chromosomes, of hereditary and acquired characters"; and it needed "a modern seasoning" of Nietzsche as well
as of biology.[28]

As Eastman understood "scientific," in the phrase "scientific socialism," it came out sceptical and positivist; and it underscored
his willingness to try new ideas. Eastman, by his definition, invited
men to have the courage to learn and to know, to examine ra-
tionally what had been taken for granted. The Marxist, to the
contrary, was "prevented by his religion from even asking a question about the natural tendencies" of men. He held to fixed articles of faith, Eastman added, and to a mythic belief in "the indefinite changeability of human nature." Since Marx's thesis "is not
scientifically defensible, an element of unconscious casuistry is introduced into the thoughts of the most single-minded soldiers of
the revolution." Subjectivist tendencies become inevitable: the
Marxist "is not engaged in scientific investigation, but in rational-
izing his motives." Such a conclusion was supported, *a posteriori*,
by events in Russia, and led to the observation that "A man who
projects his purpose into the *objective* facts is always compelled,
sooner or later, either to abandon his purpose or distort the
facts." [29]

"Scientific socialism," in summary, was anything but scientific.
Indeed, it was the sort of philosophy, he claimed, that Marx had
always denounced. The root cause of the distortion—and Eastman
continually returned to it in *Marx, Lenin and the Science of Revolution* and in *Marxism is it Science*, was the Germanic penchant
toward abstract speculation or, as he affirmed, Marx's reliance
"upon the relics of Hegelian mystic metaphysics." The outcome, as
Eastman once more asserted in *Stalin's Russia* of 1940, was a religion; it was "faith in . . . 'material forces,' just as Hegel had his

faith in the Divine spirit, by making their control immanent in the activities of men, not transcendent of them." [30]

Eastman had big game here—something even more momentous than the destruction of dialectical materialism by an examination of its origins and prophetic character: the target was philosophy itself. Eastman wished to strike a fatal blow at all philosophy which, like dialectics, had faith and anti-scientific values at its source. In an *ex cathedra* judgment, he declared: "if you adopt the attitude of a scientific investigator, no philosophy of any except a mere summary of your findings is either possible or necessary." [31]

Officially renouncing speculative thought, Marx nonetheless engaged in a dialectical parlor game of first asserting "something, and then this something passes over into its opposite." [32] He wanted to revolutionize society but "instead of presenting his thoughts . . . in simple and clear form as a specific plan for the solution of a specific problem," in the positivist, sceptical, scientifically-inclined Anglo-Saxon practice, "he started in by deciding in general what the universe is made of and how it operates, and then gradually worked down toward a demonstration that by the very nature of its being and the laws of its operation this universe is inevitably going to revolutionize itself." [33]

"Dialectics," in brief, was merely a utopian's dream superimposed upon social and historical realities, as Eastman understood it. And Marx's materialism was not "materialistic." That "much-touted" factor "was not an advance from Hegel's religious metaphysics toward a scientific empiricism." Rather, Eastman asserted, "it was a reversion from the primitive animism of Hegel to a fetishism that is still more primitive." Eastman concluded that Marx (and Engels) had been "completely hoodwinked" by this metaphysician; that dialectics "was a half escape" from metaphysics "into the scientific point of view"; and that, by it, Marx "simply replaced Hegel's World Spirit with a World Robot who performs to a different purpose, and without demanding social attentions, all the work which the World Spirit was employed to perform." [34]

Eastman never had reason to alter these conclusions; Marx, he announced in 1940, "will take a place in history not unlike that of Rousseau—a man behind the highest scientific attitudes of his time, but borne to great heights because he created a new *Wel-*

tanschauung, and one which fell in with the passions, aims, and tactics of a great social movement." But Marx's system was a disguised religion, and Eastman wrote two years later of "the religiously believing mind of Karl Marx." And, after the passage of a decade, he still pronounced Marx "a mystic believer in the inevitability of a millennium."

Dialectics was only one target of Eastman's shafts. Marx's view of history, he concluded, lacked a causal understanding of events. Nor did Marx really consider the nature of the post-revolutionary state; he only claimed it would "wither away." He simply assumed, being a utopian, "that truly miraculous things would follow of themselves." [36] In reality, Eastman declared, history seemed to have come "to a dead stop" for Marx with the dictatorship of the proletariat.[37] Marx did not extend any contradiction beyond this point in history—a fact which lent validity to Eastman's claim that Marx's own will and aspirations, not objective knowledge, dominated his thinking.

Perennial emphasis upon man's biological drives also eroded Eastman's belief in Marxism. He charged Marxists with failure to consider inherited human characteristics and biological imperatives: they "failed to allow man any biological character at all"; and their teacher "failed to realize [that these psycho-physiological factors] are hereditary." Marx, furthermore, erred in his belief that man's instinctual nature would change with alterations in his social environment. In Eastman's brief foray into organic evolution, Darwin, it should be mentioned, emerged as much the better thinker. He was a scientist; he approached his task "without any political purpose" or preconceived ends; and his books "have an objective validity which Marx could have attained only if he had recognized the role played by his purpose, and separated that part of his thought which consisted of analysing facts, from that which consisted of planning for the realizing of an idea." [38]

III   *Marxism vs. Leninism*

With Lenin's appearance on the Russian scene, Eastman found, as we have seen, his champion. Lenin typified the revolution, he stated in 1918: "its scientific spirit, its abandonment of ideologies and state eloquence, its simplicity and courage, and its generosity and consecration." Above all, Lenin was no "extreme dogmatist."

Quite unlike Marx, he offered up only rhetorical and ceremonial concessions to dialectics. For him, the term "dialectics" suggested flexibility. It meant "that ideas should be handled as instruments of action, and not actions mechanically deduced from ideas." Leninism was based upon experience as the source of human knowledge. It penetrated all sacred precincts, possessed a critical view of life, and ignored or rejected metaphysics. Leninism thus became the concretization of Marx's imaginative vision.[39]

Lenin's deviations from the major canons of Marxism were not missed by the orthodox, and Eastman took it upon himself to defend his hero—when he was denounced "by the well-trained priests of dialectic materialism." Lenin, he stated, made some significant modifications of Marxian political ideas. He announced the indispensability of the "professional revolutionist"; he rejected Menshevism and "left-wing infantilism" on psychological rather than on class grounds; and, among other things, he gave greater emphasis to the peasants and colonial peoples.[40] These deviations, Eastman makes clear, derived from Lenin's "thoroughly experimental" methodology. The chief affirmative lesson to be learned from Lenin, Eastman wrote in 1940, "is that of mental flexibility without moral compromise"—or, as he phrased it elsewhere in this same year, his adherence to a methodology that held things "subject to redefinition in the light of the developing facts"; as a result his "plan of action, will be kept in a state of development and living relevance both to the facts and to the aim."[41] Once more, the gravitational pull of instrumentalism influenced Eastman's thinking, limning a portrait—this time of Lenin—in harmony with his own wish-fulfillment.

CHAPTER 9

Dewey and Freud:
Additional Forays
into Anti-Intellectualism

ANTI-INTELLECTUALISM, the view of life as an experiment, the fevered pursuit of action, were among the shared attitudes of Eastman's generation. To radicals like him, touched by Jamesian pragmatism and sympathetic to innovation, Lenin was the hero. Time and again, Eastman noted his kinship (and that of the Bolsheviks generally) with Dewey: "I still believe [Eastman advised readers of the *Liberator*] they will find in John Dewey the best, as well as the first clear teacher of the instrumental character of true thinking. John Dewey will have his place in history among those who pointed the way to that trained and hard-headed idealism which is to distinguish the culture of the twentieth century. But in the sphere of politics it is the Russians who exemplify it." [1]

Trotsky, of these Russians, joined Dewey and Lenin as exemplars of the functioning intelligence. He shared Lenin's "purposive practicality." He also thought "with a consciousness that the world is a process. . . ."; he realized that practical science "does not consist of learning by heart a set of dogmas that are true *in the abstract,* and then making automatic and universal inferences from them"; he was the "revolutionary engineer applying the science of Marx in the manner of Lenin." [2]

Such thinking caused Eastman to avoid abstractions, to describe his response to William James, with whom he spent some hours, as "reverential love," and to champion a non-ideological brand of Socialism. "To me," Eastman recalled, "socialism was not a doctrinal belief, but a working hypothesis. I did not think Marx explained the world or told us where history was going; I thought he proposed a method of procedure by which we might make history go . . . in a particular direction. To me the procedure was experimental, and the ideas were subject to correction." Marx offered a methodology, not a blueprint. The revolution, it followed, must be "conducted in the spirit of experimental science" and by "completely flexible minds." Marx's thought, he forcefully stated in September, 1916, "was practical"; but a decade later he claimed with equal vigor that it was utopian. What is important are not the discrepancies in Eastman's statements but the standards that Eastman employed. It is significant, in this context, that Eastman approvingly contrasted Lenin, who supported only "a thoroughly experimental procedure," to Marx—to the latter's detriment, since Lenin's hypothesis always had "living relevance both to the facts and to the aim." [3]

"New events, new conditions, new inventions, new ideas," Eastman insisted, "will enter the world in the next few years, and all our plans will have to be drawn anew." Those, therefore, who advance some iron law of history should beware. "The day of the social prospectus is dead," he flatly declared; and the social ideal can be outlined only in very general terms.[4]

I *Eastman's Scepticism*

Such attitudes, we may believe, were partially formed in Eastman's days at Columbia. He had been a student of Dewey's, it may be recalled, attending his teacher's course in logical theory. Certainly the experience of having Dewey as friend, colleague, and employer was among the most meaningful of Eastman's early years, if only because it offered authoritative confirmation to his own thinking. Given Eastman's pre-Deweyan stress on the applied intelligence, his avoidance of the non-functional, his commitment to a life that was whole and natural, he would naturally respond to someone who defined human growth as process and who—in *Ethics* and in *How We Think*—emphasized adjustment to new conditions. Both men believed, as Dewey phrased it, that a program of ends and aspirations must reject apriorisms, and that ideas "must themselves be framed out of the possibilities of existing conditions."

Eastman had been groping toward such thought for some years. In a college thesis, written in 1904—three years before James'

Pragmatism was published—he identified the current thought that most attracted him. It was "affirmative agnosticism, pragmatism, socratic scepticism. . . . call it by what chill name you will, it is great! . . . I liked the new philosophy because it gave a biological foundation to my instinctive scepticism." [5]

The sources of Eastman's scepticism, as we have earlier demonstrated, are difficult to sift; they are elusive and complex and at the heart of the man himself. Possibility his scepticism was borne of his early and continuous pagan view of nature; more likely, it was grounded in the radicalism of his day. And both of these manifestations may be traced to an adolescent's awareness that he had come of an age when theology as an intellectual discipline had fallen on bad times and that religion, rather than a set of postulates to be scrutinized and debated, had become an ideal of personal conduct. In any event, it would be unwise to claim exclusiveness for any single cause, though it is clear that scepticism most fully flowered in the 1920's in his political loyalties and his hortatory appeals for scientific criteria.

Eastman's scepticism was publicly expressed as early as July, 1913, when he condemned "the preachers of emotional brotherhood" for teaching the poor to be "content with an humble lot." [6] Two years later, he took on God himself, and those servants of God who sought to make peace between capital and labor "at the current rate of exploitation." [7] The church, he claimed, was against labor's struggle; it "is against discontent, is against rebellion, is against the arrant assertion of human rights, is against clear thinking as well as heroic action toward a free and happy world"; and he charged that the pulpits betrayed Jesus himself, "whom they profess to believe divine." The church inculcated meekness and preoccupation with the next world, thereby distracting men from struggle for their material rights in this one; and he ridiculed "Rockefeller's un-Christ-like zeal to cherish the souls of his workers" which took the form of giving them churches but not a living wage or social justice. [8]

With the outbreak of World War I, the *Masses'* pages rang up all the charges against the church, mostly for its militarism. [9] Eastman attacked it as a Judas Iscariot, and he encouraged cartoons which exposed "the war-mongering Christians." [10] The monthly's virulently anti-church position transcended the war issue. In the tradition of Christian Socialism, Eastman insisted that Jesus' principles of conduct "are wholly out of accord with our industrial life"; so much so, that the clergy is "forced to deny him and betray his ideals continually." Yet Eastman blurred the case for scepticism: he never embraced an unqualified irreligious viewpoint; and, in the role of instinctualist, he paradoxically suggested that the religious emotion offered "combined satisfaction" for our instincts: "God is. . . . a refuge to our fear, a temple to our wonder . . . , an infinite companion." [11]

In a sense larger than may be imputed to political radicalism, Eastman's scepticism was the product of an insistence upon the values of temporal life—of a life organically whole and enfolded in nature. In another sense, it was shaped by his increasing awareness that knowledge is derived neither from God nor from Aristotelian logic, but from empirically verifiable observations—from applied science.[12] Eastman conceived of the mind "as *primarily* an instrument of survival in the life struggle." [13] Such being the case, "no absolute or universal truth is attainable." But, Eastman consoles us, "this need not stop us from using specific and relative truths in improving life."

II *The Pragmatic Temper*

In this manner, Eastman arrived at pragmatism. He departed from its acknowledged founder, John Dewey, only after his own brand of instrumentalism became more critical and sophisticated —when he realized that Dewey, by redefining truth, sought "to give moral judgments the same kind of validity possessed by judgments of fact." [14] But Eastman's deviation was never radical, for he had reduced instrumentalism to a non-epistemological embodiment of experience, a definition that was Dewey's and to which Eastman could give unreserved fealty. Emphasis on experience carried him, therefore, to scepticism, to criticism of Marxism, and to a functional definition of socialism, all other versions being debased.

Eastman thus made bold and inspired use of instrumentalism— a use that flowed inexorably from Dewey's own understanding that the concept would provide a basis for "social and intellectual reconstruction." [15] This view was in harmony with the experimental and improvisatory temper of the 1920's and of Eastman himself. He also opposed ultimates with expediencies, insisted on ideas as tools for the enrichment of "experience"—which word meant any direct perception of life, any perception that did not percolate down second hand—through the eyes of other percipients. He did not restrict experience to the sexual, though that obviously was present; or to pantheist immersion in landscape, though that, too, was in evidence; or to an anti-intellectual posture, though the cult of primitivism had such implications.

Eastman may have mistrusted intellection and trusted the senses, but the discord was never dramatically marked or clearly resolved. Indeed, the stress on empiricism was balanced by a near-equal emphasis on mind—rather, the role and use of it. But even this functional approach gave learning a role, and it could not be insouciantly disregarded. It is simply that Eastman rejected the view of mind as an abstraction. Thought must never be abstract; for—when it is, or when it "is cultivated for its own sake, or when an attempt is made to state the nature of certain facts independently of their relation to any specific ends"—then there is enormous difficulty, as in Marx's historical materialism. Conscious thought, Eastman repeatedly stated, was "a practical instrument"; and "logical concepts and all fixed principles are but the instruments of action." [16]

Science, too, was yoked to the practical. It "regards all valid knowledge," he declared, "as derived ultimately from experience, derived by the methods of observation, experiment and rational calculation, and subject to the practical test of action." Thus he hardly distinguished between the scientific and the "practical, between James and Dewey, or between Dewey and Lenin. Such types avoided absolutes, abandoned fixed ideas, dispensed "with universes," and remained plastic in their approach toward knowledge. These emphases gave Eastman the appearance of being anti-intellectual; and his grave lack of faith in intellectuals who, as he saw them, considered themselves a class apart, gave added confirmation. But, in truth, all it signified was his general drift toward the most militant wing of the Socialist Party—the activists who, before 1914, were mostly Wobblies. [17]

This pull toward Socialist activists had at its origins the claim that "all knowledge, even that which issues from reflection, is experimental." No one feels class hatred while sitting at home "thinking about things," he exclaimed as early as 1913: "after you go outdoors and get into the fight in a concrete situation . . . where the knife is drawn and it's a clear case of life against profits, then you begin to see red, and you forget all about your theory." [18]

This aspect of Dewey's thought, this aversion to the " 'spectator theory' of knowledge," Eastman fastened upon;[19] and nothing could shake him loose. Even in 1957, after renouncing pragmatism and claiming that Dewey had erred in identifying "truth . . . with the happy outcome of the whole process," Eastman still believed him "right in emphasizing the fact that thinking developed as an instrument for the solution of specific problems of action." [20] Eastman's rejection of pragmatism in the 1950's evolved from his harsh estimate that it was an "effort to defend the values called spiritual against a glorification of America's hard-headed practicality." Few Abraham Lincoln specialists would share his conclusion that Lincoln lacked such practicality. This claim was repeated early the following year, in the course of Eastman's running polemic with Sidney Hook, in which his major defense was a few *ex cathedra* assertions and a summary of his early relationship with Dewey, followed by the question: "can anybody believe that I don't know what Dewey's instrumental theory is and [that I] can be dismissed [as] laboring under a misconception . . . ?" [21]

The Hook-Eastman debate of the late 1950's closed a chapter in Eastman's life which had begun more than two decades earlier— in a series of bitterly personal thrusts and responses in articles. Each of the principals, both former pupils of Dewey, claimed his own brand of Marxism was truer to Dewey and instrumentalism. Eastman insisted that their teacher would balk at dialectics, that Hook had confused instrumentalism with the mystical pragmatism of William James, and that Dewey sought to give a purpose to history not confirmed by the facts.[22] This last dissonant note was introduced in the 1930's when Eastman and Dewey traveled in opposite directions on the question of the Soviet Union—with Dewey espousing a Socialist economy and organized social controls.[23]

In emphasizing an "instrumental interpretation of consciousness," Eastman never neglected Darwin's "biological psychology." Immediate sensations never captured the entire stage; there were always instinctive drives to be considered. Indeed, as a previous chapter has indicated, Marx was sharply criticized for neglecting biological imperatives. Eastman, it followed, inevitably veered to Freud; he explained so much; he offered solutions to vexing problems; he was in harmony with the "scientific" climate of the 1920's.[24]

III *Freud and His Impact*

The scientific method, it will be recalled, was a major article of radical and Bohemian faith in the first three decades of the century. It had, as Frederick Hoffman, has observed, "a prestige value in the world at large." [25] Social critics and intellectuals generally supported science since it encouraged sceptical attitudes toward church dogma, traditional morality, and middle-class values.[26] Eastman welcomed science for other reasons: science possessed an unmistakable self-serving property for him, and he came to view it as a believer did a revealed faith.[27]

Freud's propositions seemed admirably scientific, reason enough for Eastman to embrace them. And yet Freudianism appealed because unlike science, it was warmly human, and stressed irrational forces. Eastman is very much the mirror of his age. He accepts Freudian thought for the same contradictory and diverse reasons it was acceptable to the pre-war intellectual community at large—because it seemed to be a grab-bag of major trends: instinctualism, anti-rationalism, hostility to science, celebration of science. Freudianism did more than challenge established middle-class codes of conduct and morality, it was a liberating and regenerative social force.

Freudianism also reinforced the convictions of those who sought a hedonistic life style and who were in growing opposition to establishment morality. Eastman shared the Bohemian assumption, derived from Freud, that "repression" was "bad" for both society and the individual, and that it created a national neurosis and destroyed creative expression. Those, like Eastman, who were opposed to all moral overseers, were almost fanatically hostile to any monitors of sexual morality. He scorned all those who sought to codify sexual behavior, as an earlier chapter has indicated. New doctrines of psychology seemed to offer demonstrable proof that sex and sin were not synonymous. Sex, to the contrary, uncovered the mystic spring then sealed over by the heavy stone of social convention and by "bourgeois" notions of romantic love. It

opened the individual to the most exalted of feelings which, paradoxically, could best be understood by psychoanalytic practices,
the way of science. Thus the all-consuming and essentially mystical experience of romantic love was not found to be exempt from
objective clinical tests. Compounding the paradox, however, Eastman's attitude toward the sexual experience itself crossed over
into the irrational, approaching the sexual vitalism of D. H. Lawrence. For Eastman, as for many of his contemporaries, the sexual
experience was possibly the deepest and richest that an individual
could have.

Eastman's first encounter with the science of the mind occurred
less than a decade after Freud, working alone in Vienna, had discovered psychoanalysis. When Eastman, troubled by insomnia
and various physical ills, entered Dr. Sahler's sanitarium at Kingston, New York, he became familiar with a therapy closed related
to Christian Science. It was "a mixture of suggestive therapeutics,
psychic phenomena, non-church religion. . . ." Out of this
confinement and intensive reading in the doctor's library—one
rich in mystical and scientific volumes on psychic experiences—
Eastman came to have some familiarity with psychoanalytic theory. Discarding the occult aspects of Sahler's therapy, he retained
the conviction that mental healing was a valid approach to both
mental and physical ills.[28]

When the Vienna and Zurich societies met in Salzburg for the
first international congress of psychoanalysis in 1908, Freud was
joined by Stekel, Ferenczi, Adler, Ernest Jones, and others.
A. A. Brill of New York also was there. His name becomes increasingly important in these prewar years; for Brill—"the first psycho-
analyst to open an office in America," declared Eastman—helped
spur Freud's reputation in the United States by publishing in 1910
his paper on Freud's interpretation of dreams and by translating,
beginning in 1913, the master's work. Although Freud himself
stimulated interest in psychoanalysis with his visit to Clark University in 1909, Brill was the major votary working in America. To
him Bertha Eastman came at the astonishingly early date of November, 1909; and Eastman, claiming that this visit was part of
her insatiable and "everlasting thirst for experience," noted that
Brill was astonished at the boldness with which she described her
"intimate sexual life—or lack of it." Her son also went to Brill,
who quickly perceived Eastman's problem as " 'a strong mother

fixation. Your pattern is that you want to get away from your mother and yet be with her.'" Walter Lippmann invited Brill to speak at one of Mabel Dodge Luhan's salons sometime in 1915, and she herself, like Eastman, preferred Brill to Smith Ely Jelliffe who was, next to Brill, the leading exponent of Freudianism in America.[29]

By this time the cultural impact of Freudian thought had become unmistakable. Eastman wrote two articles for *Everybody's Magazine* on psychoanalytic theory in 1915, in which he explained concepts like "repression," "sublimation," "unconscious motives." [30] Elements of Darwinianism occasionally larded the exposition, but Eastman generally followed a direct line of assessing Freudianism for lay readers. Thus he likened "the mind . . . [to] a deep mine, or a mysterious well of water, whose conscious surface is not large, but which spreads out to great distances and great depths below"; he claimed that sex was first among "these trouble-making desires"; he commented upon "the fact that we *all* carry in our unconscious minds these infantile attachments"; and he defined psychoanalysis as "a technique for finding out what is in the unconscious mind." [31]

Eastman wrote about Freud as a popularizer and a journalist, a craft with which he was most at home. His tendency to glibness which made concepts seem so easy—which enabled him to avoid the deeper, more subtle analyses of ideas, and which were weaknesses in lengthy, scholarly expositions—was converted into strength. And the direct, understandable, unostentatious quality of his prose was suitable for such journals as *Everybody's* and the *Masses*.

The *Masses* columns reflected Brill's efforts and Freud's burgeoning popularity. In part, the magazine's interest in psychoanalysis suggested an age which had left behind the simple world of Jefferson and Adam Smith; in part, it reflected Floyd Dell, who was a champion of the new science; in part, it was traceable to Eastman's own preoccupation with, *inter alia*, woman suffrage and birth control—issues that prefigured the great debate on feminism which took place in the post-war decade. Eastman's absorption in these subjects was more a product of deeper impulses than a shared concern of his generation, though his interests fortuitously converged on the central themes of Village intellectual life: the

primacy of sex in human relations and the elimination of social
as well as moral restraints upon individual expression.

But, as Joseph Freeman acknowledged, these "sons and daugh-
ters of the puritans, the artists and writers and utopians who
flooded Greenwich Village to find a frank and free life for the
emotions and senses" paid the usual heavy price. They also purchased "a sense of guilt" for betraying the faith of their fathers,
and it caused them to exaggerate the importance of pleasure; they
therefore "idealized it and even sanctified it." [32] Eastman was of
this generation. Moreover, he had the benefit of Dr. Sahler, of his
own visits to Brill, and of a half-hour conversation with Freud.
Freudianism was more than the Village's fashionable parlor game
for him;[33] it was another link in the chain of romantic protest
which repudiated as unwise any effort to legislate desire or to har-
ness emotional expression to middle-class dictates. It was new, unorthodox, shockingly frank; it counseled liberality in sexual matters at a time when talk about them was at its apogee.

IV *Freud vs. Marx*

Freudianism, by the mid-Twenties, had destroyed Eastman's
faith in the majesty of Marx, but it confirmed his faith in the
majesty of Dewey and of science. It did so by emphasizing the
effort to "make the patient conscious of his own real desires,"
which was of pivotal importance to Eastman. If Eastman, with his
incurably bifocal vision, had subscribed to an uncomplimentary
view of man's nature as rooted in ineradicably aggressive impulses, he had also held a general hopefulness about mankind, one
anchored in education. A powerful agent for beneficent change,
education was predicated upon "the therapeutic importance of
becoming conscious." When a man became conscious of his "real
desires," "the ordinary process of thought and its education, is the
only cure that is offered. The cure is occasionally almost instanta-
neous, because the suppressed motive is infantile, and its irrele-
vance to the present situation is immediately recognized." [34]
Eastman, at this exact juncture, departs from his usual characterization of Marxism—which found it at the opposite end of the
spectrum from both instrumentalism and psychoanalysis—and asserted that it anticipated Freud. "Marx's word ideology," he

stated in 1926, "is simply a name for the distortions of social and political thinking which are created by these suppressed motives." [35]

Consciousness of self thus became first cousin to the familiar apothegm, "knowing is itself active," a proposition that Dewey would have admired.[36] Freud, having enormous appeal, was "the cleanest man on two continents," George Forbes proclaimed in *Venture;* ". . . he was breaking through. . . . He digs under the talk. Digs under the mind. He puts words to a new use; he may turn out after all to be the Resurrection and the Life." [37]

Eastman nonetheless hedged his conversion. He could be faultfinding. In a critical barb of 1913, he found psychoanalysis to be "a shapeless and immature science," one "that . . . has reached hardly any final conclusions of general acceptance." [38] He warned Freudians that the theory of the unconscious did not comprehend everything and that, for instance, it did not "explain" all myths (such as incest) or the existence of mythology.[39] Nor did it explain "away all revolutionary intelligence as a manifestation of the 'Oedipus complex.' " [40] "It is quite a fashion" among Freudians, he observed, "to dismiss any man who wants to cut under the plausibilities of existing law and government, as a neurotic driven on by an unconscious fixation of infantile emotion against his father."

Elsewhere, however, Eastman seems to have fallen into the psychoanalytical trap that he warned against. In *Venture,* in a passage illuminating Eastman's own doubts about his revolutionary sincerity, he described a fictional character's self-proclaimed sympathy for the workingclass as deceptive. His "real interest," Eastman revealingly declared, "was in overthrowing the tyranny of the father-image and asserting his own manhood, of which entirely unknown to himself he was unquestionably in doubt." [41] The twin addictions of Eastman's, radicalism and Freudianism were, we may believe, in some measure anchored in intimate personal problems—insecurity, an inadequate father figure, and Oedipal fixation.

Not only was psychology superior to Marxism, it took precedence over all ideologies since they were "rationalizations" that served "as concealments in consciousness." [42] Eastman, in 1942, denied substituting Freudianism for Marxism; yet he asserted that Freud was "remote historically from Marx's mind," that an "infant science [psychoanalysis] that is alive" is preferable to "a dead metaphysics [dialectics]," and that psychology's "power of fact" may be favorably compared with Marx's "system of historic metaphysics." [43] At times, Eastman varied only as to prophesy as to whether psychology would "destroy" Marxism or, in an instrumental sense, "bear out . . . Marx's generalizations about past history"; and, eventually, he embraced psychoanalytic theory because it was factual, analytical, "an exact science." [44]

However disparaging he might be at times, Eastman recognized psychoanalysis as his own and adopted it—or at least those features in harmony with his own thought. Freud, for all his lapses, "made himself a wise and wonderful scientist of sex" and gave "a gift of illumination to the world not second to that which Hobbes gave." [45] Freud could be forgiven so much, if only because he "lifted a great incubus of shame from the shoulders of humanity," because he gave "the boon of candor to a poor animal desperately endeavoring to become a man." George Forbes of *Venture*, speaking to Eastman's *doppelganger*, affirmed: "Psychology has laid the foundation. Freud has a big hand there. Do you know, Hancock, what is the chief distinguishing features of this epoch? It isn't these sky-scrapers, airplanes, wireless. . . . It's the development of a science of human nature." [46]

V *Flirtation with Behaviorism*

Eastman's attraction to data-confirmed propositions was readily transformed into a preoccupation with data alone; and, though recognizing the dangers inherent in a wholly empirical view of phenomena, he did occasionally veer into behavioristic psychology. After all, he had long been interested in "the interior causes of consciousness," having read Washburn, Watson, Munsterberg, among others; and he had wrestled with sensationalist images and motor responses. [47] Understandably, he conceived of behaviorism as a weapon of war in the hands of those hostile to "Hegel's antiquated theory of mind." [48] Behaviorists, such as Pavlov and the Russian physiological psychologists in general, necessarily opposed subjectivism. Their work on reflexes and the physiology of higher nerve centers was at variance with the theories of Russian Marxists, and they undermined the Marxist boast of being in the scientific vanguard.

Eastman, to his credit, refused to take the final plunge into the cold, unpromising waters of mechanistic materialism. He shivered on the brink, but he eventually drew back. Cutting to the heart of the matter, he recognized the "totally inadequate view" of behaviorist thought. In a vein suggestive of the humanist objections to mechanism advanced by Marx, he continued: "The interaction of organism and environment is for him [the behaviorist] carefully divided into reflex arcs all operating in one direction. A stimulus to the end-organ, a commotion in the central-nervous system, then a response in the muscles—that is the whole story of life in his laboratory. But life interflows with reality in full circles. We do things not only because we have a sensation, but also in order to make a sensation."

But Eastman nullified the pessimistic and dangerously egalitarian implications of this passage by reducing the "instinct of self-preservation" to simply "a will to live in the sense of an affirmative reaching out after life's experience." In this manner, he stated his unwillingness to transform man from creator into creature; and he inferentially rejected behaviorist theorems.[49]

Thus Eastman's encounter with Freud's propositions lit up his mind. They supported his dependence upon instrumentalism, his antagonism to dialectics, his fascination with humor, his flirtation with physiological psychology, even his affirmation of Darwin and of inherited instinctual drives. Freud also assumed an axial role in Eastman's view of literature. Psychoanalytic theories did not, to be sure, explain a work of art. "The movements of social forces that condition" such a work were "often more important than the motives of the individual which cause it." Psychoanalysis, however, could contribute to the understanding "of the uses of language in literature." Moreover, it helped shape Eastman's literary tastes. It prompted his attack on both the "Right Wing" and the "Left" among the critics: He criticized the former, led by Norman Foerster, because the group claimed that psychology was a pseudo-science, the latter, because it utterly ignored "the existence of a science of human behavior."[50]

CHAPTER 10

The Literary Mind

EASTMAN'S CULTISH ABSORPTION in science pervaded all his thinking. He had pondered its application to poetic expression while at Columbia, but he only wrote of the problem at length in 1932, in *The Literary Mind*.[1] Opening with an assessment of science and of its "invasion of the field of literature," this book adjudged such an invasion "the great intellectual event of our time"—one more so than the decline of religion, the introduction of the machine, World War I, the "breakdown" of capitalism, and other alleged sources of the "modern temper that afflicted literature in the 1920's and 1930's.[2] The resultant schism between literature and science, Eastman believed, was responsible for "the literary tendencies" of three centuries. At pains not to assign the division to any one cause, he stated: "It [this schism] has brought other things after it, or comes with them—industrial capitalism, the machine age, finance capital, democracy, sex equality, proletarian revolution, the World War. And there is always the dance of the chromosomes to remember. It would be metaphysics to exalt any one of these causes as prime mover above all the others." [3]

Confirming this dichotomy between science and literature was the distinction between the way things are experienced and a conception of them "in their practically important relations"; in other words, Eastman saw a tension between acquaintance *with* things (experience), which was at the core of poetry, and knowledge *about* things, which was the aim of science. Science and poetry could reconcile their differences since the poet employs the data of phenomena, but science drives out poetry "by ignoring the experienced quality of things." For example, in reading E. E. Cummings' poem about a mouse, scientists would despair of the poet's ignorance; but poets would "leave the business of making sense *about* mice to the zoologist." [4]

Eastman was informed; he knew his literary history, particularly that of England, and he had some knowledge of social history. He recognized the significance of the metaphysicians and of the Romantics' effort to recapture both the Elizabethan rhetoric and the kingdom of knowledge. The failure of the Lake district poets, as he understood it, resulted in "a gradual retreat, a reluctant acceptance of the steadily advancing division of labor, a search for some independent function and prestige for poetry." [5]

Eastman took the long view of literary developments. At one time, he believed, men of letters did not find knowledge either too large or too technical to grasp; Chaucer, he reminds us, had been an astronomer. But, gradually, beginning in the sixteenth century, the inexorable division between science and poetry took form. Science was gradually perceived as a separate pursuit, one wholly distinct from literature. The work of Galileo, Gilbert, Harvey, and Descartes widened the breach; and the appearance of the metaphysicians confirmed it. [6]

Eastman looked back nostalgically to the sixteenth century before poetry and science had parted, when writers "experienced the stimulus of that birth of real knowledge which has created our modern world, but without feeling pushed aside by it"—when men still held the naïve conviction, an Aristotelian legacy, "that poetry itself is knowledge and that knowledge can go no higher than the poet raises it." He endorsed Sir William Osler's address of 1919, which expressed the belief that science and the humanities needed each other. He admired the universal genius of Goethe because the latter was "the only man since poetry and science" divided "who did work and play creatively in both fields." [7]

Considering the antimony Eastman established, his choice of science or poetry was predictable. Eastman, the champion of science and of the pragmatic method was, paradoxically, also the apostle of the pure feeling. Poetry was emblematic of the latter. "Poetry is clothing life in its own form," Eastman's Jo Hancock exclaimed. "A poet lives—that is the primary thing." [8] His decision "to go away somewhere, to the mountains or the sea, and write a great poem" was shared and sympathized with by his creator. Eastman, after all, was always writing poetry and was inordinately proud of it; and his verse was irredeemably stained by a Romantic, deeply personal view of life and love. Jo Hancock's poems would be about failure, about how the poet fails of life "exactly because of the purity and greatness of his wish to live. He wishes to live all of life. . . ." [9] If Eastman failed, he wanted it to be for the same reason; and his poems were about life and, simultaneously, had a purely private dimension. In the preface to his *Colors of Life*, (1918) Eastman stated, "life is what I love. And though I love life for all men and women, and so inevitably stand in the ranks of revolution against the cruel system of these times, I love it also for myself." Significantly, he added, "my poetry has never entered even so deeply as it might into those tempests of social change that are coloring our thoughts today."

Thus Eastman identified the creative act with "life," which was coterminous with "feeling" and "experience," rather than with any socially relevant goals; the latter were supererogatory at best. "Poetry," he flatly stated, "always speaks to words that feel"; to a "thing like music or the morning," and it "stands in no need of meaning anything for those who are sensitive enough to perceive it." [10] Science versus poetry, therefore, could be transposed into other, now-familiar antitheses—thought versus feeling, intellection versus experience. Whatever the terms of the contrast, poetry was non-factual and non-scientific—and enormously attractive for precisely this reason.

I *On Poetry*

But poetry was more than an expression of organized emotion for Eastman; it was a way to "heighten consciousness"—by which he did not mean consciousness of self in the Freudian sense (whereby the laws of necessity are made clear) but of the experience described—to make it more vivid and meaningful. Such feelings were attainable and made manifest in "pure" poetry—which had its force in the "aboriginal foundations of life": pure poetry, as he defined it, was antithetical to the pragmatic; and the purest had some thing of the radiance and rhythm of the Impressionists about it. Such poetry celebrated a private experience; it was incantatory; it evolved "upon threads of connection as tenuous as those of a musical symphony." Those who practiced it abandoned the charade of calling "forth actual events and objects into the air." But they had not on that account, he continued, "acknowledged the empire of practical sense. They remain proud. They refuse to deck themselves out with meanings. They stand there, offering you nothing—only themselves, and that only if you will surrender to an invisible spell." [11]

By "pure" poetry, therefore, Eastman meant "art for art's sake" or, putting it obliquely, that tendency which acknowledged art as "independent of, and irrelevant to all practical thinking and all reliable truth." Its overseas practitioners were the French Symbolists—Mallarmé, Baudelaire, and Rimbaud—and the English literary critics of the 1890's, Walter Pater, Oscar Wilde, Arthur Symonds. The supreme exemplar in American poetry was Edgar Allen Poe, and he had a host of imitators and disciples in the 1930's—those who "are not conscious, any more than Keats was, of the break with an antique tradition." These "pure" poets take "their place more and more among the artists rather than the priests and teachers of mankind. . . . [They are] a group of extremists, excitedly modern, making a veritable crusade and consecrated glorious life work of the art of telling us nothing in their poems. . . . They belong to a different tradition.[12]

These observations, both descriptive and condemnatory, illustrated the dilemma that beset Eastman—the dualism between a socially relevant and a uniquely personal art. They reflect upon another dualism troubling his generation—that between "life" and revolution. Eastman, after all, was hardly unique;[13] for Floyd Dell and Joseph Freeman, among others, life was contained in temporal desire, individual experience, moments of "energetic idleness"; and these objectives were antagonistic to social struggle. Life, whatever it was, *was* greater than revolution—and Floyd Dell asked himself, during the *Masses* trial, what he was doing in the courtroom when he should have been at home writing a story: "How in the world did I come to be mixed up in this political cause celebre?" Yet "pure" poetry, even when it communicated and was not meaningless to the reader, left radical poets and writers discomforted. Distracting headlines, which told of social injustice and revolutionary developments, propelled the Dells and the Eastmans into courtrooms.

Eastman could hardly surrender to the tendency of poets to abdicate a role external to themselves. To the venerable truth that poetry was the sum of experience, he opposed the equally hallowed function of poet as prophet and truth-seeker. But to achieve the latter consummation, the poet "will *have* to make some genuine and verified . . . knowledge his own. He will have to read some science deeply and become at home in the temple of science. There is no way to overcome a division of labor without retrogress, but for one person to perform the whole of both kinds of labor." [14]

Eastman, however, did not sustain any clearcut preference; his own deepest impulses were too much in conflict for that. Radicalism and revolution diverted him, as they did all putative poets among Socialists; yet at times he claimed that the asocial poet, the "pure" poet, was the most gifted creative artist of his time. He could admire such poets because "their gifts and their business is all with the felt qualities of experience"—nothing more. Hence he was greatly drawn to Sergei Yessenin, "perhaps the most unconsciously melodic of all contemporary lyric voices," "that is . . . , the creative artist in his purest essence. . . ."; and, Eastman continued, "the purpose of his singing is his song." [15] Eastman, in summary, championed the scientific method and the "realistic" appraisal; yet he chose the way of poetry which was closest to the springs of his personality. The choice, we have noted, was not decisive or viable; and it reflected the contradictions that unconsciously beset him.

II *Foray Against Humanism*

The dualism between science and literature accounted for the development and transformation of literary criticism which, he insisted, was in decline. He recalled the commanding figures of the profession—Walter Pater, Gotthold Lessing, William Hazlitt, Sainte-Beuve, Ernst Renan, Matthew Arnold, Allen Tate, and Samuel Johnson chief among them—and concluded that something momentarily flared and flourished "like a comet and then died down to almost nothing." Significantly, the peak of literary criticism were years of great scientific investigation and growth, the development of psychology and the social sciences, and the schismatic years that followed. The great critics, he declared, "were, at first, forerunners of these sciences, and then afterwards mediators between them and the general body of intellectual literature." Men of letters, by a minor stratagem, sought to appropriate a little of the growing authority of science; but, as the gap between it and poetic literature widened, the gulf became increasingly difficult to bridge. Eastman noted that a "division of labor" occurred between the critics of science, such as Dewey and Bertrand Russell, and the critics of literary art, the Mores, Eliots, and Middleton Murrays; or, subsuming the latter under another rubric, the "classicists" (both poets and critics)—with Pound, Eliot, Winters, Tate and Sitwell outstanding—opposed by "an older and more solemn group" of humanists.[16]

Whatever the literary polarity, Eastman's exegesis became a two-pronged assault—on humanism and classicism. The humanist circle, he claimed, invented "fantastic theories of criticism" —strange intermediary spheres which were hybrids, belonging neither to science or poetry. For Eastman, the battle with humanism had to be held on this middle ground. The humanists—the "pseudo-moralists," as he styled them—defended "the prestige of their profession with high talk of the inner life"; they sought to convince us "that they occupy some celestial intermediary sphere." [17] From their exalted command post they strike at their adversary—the neo-Classicists. But the quarrel between them was gentlemanly, artificial, and unreal since the humanists were only peripheral enemies who had an opponent in common: science. And science was the real enemy in "a war in defense of the ancestral preserves of humane letters against the encroachment of verified knowledge." [18] Eastman derisively claimed that humanists were "fighting for the right of literary men to talk loosely and yet be taken seriously in a scientific age."

With their highly conservative vision and moral temper, the humanists provided an easy target. Their defense of humane letters, Eastman asserted, was marked by an elitist concept of knowledge —the pursuit of ideas *per se* by an aristocracy of talent. The humanist goal, as he explained it, was "an impeccable acquaintance with 'the classics' . . . [and] a mastery of 'the humanities,' as opposed to the rather low social rating of the vulgar pursuit of useful knowledge." Though humanism smacked of the rule of the gentleman—reason enough to condemn it—it was the fundamental bias against science to which Eastman most objected: "They are brandishing every weapon or idea they can lay hold on—brandishing God himself if they can still hang to Him—in a vain effort to defend the prestige of humane letters." Such hostility to disciplined and verifiable scientific procedures, he was convinced, most accurately described their motives—the need to defend their humanistic empire against "the inexorable advance of a more dis-

ciplined study of man." They invoke the name of a higher morality, or the claims of "intellect" or of a "superior order of intelligence" in defending their resistance.

Whatever the name of the game, such resistance was basically
against a force that threatened the prestige and integrity of these
humanists. Continuing to strip away their defenses, Eastman
called them "obscurantists" and "pseudo-moralists" who guarded
their citadel with "high talk of the inner life." In support of this
contention, he cited Paul Elmer More's attempt to demean I. A.
Richards, and the humanists' depreciation of Emile Zola and
Dreiser which was undertaken to preserve the domain of the gentleman in literature and to keep it free of science. Eastman,
finally, accused them of "infantilism," "loose talk," defense of the
Cult of Unintelligibility; and wryly he opined: "I do not see what
to do with the whole tribe but bundle them into a well-rotted ship
and shove them out to sea." [19]

III   *On T. S. Eliot*

Eastman was hardly more patient with the neo-Classicists. He
described Eliot's *Ash-Wednesday* as an "oily puddle of emotional
uses"; and he contemptuously dismissed the *Nation* and the *New
Republic* for their praise of *The Waste Land*. Even so thoughtful
a critic as Edmund Wilson was culpable, Eastman declared, since
he did not—could not—convey the meaning behind Eliot's vague,
allusive language. Joseph Wood Krutch was of no help when so-
licited for an explanation of the poem, nor were I. A. Richards
and Merrill More. Indeed, each of "these three skilled and sympathetic readers" presented different interpretations of *The Waste
Land*—demonstrable proof of its obscurity. Hart Crane's *White
Buildings* furnished another illustration, and Eastman cited two
"eulogizers"—Mark Van Doren and Allen Tate—who offered
varying interpretations.[20]

IV   *Quarreling with Literary Critics*

Few major critics escaped Eastman's shafts and certainly not
Krutch, Richards, or Van Wyck Brooks. Eastman revolted from
the implications of Krutch's *Modern Temper*, one of the most
celebrated books of the 1920's. In a work of almost unrelieved

pessimism, Krutch brought home the message of man's moral and social incapacity, of his inability to progress toward a more perfect society. This work disabused men of humanistic goals and it taught men that love was desolation and nothingness at the end. Krutch proclaimed that poetry was doomed, that the novel was dying, that it was no longer possible to write genuine tragedy because such a form required faith in man's nobility and in the genuineness of his suffering—a willingness to suspend disbelief in man's capacity to act heroically. To Krutch, science was responsible; but men had even lost faith in it, or rather in the power of its "findings to help us as generally as we had once hoped they might help." To Eastman, who forcefully rejected this hapless vision of life, the novel's proclaimed "dead end" was merely the sharpening of the conflict between poetry and science, "between the propagation of knowledge and the communication of experience. It is the same dead end at which poetry and tragedy and comedy have arrived, and it raises the same problem, the problem of the future relations between poetry and truth." [21]

I. A. Richards, Eastman admitted, pioneered in his *Practical Criticism,* in the attempt to formulate a psychology of poetry, and he was among the first to admit that poetry was not knowledge. But, in conceding the latter, Richards was converted to sentimentality. "He offers as I do," Eastman stated, "a definition of poetry, and his statement that 'critical remarks are merely a branch of psychological remarks' is obviously akin to the thesis I am advancing." Welcoming Richards' recognition of an "inevitable division of labor between poetry and science," Eastman lamented the fact that Richards (and C. K. Ogden) separated "knowledge from life and then declared poetry once more the mistress of life." Eastman, though admiring him, presents a bill of particulars: Richards could not explain metaphor, or even the association of poetry and meter; he was too austere and moralistic, more so even than Arnold; he erred in denying that poetry referred to things; and, finally, his doomsday view of literature was similar to Krutch's— and they were, therefore, twin prophets of literary despair.[22]

In Van Wyck Brooks, Eastman took on an even more formidable adversary. For Brooks was the leading literary radical of his day, the symbol and avatar of the creative life. He had edited the *Freeman,* a magazine that, richly and imaginatively Socialistic, was radical in art and politics; and he contributed important social and esthetic criticism to the *Dial*, another journal that helped to shape America's literary tastes. There were his now famous theses about the "usable past," about the creative personality as an apostle of democracy (in Whitman's sense), about the homogeneity of America's cognoscenti; there were his first gropings toward a psychological approach to both literary biography and the New Criticism initiated by Pound and enshrined by Eliot. Brooks was famous; Eastman, only a little less so; and they engaged in a highly publicized duel, inspired at first by Eastman's science-literature thesis.

The quarrel between them was deeply embedded in their respective views of literature. The world constantly intruded in Eastman's personal thoughts. He confessed to difficulty in combining his work for social justice and his creative writing, thereby anticipating the great debate between private and socially relevant artistic expression. He admitted to another internalized warfare—that of creative autonomy, which was immediately attractive to him, in opposition to party-imposed discipline which, as a Bolshevik in good standing in 1919, he believed the artist ought to accept. Charmed by Lenin's solutions, he chose the disciplined, "scientific," tough-minded approach—that of loyalty to the proletariat and to the immediacy of the class struggle.

The literary issues were crystallized by Romain Rolland's "Declaration of Intellectual Independence," which appeared in the December issue of the *Liberator*. Signed by the most prominent citizens of the world community of culture (and including Jane Addams, Selma Lägerlof, Stefan Zweig, Bertrand Russell, Hermann Hesse, Benedetto Croce, Henri Barbusse), this declaration invited all intellectuals—who had recently debased themselves by accepting wartime chauvinism—to write for "the whole of Humanity": "We do not know peoples. We know *the* People—one universal—the People which suffers, struggles, falls to rise again . . . the People of all men, all equally our brothers. And it is that they shall become conscious with us of this brotherhood, that we raise above their blind battles the Ark of the Covenant—the unshackled Mind, one and manifold, eternal."

Replying in the same issue, Eastman politely rejected Rolland's statement, with its misty abstraction of "the Mind," and what he conceived of as an elitist distinction between a "superior cult" of intellectuals—"a class apart" who represented "higher thought"—

and the "wage laborers of the earth." Intellectuals, Eastman insisted, must affiliate with the workingclass, not work independently of it: "There exists a science, consisting of a series of hypotheses as to the method by which this choice of ours may be carried out . . . , the science that was founded in the Communist Manifesto of 1848—the science of revolution. And almost the first postulate of that science so far as it applies to the present times, is that if we wish to achieve liberty and democracy for the world we must place ourselves and all our powers unreservedly upon the side of the working class. . . ." [23]

Four months later, Eastman, when invited to join an international order, the "League of Intellectual Solidarity for the Triumph of the International Cause," made a similar response to Henri Barbusse. Eastman approved of the order's openly revolutionary fervor, but he accused the movement—known as *Clarté*—of the same bourgeois sentimentality and unscientific thinking that he had found in Rolland's declaration. He believed that Barbusse "wanted to obscure the line of battle and weaken the revolutionary perceptions of the workers." Middle-class liberals, Eastman warned, would never rise above their class interests: "The task at hand [he continued] is the overthrow of a master class by the workers of the world. It is just as simple as that. In this operation the humanitarian intellectuals will function up to the critical moment as obscurers of the issue, and when the critical moment comes they will function as apostles of compromise and apologists of the masters."

"We literary and artistic people," Eastman maintained, "are distinguished by our ability to realize, feel and express the qualities of things. We are experts in experience but must keep poetry true to the science of revolution." [24] Both the implications and the purpose of this statement are plain: Eastman, the apostle of the spontaneous feeling, had here chosen the road of party discipline. Even experience needs to be channelled, directed, organized; and artists and writers, he lectured Barbusse, required external controls. He asked: "Is it wise for these people whose service to the revolution is inspiration—the poets, artists, humorists, musicians. . . . —to form a distinct and autonomous organization of their own?" It clearly was not, he replied, because "these particular people . . . are more in need of guidance and careful watching by the practical and theoretical workers of the movement than the members of any other trade." And he insisted that "the party is the *only organization,* the only corporate source of intellectual guidance."[25]

When Eastman's rejection of *Clarté* provoked Brooks's essay in the *Freeman,*[26] Eastman accepted the challenge. A series of exchanges narrowed the issue to the function of the writer in revolutionary crises.[27] Brooks defended the writer's power and usefulness: he could honestly present life and bring the working class to intellectual and social maturity. Eastman, Brooks claimed, had denied this role to the intellectual: "he considered them so exceedingly playful that, far from being in a position to educate the workers, they were themselves, like refractory children, in want of education."[28] Vigorously pleading the cause of revolutionary letters, Brooks insisted that literature, not science, was responsible for the partial success of Russia's Revolution; that Eastman erred in assigning to literature a minimal role—one " 'of no practical importance' "—in arousing the revolutionary will; and that Eastman, if he "wants a revolution, a successful revolution in America," "had better revise his view of literature." Because, Brooks continued, inspiration "may turn the wheel," but only " 'education' will provide the wheel with tracks on which it can revolve to any purpose." A civilization without an organized culture, he concluded, "is a hard and stony ground" for revolution. Without such a culture, people are unconscious; and only literature can arouse consciousness and guide a people to maturity.[29]

Brooks makes a compelling case. Eastman had indeed defined the field of literary expression too narrowly, and he was vulnerable to the charge of having "a deep contempt for his own vocation," of wishing to discredit and humiliate it.[30] Brooks is most persuasive when he maintains that only literature—not science—can create sentient men imbued with revolutionary zeal. He is convincing because of Eastman's simplistic and yet blurred presentation of the science-literature cleavage. Eastman's thinking, we have noted, wavered throughout. And, as we also observed, he might advocate the radical conscious self in one passage, thereby paying homage to instrumentalism and the new psychology, and then in another he could apotheosize the untamed and anarchic unconscious self. He shifted from one foot to another, advancing contrary propositions: the Romantic revolutionary and the Realistic writer; the liberated "poet" and the

Socialist artist, who was both free and unfree, who ought not to submit to party directives but who must turn to the party for guidance. Such equivocation was typical of Eastman, and it left him vulnerable to his critics.

CHAPTER 11

Art and Politics

THE DECADE of the 1930's was one of intellectual warfare for Eastman. "Instead of appreciating, encouraging and arousing," as Edmund Wilson commented some years later, "he had turned into a critic of the sidelines who guided, jeered and complained." [1] He became a literary gadfly within radical ranks; he engaged in quarrels, sporadic or sustained, with Brooks, Richards, Krutch, Hook, Trotsky, Rolland, Barbusse, and others. The wide variety of issues that provoked his shafts suggest the catholicity of his interests: Hegel's dialectic, Ernest Hemingway's virility, the role of the Socialist writer, the nature of modern literature, the significance of anarchism, and the condition of Russian culture.

Increasingly shrill in tone, Eastman's writings took on a choleric and *ex parte* quality, one reflective of the growing isolation of his position. More and more, he became the self-proclaimed trustee of the new psychology, of a modern view of literature, and of an objective approach to the Soviet Union. Frequently, his position was little more than an *ad hominen* attack delivered by a combatant always ready for verbal jousting, particularly when his *amour propre* was hurt. But, at other times, he invested issues with clarity, understanding, and a foresight that was arresting.

Eastman had devoted nearly a lifetime to speculation on the relationship of art and society. As the preceding chapter has suggested, he was torn by contrary winds—of the artist as revolutionary agent and of the artist as immune from the social storms, of art as an expression of solitary man and of art as a social expression, of literary freedom and literary responsibility. His choice was somewhat capricious, as we have seen, depending on the times and the demands of the debate. His dilemma was widely shared, for most observers were troubled by the inability to find a clear-cut, durable line between the artist as surrogate of the revolution and as dweller in a private domain. Eastman insisted in 1915 that only "a queer morality" could "escape the grip of the tragic problems of our time by turning the eyes in another direction"; six years later, he urged a "free and irresponsible literature"; and, still later, in 1934, a literature guided by party dictates and aspirations.[2]

I *The Russian Literary Scene*

Eastman's *Artists in Uniform* was written by a victim of history, one who occupied a lonely command post in 1934, an enclave under continuous sniper fire. World-wide obloquy had a deleterious effect on Eastman; it tinctured his vigorous language and made him at times intemperate and opinionated. *Artists in Uniform* was tinged by bitter and excessive rhetoric; but these qualities were venial sins, an index to Eastman's original faith. Written with fire and conviction, this book was valuable as a set of caveats. It told the whole lamentable story of Soviet cultural policies. Published in 1934, in rebuttal to *Voices of October* (by Freeman, Kunitz, and Lozowick), it arraigned Russia's treatment of intellectuals after Lenin's death and after, by contrast, the period of spontaneous experimentation.[3]

As we have noted, Eastman responded openly and with ardor to the great flowering of Soviet culture after 1920. It coincided with his own sojourn, the end of civil war, the NEP period of 1921, and Lenin's encouragement to a measure of individual freedom. Lenin instinctively knew "that art is not the business of a body organized for practical ends," Eastman stated in 1934; and, had he "deemed art a weapon to be wielded by the party or the class, he would have written fully and explicitly about it. He ignored no weapons." [4]

Given encouraging social and economic conditions in Russia, there was an eruption of fresh talent and innovation that seemed worthy of encouragement. "I once attended an evening meeting of the Poets' Union," he recalled, "and listened to the reading of original manuscripts representing fifteen separate and distinct schools. . . ." This bewildering variety of literary blocs, each claiming to speak for poetry and each driven by an irresistible desire for experimentation, reflected the health of Soviet culture. Vladimir Mayakovsky in poetry; Nicholas Tikhonov and the post-acmeists, with their insistence on the concrete individuality of things; Sergei Yessinen and the Imagists; and Boris Pilnyak, Isaac Babel, Eugene Zamyatin, Constantine Fedin in their stories were trying out new techniques; and there were the Cosmists, with their manifesto that "'the poetry of the collective principle, and of the joy of labor . . . is the pulse of the proletarian culture'"; the Serapion fraternity, that loose literary constellation emerging from Leningrad's House of the Arts; the Pereval group which flowered out of the generational ferment in two literary groups, *Molodaya Gvardia* (Young Guard) and *Oktyabr* (October)— when younger members wanted to look objectively at conditions and sought an organic relationship with the people—to the neglect of party membership and aspiration.[5]

"'Each of us has his own face and his own literary tastes,'" affirmed Lev Lunts, the Serapion's chief theoretician in *Literaturnye Zapiski:* "'Each of us has his own ideology and political convictions.'"[6] To such single-minded insistence "'that the voice should not ring false,'" Eastman had no choice but to give his endorsement. He was intrigued by the Serapion insistence upon individuality, its rejection of political interference, its emphasis upon technique, its demand that the poet has a right to dream, its yearning for freedom of expression and even its Romantic outlook: freedom and Romanticism, as he saw it, were handmaids of the revolution. Of Yevgeny Zamyatin, the Serapion's guide and prophet, Eastman recorded his heroic activities in 1905 and his insistence upon intellectual freedom and scientific attitudes. Of V. Pereversev, an absolutely independent Marxist literary critic, Eastman strongly identified with his devotion to literature as an art and with his assertion, "'The artist creates life, and not systems. He does not reason and does not argue, but lives, imagining himself to be this or that character in this or that situation.'" Of Ivan Katayev, the most talented of the Perevals, Eastman admired his belief that "life is beautiful and 'justifies itself.'" Of A. K. Voronsky, the editor-in-chief of *Krasnaya Nov* (*Red Virgin Soil*) and the Perevaltsky champion, Eastman endorsed his defense of the "right of artists to an independent vision of the world."[7] Voronsky's *Krasnaya Nov,* Eastman pointedly noted, was "inspired by Trotsky, and its policy was based upon that concept which he shared with Lenin of the revolutionary power as a gardener rather than a drill-sergeant in the field of art."

Eastman could write about these days with some authority. Although somewhat vague in his recollections, he apparently was an eye witness to the founding of *Red Virgin Soil:*

> And Voronsky himself, if I remember rightly, participated in an effort made in 1923 by a group of these poetic-minded Bolsheviks [the Pereval group, we may surmise], who were hospitable enough to include me in their number, to found a journal which should give even a wider range to literary experimentation. It is interesting, in view of the subsequent canonization of party propaganda as the sole form of revolutionary art, to remember that Demian Byedny [Bedny Yefim Pridvorov was Bedny's real name], subsequently the poetic staff-officer of the Stalin clique . . . was an enthusiastic member . . . I recall with particular pleasure his enthusiasm over the article I contributed to our first number. . . .[8]

Eastman's comments on Sosnovsky's place in Soviet letters is fully as enigmatic as those on Gorki and, once again, the omission of certain facts seemed deliberate. Sosnovsky also was a member of the Perevaltsy, as Eastman records, and he "went the way of all those Russian Bolsheviks who combine three qualities—honesty absolute, a high intelligence and extreme courage. He languishes with hundreds more of the old fighters for communism in one of Stalin's 'isolators' in Siberia." [9] Absent for reasons we may only surmise is Sosnovsky's role in those years when he belonged to the "ideologically pure" and led the anti-Trotsky On Guardists against the "petty bourgeois" Fellow-Travelers whom Trotsky supported.

These voices—Pereversev, Voronsky, the Serapions, the Perevaltsy, Kataev—gradually were silenced. Russian writers came under direct party controls; and, rather than forge a new art for a new society, they became amenable to vulgar social command and were reduced to propagandists of the state. This devolution from great diversity, which characterized Soviet literature between 1920 and 1923, to total coercive conformity has been richly documented elsewhere.[10] Suffice to say that these earlier years encompassed a period of unprecedently varied artistic activity and intellectual ferment. Eastman, however, seems unaware that the major generative force of these years, the revolution itself, contained a destructive seed. The passionate commitments on the part of writer and politician alike made artistic independence difficult to maintain; so, too, did the near-universal conviction that the man of letters was a social engineer, that the writer held the Russian future in his hands. Such an understanding tended to restrict artistic freedom and eventually—when embodied in party dogma and canons of Socialist realism—to destroy it. Freedom was increasingly wedded to social commitment and the resultant loss for Soviet letters was immeasurable: What was once Russian Realism in literature became, under the influence of Gorki, Romanticism in its gloss of facts.

II   *Creative Freedom and State Repression: The First Gusts*

Eastman certainly saw the struggle, the idealism, the clash of wills. He duly noted the gradual erosion of creative autonomy, as ardent champions of individualism joined schools and groups; and the outcome—which extinguished the gains of the early 1920's— left him with a personal sense of bereavement. Yet for Eastman the outcome was prefigured, built into Eastman's conception of the artist. Such a man must always find the state a potentially malevolent institution; he must find his own voice; he must "sing greatly"; he must understand that individual expression was inviolable—to be insulated from all external directives.[11] Matthew Josephson, whom Eastman quoted approvingly, had reduced the need of the artist to the succinct observation: " 'art demands a lonely and personal effort, rather than a collective one.' " [12] Such individuality was reason enough to admire the Serapions, Eastman stated: each of them had "his own individual ideology. Words of art organically are good with no matter what ideology. Art lives its own life and has no ultimate goal. Art is meaningless to politicians." [13] Only when its practitioner finds his own voice could an estimable proletarian art arise. At all times he must take chances, and live and write experimentally: "fear and failure of the spirit of adventure are the death of art. Recklessness is its life." [14] At all times his work must be free, irresponsible, "playful," spontaneous. But these articles of faith relating to the creative spirit and act were at opposite poles from party doctrine. In affirming as much, both Eastman and his ideal artist were headed for collision with those who authored and administered Soviet cultural policies.

The second phase of Soviet literary activity began with Lenin's death and the intra-party struggle. Eastman noted the growing ostracism of literary mavericks, their economic boycott by the state-controlled publishing house, the subordination of "every creative impulse . . . to a task described as 'organizing the mind and consciousness of the working classes and the broad toiling masses in the direction of the ultimate goal of the proletariat as reconstructor of the world and creator of the communist society.'" [15] He was, to be sure, somewhat premature in these observations. Though the "handwriting was on the wall" in these years, the relative freedom of pre-1925 still existed, as did many of the literary schools. Nonetheless, the political climate had begun to change as the party, starting in 1924, formally inaugurated discussions on the current literary scene. In this period, too, influential literary organizations were being formed, the products of mergers of previously independent blocs: MAPP (the Moscow Association of Proletarian Writers) in 1923, then RAPP (the Russian Association of Proletarian Writers) in 1925.

For Eastman, the creative outburst of the early 1920's assumed the highest importance, and the retreat from it portended disaster. Experimentation had been a fixed star, the major index of individual and ideological health. For this reason alone, these mergers were lamented; and increasingly stringent monitoring of Russian art was decried. Artists, he wrote in 1926, must "defend their independence . . . both against the attempt to organize them, and against the attempt to intimidate them with a specific practical principle parading in the guise of a general theory of the universe." [16] They may help the revolution or oppose it, or be "as indifferent to it as the wind of a spring morning." Revolutionaries, of course, should use artists; but the variety of life that they express cannot be subsumed under a simple formula: "To tell a sensuous poet that there is but one 'reality' . . . is to deny the emotional validity of his poems," cause enough to reject such instruction. It followed that the Serapions' insistence upon individuality would be lauded by Eastman and that the "office-holding bigots" who sought to use art would be condemned. Eastman would publicize and denounce any attempts to subject art to "regulation by party manifesto." [17]

III   *Terror and Suppression*

Eastman's *Artists* sounded a lonely tocsin in 1934, for his belief that matters had become urgent by this time was not generally shared. Nonetheless, there seemed to be rather compelling evidence. Sergei Yessenin, the peasant poet and Eastman's "cherubic hooligan"—possibly "the most unconsciously melodic of all contemporary lyric voices"—had killed himself by 1925. His suicide, Eastman suggested, was due to his disillusionment and repudiation of the Soviet Union, combined with his refusal to "subdue himself" by "stepping on the throat of his own song." Yessenin was one of "the purest poets," as well as a man possessed of revolutionary fervor; hence, he had demonstrated those virtues by which Eastman measured himself, and the latter unconsciously endowed him with his own values and aspirations.[18]

Then there was Evgeny Zamyatin, even more independent and courageous, who was distinguished for his artistic maturity and flawless craftmanship.[19] The spiritual father of the Serapions, he bridged the past and the future for a generation of Russian writers. He also was "a trained man of science," which evoked Eastman's admiration. Moreover, he was a working Bolshevik as early as the 1905 uprising; and he intellectually and emotionally accepted the October Revolution. But his crime, according to Eastman, was "that he kept his intellectual independence and moral integrity": "he refused to take orders from a political bureaucracy." [20] Hence the order was issued for his destruction, especially after Zamyatin's *We* appeared in *Volia Rossii*, an émigré monthly published in Prague—"at first without his knowledge, and as soon as he knew it, *against his protest*." Since *We* anticipated Orwell's *1984*, it became the focal point of attack. The charge was collaboration "with White Guard circles beyond the border," which resulted in arrest, persecution, vituperation, ostracism, and—only after Gorki's intercession with Stalin (again strangely omitted by Eastman)—exile abroad.

Another chapter of *Artists* was devoted to Mayakovsky, whom Eastman knew and liked. Strident, coarse, impetuous, the most colorful of the Futurists, the rebel against bourgeois society, "the bohemian dissenter" who "behaved discreetly," and bent to the turn of the party screws, he also broke under pressure and took his own life. Vyacheslav Polonsky, a well-known critic and writer who joined the party in 1919, was one more who aroused Eastman's concern. Like Mayakovsky, Yesenin, Pilnyak, Voronsky, and the Serapions, Polonsky was slandered by the On Guardists: he was "attacked and falsified and libelled, hammered, haunted, hounded out of office, out of press, out of all social breathing space, and out of life." [21]

So, too, was Isaac Babel, another writer with whom Eastman felt strong emotional kinship. *Artists* was published before Babel became a purge victim; but Eastman, taking note of his voluntary silence, pointedly asked why Babel, with his international fame, should "retire into the background." The answer came, an easy and bitter one: Babel refused to "submit to the demand of the hacks and hand-cut men of the Stalin regime that he write ballyhoo for the Red Army"; he refused "to surrender his incomparable pen into the hands of these new slave-drivers of creation, these brigadiers of the boy scouts of poetry, these professional vulgarians prostituting the idea of the liberation of all society by the proletariat to the task of enslaving all utterance and all creative life." [22]

Alexander Voronsky, one more cultural hero, was the publisher of Yessenin (in *Krasnaya Nov*) and the supporter of the Pereval Group; and he too became a major target of the On Guardists. RAPP writers, chiefly Leopold Auerbach, whom Eastman despised, virtually terrorized all dissenters; he waged unrelenting offensive against Pereval and *voronschina*—Voronsky and his protégés, the Fellow Travellers. Voronsky believed that Russian proletarian art was not only non-existent but was also impossible "until the creation of adequate material and cultural conditions." Thus he shared Trotsky's sentiments, reason enough for criticism to fall on his name; but that he also stressed artistic qualities, rather than ideological content, was another sin against him. He "was defending the right of artists to independent vision of the world," Eastman declared; and thus he had to be "beaten down, slandered, vilified, misquoted and misrepresented, his great prestige, resting upon party membership and association with Lenin since 1904, reduced to vapor and destroyed, his name and the name of his strong group 'pereval' identified with counter-revolution, his editorship taken away from him," and he himself sentenced in 1928 to Siberia. When Voronsky returned from exile to

Moscow, Eastman reported, he squandered his rare gifts in editing the classics, a safe occupation.

For every Yessenin who refused to surrender his lyre to the party and who took his life, there was a Mayakovsky who "bent his lyre to this storm and behaved discreetly." For every Zamyatin, there was a Valentine Kataev, whose belief "that life is beautiful" was "scared out of him by the inquisitors"; and a Romanov who repudiated the novel which he wrote—" 'a politically mistaken book' "—and the essence of "poetic art" in the process; and a Gorki, who was chastened by the charges against him; and a Pilnyak who also lacked moral stamina and buckled under pressure.[23]

Boris Pilnyak, a special case to Eastman, merited an entire chapter in *Artists*. Pilnyak was the peasant poet, the Romantic without a political credo. He was also the author of *Mahogany*, a novel that provoked a violent reaction. The victim "of a veritable pogrom, a literary lynching at the hands of a mob instigated and egged on by the state power," the frightened Pilnyak revised his novel; and he thereby, according to Eastman, became "Russia's leading expert in recantation, abjection, self-repudiation." [24]

IV   *Communist Literary Policy: The Arraignment*

The primacy in Russia of politics in letters—the drive for conformity—was apparent to Eastman by the mid-1920's. Zamyatin's suicide had sealed it. By November 1930, therefore, with the Second World Plenum of the International Bureau of Revolutionary Literature—the Kharkov Congress—Eastman's hostility to Stalinist cultural practices was markedly abusive. *Artists* opened with this Congress and with criticism of the American delegation, which included Mike Gold, Eastman's former colleague on the *Liberator*. But even earlier, in "Artists in Uniform" of 1933, Eastman hammered at the "American pilgrims" who slavishly submitted to "those fervently sophomoric under-Y.M.C.A.-secretaries of Stalin's bureaucratic church" who dominated the sessions.[25] Leopold Auerbach, Stalin's young adjutant who already headed RAPP (Russian Association of Proletarian Writers), received his first adverse criticism from Eastman for his resolution that " 'every proletarian artist must be a dialectic materialist.' "

Eastman, in all likelihood, was not among those who hailed

RAPP's liquidation in 1932, for he claimed that the event would merely substitute "socialist realism" for "dialectic materialism." Once again, he stated, America's left-wing intellectuals swallowed the Communist line, remaining subservient; and he concluded that the American people were "quite right not to trust them. No man possessing the mind and will to revolutionize America will express it by wallowing at the feet of some almost second cousin of the nephew of someone who sat on the knees of a man who helped to revolutionize Russia. . . ." Herein was a viable criticism of the American Left; its tendency to grovel before Moscow's dictates, to take orders, to kneel "in a position which leaves nothing visible to the American worker but his rump."

For Eastman, the performance of the American delegation and Auerbach's nostrums—that "art is a class weapon," that "artists are to abandon 'individualism,'" that "artistic creation is to be systemized, organized, collectivized;" that the party would give "'careful and yet firm guidance'"—were to be abjured. "This new religion of the Holy Land," he exclaimed in conclusion, "is what explains the crude humiliation of arts and letters" of which Kharkov was a dramatic example.[26]

Conditions worsened in the Soviet Union after *Artists*, but Eastman had seen enough: Yessenin was dead; so was Bely; so was Mayakovsky; so were the Serapions after Trotsky's banner fell in the dust with such heartbreaking suddenness; and the Imagists, Biocomists, *nicheivki*, Constructionists, etc. had been liquidated; Mandelstam was in exile; Babel had disappeared, after announcing at the Kharkov meeting that he had become master of the "genre of silence"; the Pilnyaks had "castrated" their harshly honest work. And Zhdanov had emerged from the wings and proclaimed the shape of things to come—a Socialist Realism which promised to be more confining than anything RAPP had ever proposed.[27] *Artists*, the outcome of the situation, was an abrasive commentary. It documented in characteristically polemical fashion the destruction of those creative impulses which would not submit to state dictates—"the systematic effort of the bureaucratic political machine . . . to whip all forms of human expression into line."[28]

Artists, therefore, became an inquest, an accurately informed commentary that signaled the end of Eastman's lofty hope for Russian literature as a humanizing force, as an agency of social resurrection. The theme of the book was simple and direct: "what with bigotry of Marxist metaphysics and brutality of Stalinist bureaucratism, literature as a vitally incisive thinking human function with the push of growth in it, has been silenced, watered down, or banished, or destroyed." [29] But *Artists,* though it exposed these practices, was not simply exposure for exposure's sake. It was a caveat to the effect that the arts must be approached affirmatively; it proclaimed that art must present only " 'the reality of life' and that the artist's right to 'an independent vision of the world' " was inviolable; it admonished American writers to avoid "a fanatic 'duty' toward the Holy Land, a praying eastward, a hasty dipping of the pen at the bidding of any ignorant whipper-snapper Stalin appoints to wield the knout over them"; it was another sermon in behalf of the proposition that "art is recreation, venture, life itself." [30] For, lest we forget what its author never forgot, Eastman was a child of ministers; and his little tract waged holy war against Soviet cultural repression. The religious stamp of his early upbringing marked all the writing of this atheist; and it was never more apparent than in this little book.

CHAPTER 12

The Pre-War Years:
Traveler and Apostate

EASTMAN'S TEMPER remained that of a proselytizer—only now *against* Soviet art and politics; his strictures on these subjects in the late thirties continued to be fervently ethical, to sound more than ever like sermons. He acted out of a certitude that smacked of theology, but a certitude confirmed by almost every development in Soviet society. Trotsky's famous prediction had come true: the Communist party became surrogate for the working class; the Central Committee for the party; and, finally, the General Secretary for the Central Committee. A single, all-powerful leader was now the voice of Russia's workers; and, as Eastman had repeatedly warned, the revolution was devouring its children.

The nightmare world of Soviet culture made *Artists* appear possessed of a dreadful *déja vu*, a brilliant projection of future developments. With Andrei Zhdanov as chief watchdog over arts and letters, a new wave of regimentation swept across Russian culture. Trotsky's elimination was paralleled by the liquidation of the Fellow Travellers and of the Smithy and Pereval groups. Hard-line political orthodoxy reached its apogee as hundreds of artists and writers disappeared.

Neither Soviet culture nor Eastman's reaction to it can be entirely meaningful without reference to extra-cultural factors. The bureaucratization of the arts; the strait-jacketing of letters; the systematic pressure upon novelist and playwright; the insistence upon Socialism Realism as *the* official creed; the liturgical epithets of "the indestructible Party," "Stalin, our sun," "disintegrating capitalism"; the strident warnings about counter-revolutionary conspiracies; the daily arrests—all developed out of Stalin's attempt to consolidate his personal power. Hence, the destruction of creative freedom was matched by ruthless suppression of political opposition.

The major event of the late 1930's was the purge, beginning with the Moscow trial of 1936 that convicted the "Trotskyite-Zinovievite terrorist group." This development struck Soviet intellectuals like the whiplash of a hurricane, and it produced a convulsive shock among European and American liberals. Other trials followed; and then came wholesale campaigns against suspect editors and critics, the secret police of Yezhov and Beria, the mechanism of terror which worked with impersonal efficiency, the bullying arrests of writers, the elimination of "Trotskyites" and their "abettors;" the endemic fear which crippled the creative spirit, and the prison terms and death sentences for political and military leaders.

Thus Stalin, by blood and intimidation, was cementing his power and making a reality of Eastman's dreadful vision. Slowly and almost unconsciously, owing as much to personal preferences as to desperate realities, Eastman turned from Russia and even for awhile from political affairs. Gripped by malaise during his self-styled "Blue Period," which lasted from 1937–1940, he circled around social affairs, so to speak, but was unable to address himself to major issues. His pessimism had formed slowly, though it was embedded in the belief that there is "much infantile and primitive savage yearning for dependence for external authority, for the sovereign-father . . . in the average human heart." [1] Hobbesian and Darwinian views had been locked within Eastman in deadly combat with revolutionary-Romantic optimism; and only gradually, with each turn of the Russian screw, did the negative strain become dominant. Eastman, who had been long torn by these ambiguities, was drawn to Bill Haywood's "new society" and his own "high-reaching dreams." But as early as 1921, after Moscow gave "the Russian Party" voting control of the International, he expressed reservations about the "Bolshevik, or any other new religion." [2]

This event marked the initial breach between Eastman and Lenin: "This was the date of its beginning, and this the point on which it began: the crude instinctive nationalistic bossism of the Russian leaders." [3] Eastman's first impressions of Revolutionary Russia had relieved some early doubts; but burgeoning interparty struggle revived them. Lenin's death, the growing bureaucracy,

Stalin's initial drive to power by means of the Triumvirs, and the conspiracy to falsify and destroy Trotsky betrayed Eastman's high hopes, as *Since Lenin Died* bears witness. Writing in *Venture* in 1927, Eastman, through Jo Hancock, expressed dismay about America's Socialists: they were "a good safe distance from the poor, in the first place, eating a four-course dinner in conventional style"; and George Forbes was the medium for the ridicule which he splayed on young lawyers and middle-aged ladies who belonged to Socialist groups which, at the first hint of a revolutionary seizure of power, would "barricade themselves behind the solid mahogany pianos in their front parlors." [4]

The Russian scene, however, retained its terrible fascination; and, returning to it, Eastman voiced serious doubts about Soviet political developments. Nonetheless, writing in the mid-1930's, he described "the situation as highly satisfactory in the economic and cultural fields"; and several speeches of this period were notable— in the light of what he had witnessed—for their moderation and his barely disguised search for assurance of the merit of the Soviet experiment. In order to place a pleasing gloss upon events, he usually emphasized Russia's economic progress, though in a notable talk—entitled "Present Trends in Russia"—before the Foreign Policy Association, he found "more initiative in Soviet Russia, more pep in every sphere of creative activity than there is anywhere else in the world outside the United States." [5]

And he concluded on an exultant note: "The Bolshevik Revolution thirteen years after its inception is still going forward on the original lines. The world has never seen anything like that before. It is almost a miracle, and like all other miracles which are taking place around us, it finds its explanation in scientific knowledge. The Bolshevik Revolution is the first revolution which has been guided by a scientific analysis of social forces and led by engineers who are expert in sociology and economics." [6] Elsewhere in this address Eastman expressed some reservations about Stalin's rule. He pointed out the flaw in Lenin's concept of party rule; indeed, he assigned the major share of blame to Lenin's methods rather than to Stalin's motives. Nonetheless, the generally affirmative character of his remarks remained an astonishing production from the author of *Since Lenin Died*.

The strongest impression that emerges from a reading of Eastman's literary and political chronicles seriatum in the 1930's is that of a man under seige. The smoke of battle hangs over his writings. *The Literary Decade* opened the 1930's; and, as we have noted elsewhere, in the quest for a modern synthesis of science and literature, it dismissed the most exciting contemporary experiments in letters as attempts to thwart the onrush of science. Concerned with the state of literature, it had little to say about esthetics, for example, and was mostly a sustained diatribe. It is almost as if the course of contemporary letters was inimical, at some deep level of consciousness, to what Eastman desired from existence and to the way he wished to use his powers.

I   *Eastman Strikes Against Left-Wing Orthodoxy*

Literature, to be sure, was not alone subject to critical treatment. There were the quarrels with Mike Gold, Leon Trotsky, Sidney Hook, and others. These had a personal, querulous, splenetic tone to them. Eastman seemed to be on the defensive, responding to criticism. *Voices in October* by Joseph Freeman, *et al.* evoked *Artists in Uniform* in rebuttal. The debates with Freeman and Gold in the *Modern Monthly* were also in the nature of thrust and riposte. Under attack by the John Reed Clubs, Eastman scored their unthinking acceptance of Marxist jargon, Soviet propaganda, and Stalin's growing tyranny. The *New Masses* policies, he declared, were being dictated by Moscow; and the publication therefore remained silent when confronted with "the arrest and banishment under police surveillance of the entire opposition in the Russian Communist Party." [7] He refuted the magazine's flimsy and unwarranted charges that no Socialist literature had come from him in a decade and that he was no more than a Bohemian radical.[8] He criticized the Soviet Union, but objected to being associated with its detractors; he apologized for his apostasy and resented the attacks of Russophiles. Sniped at from all sides, Eastman became at times bitter and intemperate, and appeared to be very much at bay.

II   *Eastman vs. Hook*

Victor Calverton's *Modern Monthly* served as the major vehicle of Eastman opinion in the mid-1930's. From this platform, he upheld his critique of Marxism in his running debate with Sidney

Hook. There was a certain irony attached to their quarrel, not only because both men were former students of Dewey and disciples of the pragmatic method, but because both championed experimentation and applied science; both were committed to the cause of socialism as a practical and moral necessity; both were Marxists, unanimous in their desire for a radical alteration of society; both insisted upon the need—as Eastman stated—for "a special kind of thinking [that] ought to prevail in the social, moral, and political fields." [9]

In other ways, of course, they were very different: Hook, humorless and never the hedonist, was stubbornly set against emotional appeals; Eastman, usually puckish and self-centered, was always ready for momentary emotional pleasures. Moreover, they disagreed bitterly as to the scientific properties in Marxism. Eastman stood on his usual grounds: Marx made a vain but laudatory attempt to free himself from German idealism, and his debt to Hegel was obvious in his metaphysical faith in historical inevitability. Finally, Eastman rejected Hook's contention that their teacher, John Dewey would have embraced dialectical materialism.[10]

Rather, Eastman charged, Hook had reshaped Marxism into a philosophical system that was logical, experimental, and acceptably scientific. Balking at the transformation, Eastman even accused his opponent of borrowing his ideas. "Not only is Eastman unable to do justice to the thought of Marx," Hook replied; "he cannot be trusted to give an elementary honest account of any man with whom he disagrees." [11] In rebuttal, Eastman described Hook as "superficial," as a casuist possessed of a "Talmudic infatuation with the mind of Marx," as a pedant guilty of "academic Schrecklichkeit." [12] Hook, who retorted in kind and gave more than he had received, accused Eastman of incompetence and of an unacknowledged indebtedness to Hook's work. He possibly got the better of the argument since he was a devastating logician. But Eastman's intellectual passions served him well; Hook certainly did not overwhelm him.

Eastman's argument may be interpreted as additional evidence of his disenchantment with Socialism. Still seeking to separate the positive social achievements of Russia from the deepening dictatorship, he never entertained any doubts about Stalin himself— "the schemer of unflagging zeal and genius" who had, Eastman wrote in 1934, "converted Marxism from a science of international proletarian revolution into a religion of the Holy Land." [13]

Eastman, however, remained intermittantly caught up by the promise of Revolutionary Russia. Even in 1936, on the eve of the purge trials, he had not come full circle. Despite the state's rapacity and the terror, "the wild hope of a totally new society . . . was dying hard" in the minds of people like Eastman, as Alfred Kazan recorded, after meeting Eastman at Calverton's home. "For these thinkers and scholars," Kazan observed, "natural opponents of Stalin the despot and philistine, there was still more belief in the Revolution than not; its positive value was not yet in doubt." [14]

III   *Eastman, Trotsky, and the Gods That Failed*

Eastman, by this time, had been Trotsky's American publishing agent for some years. He had translated the exile's *Real Situation in Russia* (1928), *History of the Russian Revolution* (1932), *The Revolution Betrayed* (1937), and several magazine articles. Their friendship was an outgrowth of Eastman's early and active defense of Trotsky whom he believed was Lenin's natural successor and whose "superior moral and intellectual revolutionary greatness" Stalin had recognized and clubbed down.[15] But relations between Eastman and Trotsky had cooled in the late 1930's. Eastman, characteristically, could not unqualifiedly champion the old Bolshevik; and he had early recognized the Russian's deficiencies: his failure to act decisively in 1923 and 1925, his underestimation of Stalin's will and shrewdness, his insistence upon intellection, and his lack of personal warmth. During a visit with Trotsky in Prinkipio in 1923, Eastman repeatedly argued with his host over dialectics, to which Trotsky still firmly adhered. Trotsky's unwavering claim that Russia was a proletarian state elicited Eastman's hostility. Eastman even questioned Trotsky's position on the Kronstadt rebellion by 1937; moreover, what was striking, he likened it to Stalin's practices.[16]

By 1937, therefore, Eastman had ceased his simultaneous defense of the Russian Revolution and attack upon its bureaucratic betrayers. By then, he no longer argued that the Revolution might succeed if Lenin's tactical expertise prevailed over Marx's metaphysics. By then, in a book with the apt descriptive title, *The End of Socialism in Russia*, (1937) he announced that "his God" had failed. Comparing this failure to that of Christianity, he stated: "The words socialist and communist are changing their meaning, just as the word Christian did. Just as the heretics were burned by thousands in the name of 'love thy neighbor,' so peasants have been starved by millions in workers' and peasants' Republics." [17] Eastman now confessed, in lamenting upon the rebirth of a capitalist class in Russia, that "the battle is definitely lost."

Eastman had crossed the Rubicon against Soviet policies in 1934 with *Artists in Uniform;* by 1937, with *The End of Socialism,* he had widened his frontal assault. In it the Russian government was arraigned for abandoning every vestige of Lenin's policy of Socialist internationalism. Eastman even claimed that all of Lenin's high public policies—of war, peace, and patriotism—had so disappeared that not a vestige remained. He duly noted the palpable idiocy of proclaiming one's fealty to the doctrine of "withering" while, in the same breath, exulting in the power of the Soviet state. He repeated his accusations that the Soviet Union had reestablished class divisions (if only by returning seven to eight per cent on investments) and that claims for "a classless society" were "sublime 'applesauce.'"; and he referred to his favorite *bête noire* of unrestricted population increases, claiming that the "madness of military nationalism was responsible, that a power clique looked upon the masses as its cattle and its cannon fodder." [18]

No area of Soviet life was exempt from attack by 1937. Pervaded by a bitterness that had become irreversible, *The End of Socialism* signalled the end of Eastman's ideological journey. The dream of revolutionary possibilities had fully receded. Policies were being implemented in the Soviet Union that "would horrify enlightened opinion" everywhere, and the way was being prepared for "a totalitarian state not in essence different from that of Hitler and Mussolini." So complete was Eastman's devolution by 1937 that even collectivization of agriculture was denounced—on what were rather unusual grounds for a Socialist: that the state had "given away franchises to vast farming corporations, deeding them the hereditary right formerly possessed by the aristocracy to cultivate for their own profit. . . . It is a consistent step only in the building up of social support for a Bonapartist clique." [19]

Eastman's views did not change in the years immediately preceding World War II; they were merely enlarged upon. *Stalin's*

Russia of 1940 ranged over the same ground: Stalin's domination of the immense party apparatus, his extermination of Leninist doctrine, his investment of the General Secretary with absolute powers, his "passionately vindictive character." Eastman reminded his readers of "the punitive expeditions against peasants, the campaigns of state-planned starvation, the war of extermination against thinking people generally. . . . His work makes that of the guillotine . . . look pale indeed." And he also reminded them that the inner-party fight waged by Lenin against Stalin had been fully set forth fifteen years ago, in *Since Lenin Died*.[20]

The accusations were again stroked in acid, often in rhetoric identical with that of earlier texts: Lenin's "monument of genius, the Soviet system" had been destroyed"; his policy of internationalism abandoned; Stakhanovism had created "a new privileged caste"; Stalin gave away the land to "vast farming corporations" [collectives]; a bureaucratic pyramid had betrayed the Revolution, making Russia into "a nation of informers, spies, hypocrites, lickspittles and mass-murderers. Her men and women of most noble and humane feelings are in jail, or in exile, or in concentration camps, or in hiding, or in traitors' graves, or cowed into absolute silence." [21]

IV *Marx, Lenin, and Trotsky: A Last Look*

Both *Stalin's Russia* and *Marxism is it Science*, each published in 1940, reaffirmed earlier conclusions. Both, for example, attacked "the utopianism inherent" in the "religion" of Marx and Engels which, declared Eastman, deceived them into ignoring the "all-important problem" of population controls. Engels was depicted as a "dreamer" who discoursed upon an "ideal state of things, which must come in due course, if the universe continues its 'endless ascending from the lower to the higher. . . .'" Marx, equally the utopian, "believed that truly miraculous things" would happen in human history; and he, too, founded his dreams upon "this myth of the infinite changeability of human nature." Not even Lenin entirely escaped the utopianism that inhered in dialectics, for even he ignored "the data of psychology" and put "a completely metaphysical faith in the place of this science."

But, Eastman, as late as 1940, continued to vacillate, as he sacrificed something by way of accuracy to the needs of the debate, since he denied that "shrewd and hardheaded realists like Marx *and* Lenin" believed in such myths as "the withering away of the State"—of which there was no "more preposterous notion in the history of religion"—or "from each according to his abilities, to each according to his needs"—which was "almost as utopian as the Golden Rule." Elsewhere, however, he inconsistently advanced the usual distinction between Lenin and Marx: "Lenin's mode of procedure" departed from Marx's thought "in the direction of scientific method." [22]

Eastman is not, however, wholly repetitive. *Stalin's Russia* goes beyond previous studies in acknowledging that Lenin's brilliant device for seizing power, though effective in overthrowing Russian capitalism, was fatally flawed by "utopianism"; "it trusted too much in education, too much in the reasonable and kind and tolerant and freedom-loving qualities of human natures." Such trust was the basis for Lenin's belief that the state would "die away," but it did not; rather, an armed seizure of power "by a highly organized minority party . . . will normally lead to the totalitarian state." If anything, "the machinery of education" would accelerate totalitarianism. Eastman then came to the harsh conclusion that Lenin's "revolutionary engineering" led the toilers, "with the red flag flying down the road to a more dreadful tyranny than he or they had dreamed of. He died, saddened by the first intimations of this tragedy." Stalin's bureaucrats, it followed, did not simply betray a successful revolution; "they are its outcome." [23]

These books differed from earlier studies in another way: Eastman's enmity toward Trotsky was now publicized. He reminded his readers of Lenin's admonition that Trotsky was inclined to be "'carried away by the administrative aspect of things'"; he again found Trotsky deficient in feeling, particularly feeling rooted in social realities; he charged him with transgression "not only [of] the intuitive wisdom of Lenin, but his actual principles." Eastman, who repeated the assertion that Trotsky underestimated Stalin's power, rejected his twofold contention that (1) Russia is a "'workers' state'" because he "blandly informs us" as much, and (2) that Russian Socialism failed because of industrial backwardness, which Eastman countered by the old chestnut of man's "hereditary nature." [24] Trotsky, he declared, ignored psychological and biological realities.

Eastman, by 1940, had passed beyond all possible illusion.

Since Trotsky still maintained a tentative belief in Russian Socialism as an agency of social resurrection, an irreparable divison was in the making. And Eastman found Trotsky's deeply emotional pull toward Russia intolerable. At one point, he called Trotsky a "dialectical Jesuit"; at another, when Trotsky urged proletarian "ruthlessness," he found this "proclamation of immoralism . . . a proletarian paraphrase of Dr. Funk and Goebbels." [25]

For Eastman, the Revolution was in its dying cycle; and he had emerged from allegiance to it as the chronicler of its illusions and futilities. "The failure of the Russian revolution," he wrote, "is perhaps the greatest tragedy in human history, terrible in the breadth of its impact, terrible in the depth of its significance, terrible in its personal details." It followed that this failure would also be terrible for him—that, when the splendid dream receded, he had to become something more than a sadly detached observer. He had known the great Bolshvik leaders; he had had a rich opportunity to bear witness to their first frenetic years in power; he had grown to maturity in a time of idealism, when the dream of human equality dominated; and, as he wrote, he had lived "these twenty-five years as a Marxian socialist," being as fully engaged as his temperament permitted.

Given Eastman's past and the personality, an unruffled announcement of the failure of Socialism was impossible. His retreat into the Russophobic camp was prefigured; so, too, was his facile slurring of any distinctions between Russia and Germany; they were alike in their militarism, their control over the economy, their barbarous authoritarianism—alike, indeed, in most every detail. Stalinism "contains all the evils of Naziism" and often "in extremer form"; it was more savage, "more ruthless, barbarous, unjust, immoral, anti-democratic, unredeemed by any hope or scruple." [26]

V   *The Purges*

Russian events confirmed the correctness of his position. As we have noted, earlier in this chapter, there were the great purge trials which resulted in execution or labor camps for Zinoviev, Kamenev, Radek, Rykov, Tomsky, Rakovsky—whom Eastman had so admired—and Serebriakov, among the "most courageous victims" of Stalin. Their very names, which read like a roster of the Russian Revolution, produced consternation and astonishment among America's intellectuals. That these old Bolsheviks should pour out a stream of confessions of sabotage and treason at German direction deeply disturbed the liberal image of Russia; and, for Eastman, these purges signalled the "bloody punctuation of a twelve-year period of counter-revolution. It meant that the experiment in socialism in Russia is at an end."

This Russian situation was additional proof, if it were needed, that one could not morally distinguish between Russia and Germany. The trials, as Eastman depicted them, were a monstrous frame-up. It was simply too improbable that seventeen men, "having entered a desperate plot, and having got caught, would all behave in exactly the same way." He surmised that their public recantation was due to Stalin's promise that their lives and those of their families would be spared. Three years later he turned to subtler and more compelling explanations: "The scheme of making them promote the counter-revolution by a death-hour declaration that *they were* the counter-revolutionists, could hardly have arisen except in a party where loyalty to factual truth had already, on theoretical principles, been subordinated to proletarian party loyalty. The victims had no principled objection to dying with a lie upon their lips. They had only to be reduced to believing that it was still the Party of the proletarian dictatorship."

Accurately comprehending the revolutionary mind, Eastman incisively and brilliantly explored the mechanics of confession:

> It was generally understood that personal predilections in the matter of honor, as well as life, ought to be sacrificed as 'bourgeois,' . . . I think it is indubitable that the majority of Stalin's victims made their 'confessions' and went to their deaths with a feeling that as loyal soldiers of the Party they were justified, and, so to speak, redeemed. . . .
>
> It is easy to confuse a man's mind . . . by holding him in absolute solitude except for the pressure of certain strong and convinced personalities. And when that pressure is preceded by an application of the 'conveyer system' of mental and physical treatment, it takes not only a robust, but a pugnacious nervous system to resist it. . . .

In the light of what later became known as "brainwashing," Eastman's hypothesis seems startlingly prescient. It was indeed "difficult for a man to say that the cause to which he gave his whole life had failed. It is especially difficult when he gave it in a religious belief that the process of all history and Being Itself were on his side"—particularly so, when one could point to areas, such as economic planning and the elimination of unemployment, where it apparently had not failed.[27]

If the old Bolsheviks were confronted with only one alternative, as Eastman suggests—"either to pronounce their life work a failure or to admit that there was *some hope* for socialism"—the same dilemma confronted America's liberals. Their problem, in a sense, was more difficult; for their wills had not been weakened by "the long months of solitude, and the long hours of torment"; there was no OGPU (the Unified State Political Administration, the dreaded secret police) to assist in the work of persuasion. Nonetheless, some of the most prominent intellectuals joined Eastman in denouncing the purges—John Hayne Holmes; Oswald Garrison Villard; and, happily, John Dewey. Earlier, Eastman had been pained by Dewey's "ecstatic testimony" of 1926 about the Russian educational system and, in the 1930's, troubled by Dewey's support of organized social controls. Eastman had also been critical of "naïve" non-Communist observers such as Louis Fischer, Harold Laski, Anna Louise Strong, Ella Winter and her husband, Lincoln Steffens.[28]

The trials steeled Eastman, made him more impatient of liberal vacillation. Their political lessons seemed obvious and urgent. No sane observer, he believed, really should be fooled by them; and anyone who was might be ignored either as a Communist or as hopelessly naïve. The *New Republic*, with a firm "know-nothing" attitude and a plea for suspension of judgment was, Eastman concluded, "supporting the prosecution"; so was the *Nation*, since it tended to give Russia's leaders the benefit of the doubt. Both magazines sympathized with the Bolsheviks in inverse ratio to the "decline of proletarian class power"; both "became our chief apologists for the most unliberal, unprincipled and bigoted and bloody tyranny in modern history"; and both, Eastman suggested in a letter to the *New Republic*, ought to confess: " 'We were wrong, you cannot serve democracy and totalitarianism.' "

Max Lerner of the *Nation* and George Soule, the liberal economist and reformer, were particularly objectionable. Lerner, Eastman charged, was "willing to give this same name, 'socialist,' to

Russia's systematic exploitation of the workers"; and, like Farrell, Eastman accused this "soft-headed liberal" of publicly defending the trials. Soule, who had been equivocal, believing the defendants guilty and yet condemning the whole apparatus of secret police and trials, was charged with subordinating liberty to a common goal which might be "a Totalitarian State or Monolithic Party." Time and again, Eastman criticized the "neo-Marxian ex liberals"—they were a greater menace than the Stalinists because they abandoned "their faith in popular intelligence, in open and complete debate, by lending their pages to the manipulation . . . of public opinion." [29]

Eastman did not stand alone. Defections from liberal-Communist-Russophile ranks mounted as the purges widened in scope after the Kirov executions of 1935. Eastman's position hardened, and it also became notorious. On March 7, 1938, Christian Rakovsky named him as accomplice in ten years of revolutionary betrayal, and he went on to accuse Eastman of being the intelligence agent who introduced him to the British secret service. A page-one streamer in the *Daily Worker* proclaimed, "Max Eastman is a British Agent," which brought additional obloquy and a libel suit against Earl Browder and Clarence Hathaway, the *Worker*'s editor.[30] "I'm suing," Eastman declared, "because I consider it my duty. Every man who believes in democratic civilization as against tyranny and barbarism ought to fight with every honorable weapon in his grasp."

Meanwhile, the purges abroad splintered the Popular Front of liberals, Socialists, and Communists at home. The formation of the American Committee for the Defense of Loen Trotsky widened the schism and produced a debate of unprecedented virulence. On August 24, 1939, the Nazi-Soviet Pact was announced, followed by the Russian invasion of Poland; and the breach was irreparable. Members of the Committee for Cultural Freedom —including Villard, Dewey, Carl Becker, Horace Kallen, John Chamberlain, George Counts—now joined Eastman in denouncing *all* forms of totalitarianism, and they also identified Russia with the German and Italian regimes.

The trials had produced defections but not a massive shift in liberal opinion, for magazines like the *New Republic* continued to maintain a double standard of judgment toward Russia and Germany; but the Pact was something else again. Once the ugly rumors were confirmed, the challenge to the liberal conscience was unavoidable and the Popular Front collapsed. Its end brought a convulsion in traditional liberalism, fracturing it into fellow travelers, Soviet apologists, and anti-Communist intellectuals—which would remain the ideological counterpoint for decades.

Foreign policy developments provided other ammunition for Eastman. Now completely alienated, he broadened his attack, accusing the Russian leaders of renouncing internationalism. The Bolsheviks, he declared, were primarily concerned with Russian successes and the Comintern, rather than being an instrument of international Socialism, was a reflection of Soviet parochialism. For instance, the Russians failed to assist "the fighting proletariat of the whole world," the Spanish loyalists in particular, to whom "Stalin gave a disastrously belated and fully inadequate aid." Or, for another example, Litvinov's announcement of May, 1934 which stated that Russia would "play the game of military diplomacy with the capitaist nations." Shortly thereafter, Eastman observed, the joint Stalin-Laval statement was issued, with its approval of French " 'national defense policy . . . in keeping her armed forces on a level required for security.' " Then there was the Pact, final proof that German and Russia were ideologically twinned.[31]

CHAPTER 13

The Native's Return

LIKE SO MANY OTHERS, though coming earlier to disenchantment, Eastman had invested heavily in one experiment. Its failure, without any hopeful substitute, awoke a malaise which deepened with every successive tremor registered on the Soviet landscape. The shocks ranged widely: measures raising the costs of divorce and alimony, a law that made abortion ("one of woman's few real guarantees of liberty") a crime; the abandonment of the doctrine of the "withering away of the state" in favor of a monolithic totality; the encouragement given to population growth; and the maintenance of the wage system and of classes. Without forsaking "the general aim of a more free and equal society," Eastman now unhesitatingly rejected Lenin's "conception of the role of the party and its relation to the masses." He reached even the point of declaring that a revolution "led by the industrial proletariat in an advanced capitalist country is [not] impossible" but that it would most likely lead to "a theory-blinded minority, agitating for it" and seizing "power on the Stalin-Hitler plan." He invoked the old criterion of instinctualism; or, in May 1938, he approached the near dead-end of speculation: "we have no certain knowledge where the world is going whether higher or lower." [1]

Eastman was too emotionally detached and too self-centered to remain loyal to an unjust system; too much the activist and too personally honest to endure captivity to an erroneous or unrealistic social analysis. He felt there was no choice—except to return to the old familiar canons of free enterprise, tempered somewhat by the very modest use of federal regulative power. [2]

Once again, therefore, Eastman was doing the unprecedented. Of the Socialists and putative liberals, who had been traumatically jolted by the events of the late 1930's, some maintained their faith (like Max Lerner and Frederick Schumann); some turned to despair; some (such as Silone and Richard Wright) never wholly escaped from Communism and "their lives will always be lived inside the dialectic and their battle with the Soviet Union will always be a reflection of searing inner struggle"; and some, like Eastman, came to patriotism.[3] But, with the exception of James Burnham and John Chamberlain, few followed him; and even among the Trotskyites, Dwight MacDonald's choice was more characteristic than Eastman's; that is, condemnation of Marxism, the Revolution, *and* American society.

Thus the Pact hopelessly divided liberal opinion, drove scores of independents to a belated repudiation of values they had formerly lived by. Some of them eventually would find another equally emotional outlet by rechannelling their near-religious fealty to Russia into self-accusation, repentence, and incrimination that also bordered on ecstasy. Eastman, however, customarily found non-political safety valves for such emotional drives; but the Pact did serve to quantify further his need for vindication and his near-blind anti-Sovietism. Pained and frustrated and outraged by the failure of so many liberals to see the intimate connection between red and brown dictatorships and by their continuing susceptibility to Communist arguments, Eastman remained a soured outsider. A steadily growing group now shared his ideological posture, and his early conviction that the Bolshevik revolution was not his revolution at all—but a gross betrayal of it—and they proclaimed as much with great rancor, relying for their defense upon an emotionally colored and highly selective view of the recent past.

Critical intelligence, the old-fashioned kind based on solid moral values, all but deserted them. Where once the ex-radicals enthusiastically if somewhat nearsightedly subscribed to the Soviet experiment, they now, possessed of a different epiphany, turned against it. And they did so with such rhetorical violence and evangelical zeal that, on issues involving Russia or Socialism, objective analysis became impossible. The battles had been too fierce, the polemics too lacerating, the casualty lists too long, and the debate too violent for men in either set of trenches to see things straight.

Eastman, in sum, paid the price of ostracism and of distrust by people who normally would be friends. The penalty, by the early 1940's, had become severe: the mental resilience which he extolled hardened into something else, a liberating doctrine became a contracting one, and bitterness distorted both vision and human relationships. Eastman, for instance, could no longer admit an appreciation of the Communist party's role in the 1930's, or of the impact of depression upon America's intellectuals—which saw so many swerve toward an endorsement of Russia and Communism. The hunger marches, the Hoovervilles, the Oakies, the joyless youth, the surrender of childhood, the sense of belonging to an edifice dedicated singularly to the ending of all injustice and human suffering—these had been known to Eastman; and they were forgotten.

Forgotten, too, by Eastman was the ineluctable fact that Communists frequently had had prominent roles in this hungry and embattled America, that they had been well equipped to hammer home the meaning of Fascism to Americans, that for awhile they had managed to break away from sterile polemics, that they often had been beaten and jailed, and that those who joined them formally or who lent their names and their pens had been driven by generous impulses. Caught up in an anti-Sovietism that rendered the entrapped blind to issues involving Russia and Communism, Eastman could not admit that the liberal response had really been both subtle and complex. He could not acknowledge the obvious —that many liberals had found in Russia and in the American Communist Party (CPUSA) an emotional support for their hopes; and, hence, he could not admire Steffens' decision to identify with "communist party leaders whom I can follow" "out here on the picket lines of the actual struggle." [4]

Nor could Eastman concede any dissimilarity between Germany and Russia—only the similarity, which was inflated out of all true proportion. Thus he interpreted the Pact not as a "temporary maneuver," but as "a vital union of two profoundly similar regimes"; and he was driven to the absurd prediction that German "capitalists and landlords . . . will suffer under Stalin's influence and perhaps even be swept away." [5] Only a sightlessness born of intellectual isolation and of the warping necessity of Russophobia convincingly accounts for such prophecy; only these facts—in matters pertaining to Russia—explains the lapse in Eastman's vaunted sense of social realities and the loss of acuity which normally characterized his judgments. Responding emotionally to

Stalin's endorsement of French defense policies in 1934-35, he never appreciated Russia's desperate need for a détente which, whatever the motives, might have effectually thwarted Germany's Continental ambitions.

I *Completing The Circle*

Eastman had long deplored moralism and sentimentality in making socio-political assessments, but he was at times most susceptible to these egregious criteria. For example, notwithstanding his pleas for political realism—for judgments based on solid empirical observations—the Soviet Union in Eastman's eyes had been transformed from a qualitative good to a total evil; and this transformation colored his capacity to make relevant and objective judgments.

The change did more; it turned Eastman into an ideologue. There seemed to be only one conclusion: to "chose" the West. Increasingly concerned with domestic affairs and with security measures, he proceeded to recast his thinking into an ideology which, for a pragmatist, was unexpected. He turned into something of a prophet, needing to exhort as well as persuade, and a conservative one at that. His metamorphosis was obvious by June, 1941, when he wrote for the *Reader's Digest* an article entitled "Socialism Does Not Gibe with Human Nature." The platform that Eastman chose, even more than his public disavowal of Socialism, resulted in a fusillade directed against him: "The *Socialist Call* held a three-column funeral service: '*In Memoriam—Max Eastman*' and Dwight MacDonald, an editor of *Partisan Review*, wrote: "Max Eastman, hero of the old Masses trial . . . publishes an attack on socialism which Wendell Wilkie implored every good American to read, and which is the low-water mark to date in such affairs for vulgarity and just plain foolishness." [6]

The radical who had scorned commercial journalism, struggled for artistic freedom, championed the non-conforming individual in the *Masses*, became a roving editor for the *Reader's Digest* who submitted his articles to a careful screening by senior editors whom he had once despised. But, he explained, such work is no violation of any sacred shibboleth. "I have thought of it as teaching when writing for these millions," he lamely stated: "I am a teacher and I love to teach." [7] In a series of articles in the *New Leader*, which was a more appropriate rostrum for his serious commentary, he wrote still another epitaph on Socialism.

In the course of this article, Eastman again revived his old proposition: the impossibility of Socialism because of man's instinctive belligerence and his disposition toward domination or submission.[8] Marx, whose work appeared before that of James and Freud, was ignorant of modern social and individual psychology; and this deficiency, Eastman once more asserted, accounted for the failure of Socialism. Indicative of Eastman's apostasy, he even denied a major Marxist canon—that social consciousness produced social being. More than ever, he emphasized somatically-formed personality traits and, rejecting environmental determinism, insisted that man existed outside of his social milieu; more than ever, therefore, hereditary traits took precedence and man was inevitably reduced in stature.[9]

II *Champion of Capitalism*

Eastman, seeking "a more scientific dynamics," wholeheartedly endorsed capitalism. It was now most compatible with "human freedom" and its economic laws—private property and "a genuinely competitive market." He would allow public ownership in certain areas, such as roads, schools, post office, national parks, utilities (and he commended the "brilliantly successful" TVA); but these state-run undertakings must be *within a system* of private enterprise." Only such enterprise, he declared in January, 1945, could triumph over totalitarianism. "It is not 'capitalists,' but a capitalist economy on which we base our hopes," for only such an economy made political freedom possible. Returning to the same theme seven years later, he declared that "there has to be a boss, and his authority, within the business, has to be recognized, and when not recognized, enforced." [10] The choice seemed simple and clearcut: at bottom, it was between "a system in which the amount and kind of goods produced is determined by the impersonal mechanism of the market [or] . . . in which this is determined by commands issuing from a *personal* authority backed by armed force." Those who endorsed the latter alternative—and Max Lerner, G. D. H. Cole, Harold Laski, and Julian Huxley were among them—and who believed a totalitarian state would be democratic, were dismissed as "pious believers." [11]

Eastman inferentially admitted the influence of the new "neo-liberal" economists—Friedrich Hayek, Ludwig Van Mises, Wilhelm Roepke, and William Chamberlin. They maintained that any regulated economy inevitably evolved into totalitarianism, and they invoked the democratic heritage in contrast. Resurrecting Jeffersonian laissez-faire doctrines, Eastman pressed home his plea for free buying and selling, free trade, "free movement of prices and no control on the quantities of goods produced"; only these conditions, which were intimately related to private property, could produce "that limited amount of free and equalness" which Marx—with his "metaphysical pontifications"—had hoped to render by abolishing private property. But Marx might have been, opined Eastman, less recklessly anti-capitalist had he understood "the historic relationship" between capitalism and democracy. That the word "socialism" "turns up Hitler's lips" was no coincidence; he had sought to suppress it by totalitarian rule, only to discover that the latter "leads toward socialism." [12]

III *Anti-Stalinism: From Reality to Myth*

In a series of articles in the 1940s for the *American Mercury, Reader's Digest,* and *Saturday Evening Post,* Eastman returned to another old theme—Stalin's guile and treachery.[13] Many of his comments were a stale rehash of earlier observations; but quite new were the admonitions accorded increasing American sympathy toward Stalin during World War II. "Stalin has two foreign policies," he warned: "one conducted by his diplomatic corps. The other by his secret agents." [14] His invasion of Poland must be kept in mind; his assertion, " 'it is inconceivable that the Soviet Republic should continue to exist for a long time side by side with imperialist states,' " should not be forgotten. Stalin continuing, candidly declared, " 'ultimately one or the other must conquer' "; and, Eastman insisted, this strategic intent was one of the "unpleasant facts" that democratic leadership had to face; otherwise, it could be accused—and Eastman so accused it—of lacking in fortitude and "manly nerve." For Stalin was to be believed. His foreign policy was based on the presumption of additional wars and, as Eastman cautioned the Western war leaders, upon the "overthrow of democratic government." [15] Hitler, to be sure, was the main opponent—"the arch-enemy of civilization, and we must marshall against him all the forces that can be gathered in the world, and that includes at the present moment Stalin's Russia." [16] But he exhorted, "keep your head," maintain democratic objectives, do not "permit the Stalinists and their stooges, dupes and fellow-travellers . . . to employ this opportunity to spread the power and the prestige of totalitarianism, and the mental and social habits which are its essence, on the home front." [17]

For Eastman, there was never an occasion, not even in wartime, when one could have faith in the Soviet Union. He recoiled at Eleanor Roosevelt's simple suggestion that, " 'if we trust the Russians, perhaps they would trust us' "; and he cautioned that Stalin had never ceased agitating "what he calls 'the world Communist revolution.' " [18] Somewhat later he maintained that had the democratic leaders read his chapter, "Stalin Beats Hitler Twenty Ways," they would have avoided the Yalta fiasco and possibly altered the course of history. Commenting on the United Nations, he charged Stalin with "sabotage" of the "effort to form a world government." And he also deplored the right of Security Council members to use the veto—"a sly device," he called it. He urged that "the language of power" be employed against power; yet he inconsistently combined this appeal to *realpolitik* with insistence upon "a moral sense." [19] Divulgence of "the bomb secret" to Stalin would be disloyal to this sense.

Eastman's splenetic forays were often justified. For instance, there is his vigorous and persuasive attack upon the Russian law sentencing children (under twelve) to death for petty larceny. But it is a matter of record that nothing the Soviet Union might do in the late 1940's or the 1950's could satisfy him. When, for example, the measure was repealed, he found that it meant instead "a slower and more profitable death at hard labor in slave camps." [20] Again and again, he tilted at the windmills of Russian repression: the continuing cultural purge (of Mikhail Zoschenko); the "silenced or exiled opposition"; the Russian slave empire of fourteen million; the enslaved proletariat; the unshakeable Soviet belief in world conquest and supremacy; the failure of nerve of democratic leadership; the inability of people like Vera Michaels Dean, Owen Lattimore, George C. Marshall, and Frank-

lin Roosevelt—a "pushover" for Stalin—to face political realities;
"the fellow-travellerism" of Harry Hopkins, already apparently a
sinister figure in conservative demonology; and the self-willed
"ignorance" in Washington by those who wished to be duped and
those who lacked "force of character." [21] Eastman's claim that a
"master dupester" was at work and that Stalin made distracting
noises in Berlin "while he consolidates his hold on Manchuria"
were some of the caveats of 1948; another described the "gangster
God" who was aggression personified; and, he flatly declared,
"there will be no peace in the world so long as the Stalin regime
survives in Moscow."

IV *The Communist Conspiracy*

Not limiting his critical shafts to the Soviet Union, Eastman
interpreted all manifestations of Communism as evidence of conspiracy. Hence he steadfastly repudiated the idea of peaceful coexistence. He had warned of the dangers of a wartime alliance in
the early 1940's, and depicted the post-war world in terms of a
series of relentless confrontations.[22] Eastman, the moralist, saw no
intervening choices—only antinomies. "To avoid war with Russia," he declared, "we must substitute for the policy of self-deceit
and appeasement a brave facing of the facts and an all-out effort
by every other means in our power to defeat the spread of the
totalitarian system." [23]

Equally fearful of internal subversion, he warned about cooperation with Communism at home. He further alerted his readers
about the "process of boring from within"—by which Communists
placed "party members in key positions" and thereby laid "the
foundation of a totalitarian state." He sounded the alarm for
American labor: Communist infiltrators were working in the Congress of Industrial Organization's Political Action Committee
(C.I.O.-P.A.C.). He also supported the *New Leader*'s denunciation of Sidney Hillman, for "his treachery to democracy in joining the Communists to capture the American Labor Party." [24]

Before the war ended, even before Yalta, when military and
strategic considerations demanded cooperation, Eastman exhorted policy-makers to use their "dominant diplomatic position"
in a hard-headed attempt to halt the march of global Communism; and he in effect accused Roosevelt of appeasement. Swing-

ing to the Republican party in the 1944 Presidential campaign, Eastman endorsed Thomas Dewey's attack on the foreign policy of the administration, finding its softness on Communism the reason for Stalin's desire to have Roosevelt reelected.

V *Eastman Joins the Radical Right*

There was never a season for Eastman to revise his views. If the wartime alliance did not soften his distrust of Russia, postwar conditions clearly would not. The idea of a détente, an accommodation with the Soviet Union, was out of the question. More than ever, Eastman seemed to have hit on what was an unquestioned truth: the utter evil of the idea of Communism and the near-perfection of the free-enterprise system. His defense of the "tough" line grew steadily more insistent. But he went beyond it—to the messianic demand for a holy war against Communism, investing it with a moral indignation peculiar to the religion which he had long abandoned. His aim was not merely peace, security, the extension of democracy, the thwarting of the Communist legions, but an ultimate total victory. Thus he moved gradually closer to the paranoid right in his admonitions about domestic and international Communism.

Eastman had been justly proud of his earlier commitments. "These were great days," he recalled, "when the dream of universal freedom under a state-owned economy was still in the sky, when the down-to-earth experiment was still untried." And, he continued to affirm, in December 1948, "I am not ashamed of my loyalty to that dream." [25] Nor, he added, was he ashamed of that fact that, "when the experiment was tried, and instead . . . produced the most perfect tyranny in all history"; he "was still young enough, or honest enough" to admit as much. But he would not be satisfied with exposure *per se* and the later vindication that came to him. Driven by the same purblind necessity that propelled many anti-Communists, he was converted from one set of polar beliefs to another. The same virile fraternity of attitudes and rhetoric that had been invoked by Bolshevism was expropriated for the fight against Bolshevism, at the opposite end of the messianic spectrum. He continued to use the language of idealism, frequently ignoring the considerations of power, and affirming that the whole problem of coexistence with "criminal," "promise-breaking" Communist was ultimately a moral question. Thus he traveled a familiar road, and a predictable one—given developments in Russia and Eastman's tendency to regard truth as being defined by action. Eastman, like a true disciple of John Dewey, came alive in doing—not in contemplation. The function of ideology was to tap emotion, to channel it into politics, and to invest issues with passion; Eastman turned to it easily and unconsciously.

Eastman's new ideology not only aroused emotion; it simplified ideas, preempted the domain of "truth" to itself, and presented a universally applicable set of canons. For instance, the need to counterpose America's force to that of Russia's distorted his assessment of domestic policies. It evoked concern lest labor kill "the only creature [capitalism] that ever laid golden eggs." This same pietistic fear of Communism was transformed into illiberalism at home. During wartime, it had prompted him to urge suspension of basic civil liberties on the inevitable grounds of necessity: "When American boys are dying for democracy on foreign battlefronts, it is no time to coddle totalitarians of any stripe at home." [26] Prematurely right-wing, he charged those who embraced the "party line" with "treason"; and he accused former New Deal administrators of "fellow-travellerism."

His explanation of the Amerasia case—a 1945 scandal in which the loyalty of some highly-placed federal officials was challenged (after top secret government documents were found in the New York office of *Amerasia* magazine)—further suggests the convenient marriage of journalist and ideologue, combining as it did the facile talents of the one with the simplistic formulae of the other. It was the result of the "coddling of traitors"—while, he acidly added, the "government was riding . . . rough-shod over the economic rights of Americans." [27] It enhanced the sense of urgency with which Eastman viewed the post-war threat of Communism and which found him, the former hero of the *Masses* trial, now arguing for suppression of Communism at home. "Toeing a Party line is treason to democracy," he had declared. "Tolerating those who toe a Party line is tolerating treason to democracy." [28] This primitive, categorical formula was a wartime judgment, to be sure, but war and peace were indistinguishable for an Eastman whose thinking was blurred by the immediacy of the menace of Communism. Hence he declared eight years later, "a government which fails to suppress a conspiracy to overthrow it is not democratic but weak." [29]

By 1952, in the midst of McCarthyism, Eastman made a distinction that was illuminating and suggestive: "Why should this esteemed journal of information [*Reader's Digest*] devote a whole elaborately dispassionate and highly good supplement to the question about Owen Lattimore and devote nothing but a few snide epithets to Senator McCarthy who succeeded when all others failed in smoking Lattimore out and making such supplements conceivable." [30] Thus fear of the conspiratorial left, the fear of being betrayed, plotted against, spied upon, brought Eastman to an endorsement of Joseph McCarthy. But he was not driven merely by anxieties over Communism. Sharing the larger conservative beliefs in individualism, he claimed that "bigger and bigger government" was destroying it and arbitrarily threatening his liberties. He even worried about America's participation in world organization.

His attention, however, was focussed primarily on Communism. He added his voice to those making the disquieting accusation that subversion was being plotted, and he felt that every good cause could be corrupted by Communist participation. Belief in the largely fictitious dangers threatening America prompted his contributions to the compulsive Americanism of the 1950's. It also caused him to hedge his defense of academic freedom and to raise a largely artificial issue. "The principle of academic freedom," he declared (in a review of William Buckley's *God and Man at Yale*), "does not give teachers the right to join or support a conspiracy to overthrow our government and end all our freedoms." [31]

VI *From Left to Right: An Explanation*

Before arriving in the camp of "Bill Buckley," whom he admired, and of the *National Review*, Eastman passed through successive stages of political disillusionment. Each one brought additional disorientation and frustration; each contributed to the melancholy end of a long journey down the road away from Marx. A tortuous but familiar road, it would be followed by many others who had also championed radical social change and supported the Bolshevik cause. Changes occurred which were at once striking and understandable; and only by reducing Eastman to a flat line drawing is he open to the charge of inconsistency. He changed, to be sure; but so would anyone who was not doctrinaire; so did the world over the passage of years and of a career that spanned two very different epochs—one in which the remission of capitalism seemed imminent and one which saw a post-war thermidorian reaction.

Before World War I, Eastman had been part of a "Little Renaissance" in which a radical Bohemia engaged in an imaginative quest for the good life and in which the national culture seemed once again so original and so energetic that it would sweep away the constricting aspects of capitalist society. Then there were the successive shocks of the Russian Revolution, Hitlerism, the Spanish Civil War; and, confronted by them, Eastman joined an intellectual community which found an inspirational model in Russia and which maintained sympathy for radical causes long after his own apostasy. Like many ex-radicals, the combined impact of the purge and Russian-German pact isolated and frustrated him. It also brought growing resentment against liberals who refused to admit the danger of Communism or at least to grant him the honorific title of "expert" when it came to Stalinism; and he concluded that they were servants or sympathizers of international Communism. By the time of the Russo-German alliance, Eastman was formally estranged from the main body of America's liberals, owing to the monomaniacal fear of Communism which had seized him.

VII *Eastman as Writer and Poet*

Such fears blinded him to changes that had occurred in the 1950's. To characterize the Soviet Union as a monolith, obedient to some immutable gravitational law of authoritarianism, was to miss the flux below the apparently adamantine surface of reality. But Eastman did miss it. He ignored the rise of a pluralistic world order. He limned an unchanging antagonism: America, the unambiguous leader of the "free world" locked in mortal combat with Russian "despotism." Mesmerized by these antinomies and beguiled by the cult of the hard-boiled, he would also disregard McCarthy's very real threat to the democratic fabric; he would neglect the need to maintain conventional libertarian safeguards.

His vision was limited to the many instances of Communist sub-version and to the flaccidity of "free world" leadership. Galva-nized by the need to defend the fashionable clichés of "realism" and "freedom," he found in them a meaning comparable to what such words encompassed for him in the 1920's—something enor-mously attractive because they encouraged an unequivocal loy-alty, the kind of total political commitment that he was eager to make and urgently needed. To claim as much for Eastman is not to contradict the earlier observation that he was a revolutionist manqué—one in whom the pull of doctrine was never so strong as the tug of his own personality. He gave readily within emotionally fixed limits, and these inhibitions, this restrictive giving, enabled him to retreat when occasion arose. But he had, as Edmund Wil-son has noted, a natural genius for stimulating the thinking of others. He was an elegant stylist, to be sure, with an unerring gift for the right phrase, the graceful passage, the bon mot. The *En-joyment of Poetry* of 1913 suggests as much. It defended those bold and serious writers who were carrying on the great traditions of literature—Whitman, Blake, Homer, and Shakespeare who "is, with Shelley, the supremely poetic genius of the English lan-guage." [32] Its exalted and exhilarating spirit was undoubtedly transmitted to students and adult readers alike, giving them the benefit of a book uniquely different from the dreary and uninspir-ing literary texts then flooding the publishing marketplace.

The *Enjoyment of Poetry*, however, is ultimately disappoint-ing—and not only because Eastman continues to employ the simplistic dichotomy of poetic versus practical, as the ways of looking at the world (a strange, non-class approach for a Social-ist) or because he continues to idealize the strong emotion and give it a transcendent value. (E.g., "Emotion is the sweet arbiter of a poetic choice.")[33] Rather the book disappoints because it is mostly surfaces. These are admittedly glittering, rich in fluent and graceful phrases, filled with heady and elegant passages; but there is little more. The meaning of these phrases and passages is elusive and thin, and the *Enjoyment of Poetry* finally adds up to little more than a stringing together of non-specific thoughts decked out in the rhetoric of a lover of lyric verse.

Eastman's lyrics, which dot his early years, share the same de-fects. They are inevitably trapped in sentimentality, the romantic thought and phrase. Whenever Eastman's poems deal with the emotions, and they almost always do, they are rhetorical and turbid. The lyric line, the original image, the volatile temperament of the poet occasionally appear, but too infrequently to sustain the poem itself. And the impression of Eastman's style that remains, whether in his poetry or his prose—the prose of the *Enjoyment of Poetry*—is of a writer possessed of great and unsystematic amateur enthusiasms.

Eastman's novel, *Venture*, also leaves this impression. There are brilliant things in this book: acute aphorisms on human experience, the characterization of a Platonic-Nietzschean, the presentation of the values of a superior caste. But one tires of the idea-novel that continually parades Eastman's views, that is remorselessly unilinear, and that provides a platform for an overly simple emphasis on "living." Perhaps, as Edmund Wilson speculates, this continual stress on "life," on "experience," may be in compensation for Eastman's failure to cultivate intensively the several vocations—of poetry, philosophy, revolution—in which he worked.[34]

VIII *Summary*

In any case Eastman was not a finished craftsman or, as noted earlier, a profound thinker. His mind was inquiring, as befits the journalist-observer, rather than systematic; and his views were often governed by emotion, however much he abhorred such domination. Emotion also had substantive importance since Eastman rejected the authority of reason. He symbolically capped this rejection by making Freud the presiding figure in his gallery of heroes. But Eastman was fickle: Marx, Darwin, Freud—none was unconditionally accepted. Sceptical of the claims of rationalism, doubting the transcendent powers of mind, he had, at the outset, sharply qualified the vast analytical system of Marx. Eventually, all systems of thought were partially excised. But Eastman did not find anything of comparable magnitude to replace them. He never felt any compunction to do so, and we do not find an equally inclusive and deep set of analytic ideas that substitute for the arcane ones which were repudiated.

From Eastman's perspective, the first three decades of the twentieth century surely seemed like a happy time: hope was still possible; the great historical system of Marx was regnant; man's reach might still exceed his grasp without cynical commentary. That time vanished; so, too, the innocence of youth.

But Eastman's was not merely a fall from innocence—the youthful and uncritical belief in Marx's doctrines and Lenin's tactics—to experience of the dream perverted. Eastman had a ranging and universal mind—almost that of a modern Leonardo in its sweep. His views, to be sure, seemed to suffer from a congenital weakness of American radicals when seen *sub specie aeternitatis;* they dealt with abstract people acting in accordance with deductively formulated principles. But these views placed him instinctively on the side of the angels, fighting for individual freedom and for economic and social equality. His loss of innocence derived from loss of firm belief in these possibilities: in other words, from loss of hope. It also derived from the conviction—unshaken in the face of sanguine revolutionary upheaval—that men had inextinguishable aggressive drives and also from psychoanalytic theory which, whatever its immediate and enriching benefits, ultimately was impoverishing since it limited one's appreciation of Marxism.

Edmund Wilson, with his customary acuity, has commented on these limitations as they are made manifest in Eastman and his circumscribed understanding of Marx: "How strange that this student of Marxism should never have learned from Marx what is clearly the most valid in his system, the class analysis of historical happenings. He tends to talk as if the failures of Marxism had by themselves wrecked the Leninist revolution and is not interested in finding out how the development of social forces has affected the application of ideas." [35]

Finally, Eastman's fall from innocence was a result of the very wrecking of this revolution—the result of historical conditions over which he had no control—and the prodding conscience of a minister's son who had abandoned the otherworldly preoccupations of religion but not its moralism. Notwithstanding his sustained chant to realism, by which he meant hard-headed empirical analysis, his best thoughts were invested with a powerful emotional thrust. His social criticisms, indeed everything that he observed, was mainly in terms of morality—combined with psychological motivation and philosophy. This moralizing tendency served him well and, coupled with the afflatus of youth that rarely deserted him—a sense of unique worth which denied the finality of failure—it helped see him through years of bone-crushing defeat. This same tendency, while it eludes measurement, was as responsible as anything for his loss of social idealism. Granted that the smell of corpses in Russia's Lubianka prison was an objective reality, it was Eastman's moralism which, serving as anvil to the forge of history, hammered out a transformed man, one without the humanism, the benevolence, the reasonable pragmatic wisdom of his earlier years, one who no longer viewed life as an experience or who identified with society's outcasts.

There are some writers whose lives and whose works run together, as it were, so that it is the man we read in the works. With Eastman, we find that rare thing—the fusion of the life and the letters, the thinker and the doer, the artist and the revolutionary, the Darwinian who, in his richest years, knew life and yet loved it, knew men and yet loved them. He may have vehemently denied these affections, but no matter; he was, before the loss of hope, like Sherwood Anderson's gnarled apple which had the sweetest taste.

Notes and References

Chapter One

1. Max Eastman, *Enjoyment of Living* (New York, 1948), 55.
2. *Ibid.*, 51.
3. *Ibid.*, 79.
4. *Ibid.*, 344.
5. *Ibid.*, 81, xiii, 97.
6. *Ibid.*, 119.
7. Eastman, *Venture* (New York, 1927), 3, 4, see also *Enjoyment*, 112.
8. Eastman, "Rebecca West," *Masses*, January, 1914.
9. Eastman, *Enjoyment of Humor* (New York, 1921), *passim*, see also Eastman, "Mark Twain: Representative American," *New Leader*, Sept. 26, 1960.
10. Eastman, "Mark Twain," *op. cit.*, see also, *Venture*, 2.
11. *Enjoyment*, 290, 330.
12. *Venture*, 5.
13. *Enjoyment*, 152.
14. *Ibid.*, 136.
15. *Ibid.*, 197.
16. "Jo did not like his father," Eastman stated in *Venture* (5), "and he did not like Bible Class dinners, and he did not like the Episcopal religion . . . and he was entirely cut off from the beauty and significance of the best parts of the Hebrew Bible by being compelled to learn them by heart."
17. *Enjoyment*, 110, 198, 346, 347.
18. *Ibid.*, 220, 237.
19. Eastman, *Marxism is it Science* (New York, 1940), 162.
20. *Enjoyment*, 133.
21. *Ibid.*, 133, 191, 189, 194.
22. *Ibid.*, 194.

Chapter Two

1. *Enjoyment*, 232, 144, 217.
2. *Ibid.*, 240.

3. *Ibid.*, 262, 266.

4. *Ibid.*, 284.

5. *Ibid.*, 285.

6. *Ibid.*, 57, 186, 85.

7. *Ibid.*, 306.

8. Eastman, "Knowledge and Revolution," *Masses*, April, 1913.

9. Eastman, "A Militant Suffrage Victory," *Liberator,* March 1918. This army, he later wrote, was composed of "the only Americans who kept up the banner of revolt throughout the reactionary hurricane of the patriotic war," Eastman, "Feminism," *ibid.*, June, 1919.

10. Eastman, "Knowledge and Revolution," *Masses*, January, 1913.

11. Eastman, "Concessions of a Suffrage Orator," *ibid.*, November, 1915.

12. Eastman, "Knowledge and Revolution," *ibid.*, January, 1913.

13. Eastman, *Value of the Vote* (New York, 1912), 3, 7.

14. *Ibid.*, 11, 3.

15. *Ibid.*, 4.

16. Eastman, "Concessions," *op. cit.;* Eastman, "Feminism," *op. cit.*

17. *Ibid.*

Chapter Three

1. Louis Untermeyer, *From Another World* (New York, 1939), 42; Joseph Freeman, *An American Testament* (New York, 1936), 266; Bourne to Prudence Winterrowd, April 28, 1913, Bourne papers, Columbia; Henry May, *The End of American Innocence* (Chicago, 1964 ed.), 288; Floyd Dell, *Love in Greenwich Village* (New York, 1926), 31.

2. *Venture*, 110.

3. *Ibid.*, 127. See also *Enjoyment*, 4, 436.

4. *Enjoyment*, 137, 64. See also Malcolm Cowley, *After the Genteel Tradition* (Gloucester, 1959), 216, and Eastman, *Love and Revolution* (New York, 1964), 517.

5. Eastman, *Marx, Lenin and the Science of Revolution* (London, 1926), 107.

6. *Enjoyment*, 248, 194.

7. *Ibid.*, 174, 136–37, 311, 247, 266.

8. *Ibid.*, 121, 246.

9. Van Wyck Brooks, *The Confident Years* (New York, 1952), 371.

10. *Enjoyment*, 356; *Love and Revolution*, 435.

11. *Enjoyment*, 360–1, 518.

12. *Ibid.*, xiv, 194, 94, 528.

13. Eastman, "Revolutionary Birth Control," *Masses*, July, 1915.

14. Eastman, "Is the Truth Obscene?" *ibid.*, March, 1915.

15. *Ibid.*

16. Eastman, "Knowledge and Revolution," *ibid.*, January, 1913. See also *Venture*, 42.

17. *Venture*, 100.

18. Qt. in *ibid.*, 162. See also *ibid.*, 348.

19. Eastman, "Knowledge and Revolution," *Masses*, November, 1913.

20. *Enjoyment*, 548.

21. *Venture*, 162.

22. *Ibid.*, 129.

23. *Ibid.*, 128.

24. *Ibid.*, 349–50.

25. *Ibid.*, 222.

26. *Ibid.*, 252.

27. *Ibid.*, 243, 244.

28. *Ibid.*, 252, 253.

29. *Ibid.*, 350–51.

30. *Enjoyment*, 548.

Chapter Four

1. May, *op. cit.*, 351.

2. E.g., Norman Thomas, *A Socialist's Faith* (New York, 1950), 11.

3. Eastman, "What Nietzsche Really Taught," *Everybody's Magazine* (November, 1914), 704, 701. See also Eastman, *Understanding Germany* (New York, 1916), 60, 66–67.

4. *Ibid.*, 703 (ital. added), 704. See also Eastman, "Nietzsche, Plato and Bertrand Russell," *The Liberator*, September, 1920.

5. *Understanding Germany*, 67.

6. Eastman, "What Nietzsche Really Taught," *op. cit.*, 704. See also, Eastman, "The Only Way to End War," *Masses*, December 1915, and *Understanding Germany*, 82.

7. *Understanding Germany*, 90, 91. Generally Eastman believed that "wars will be less frequent" if social reforms are undertaken. "But the perpetual menace and the occasional calamity will not be removed," *ibid.*, 108. The impact of Darwinism and Nietzschean thought were durable factors. For a late expression of the view that man inherited crude and ineradicable impulses, one of which is pugnacity, see Eastman, "Socialism and Human Nature," *New Leader*, January 31, 1942.

8. Eastman, "Socialism and Human Nature," *op. cit.* See also, "What Nietzsche Really Taught," *op. cit.*, 704.

9. Eastman, "War Psychology and International Socialism," *Masses Review*, August, 1916.

10. *Understanding Germany*, 159 (ital. added), 124.

11. *Ibid.*, 118, 119, 89. See also Eastman, *Stalin's Russia* (New York, 1940), 256.

12. *Understanding Germany,* 85, 159.

13. Eastman, "Religion of Patriotism," *Masses,* July, 1917.

14. "A swarm of people," Eastman continued, "trained by custom and habit to think themselves one—one family, one fraternity, one church, one clan, one tribe, one nation. Love me, love my dog. Love my dog, love the whole pack. That is the way we work." *Understanding Germany,* 101. See also *ibid.,* 106, 102.

15. For Socialists' vacillation and conflict on issue of causation of wars, see Freeman, *op. cit.,* 74; *Enjoyment,* 529; *Appeal to Reason,* March 31, 1917; Walling, "The Great Illusion," *New Review,* June 1, 1915; *American Socialist,* January 9, 1915.

16. *Understanding Germany,* 22–23. See also *ibid.,* 20; *Enjoyment,* 529; Eastman, "Knowledge and Revolution," *Masses,* September, October, 1914; Eastman, "Socialists and War," *ibid.,* June, 1917. "They are supposed to be so revolutionary, these Socialists," Eastman continued, "and they arrive at so extreme and to me repellent a national military position, that I have to smile at them in order to keep my tolerance."

17. *Understanding Germany,* 24, 70. See also "Knowledge and Revolution," *Masses,* October, 1914.

18. Eastman, "The Uninteresting War," *Masses,* September, 1915; Eastman, "A Separation," *Masses,* May, 1917; Eastman, "Let the War Go On," *ibid.,* October, 1914.

19. Eastman, "The Uninteresting War," *op. cit.;* Eastman, "A Separation," *op. cit.; Understanding Germany,* 166–67.

20. *The Call,* August 28, 1914. See also *ibid.,* August 13, 1914.

21. Eugene V. Debs in, *The American Socialist,* January 9, 1915.

22. L. Boudin, "Current Affairs," *New Review,* May 1, 1915.

23. Eastman, "Let the War Go On," *Masses,* October, 1914.

24. Eastman, "Knowledge and Revolution," *Masses,* September, 1914.

25. Walling, *The Socialists and the War,* 6.

26. Eastman, "Conscription for What," *Masses,* July, 1917.

27. Eastman, "A Separation," *op. cit.* (ital. added). See also *Enjoyment,* 579 and *Understanding Germany,* 143.

28. Eastman, "A Tribute," *Masses,* December, 1914. See also Freeman, *op. cit.,* 76.

29. For Eastman's pre-war impressions of Wilson, see *Enjoyment,* 125, 385, 546–47. See also *ibid.,* 547 and Eastman, "Comment," *Liberator,* January, 1922.

30. Eastman, "Sect or Class," *Masses,* December, 1916. For a relatively late expression of approval of Wilson, see "President Wilson's Letter to the Pope," *ibid.,* September, 1917.

31. *Ibid.* See also Eastman, "Wilson's Failure," *Liberator,* May, 1919, and Eastman, "A Separation," *op. cit.*

32. *Understanding Germany,* 108–09. For a further statement of the "bellicose and herd instinct" view of wars' causation, see Eastman, "The Religion of Patriotism," *Masses,* July, 1917.

33. Eastman, "Revolutionary Progress," *Masses,* February, 1917. In the light of such sentiments, Eastman's statement, "I never championed Woodrow Wilson" of five years later is unconvincing. Eastman, "Comment," *Liberator,* January, 1922.

34. *Enjoyment,* 529. See also Eastman, "War Psychology and International Socialism," *Masses Review,* August, 1916, and Eastman, "Revolutionary Progress," *Masses,* February, 1917.

35. Eastman, "War and Politics," *Masses,* August, 1916. See also *Love and Revolution,* 22.

36. "But to draft me," he continued, "in a war whose purposes it will not so much as communicate to my ear, seems an act of tyranny, discordant with the memory even of the decent kings." Eastman, "Conscription for What?", *Masses,* July, 1917.

37. Eastman, "War and Politics," *Masses,* August, 1916.

38. *Love and Revolution,* 30, 123.

Chapter Five

1. Van Wyck Brooks, *Autobiography* (New York, 1965), 206.

2. Granville Hicks, *John Reed* (New York, 1936), 93.

3. *Enjoyment,* 394. For a powerful affirmation of the I.W.W. and the weapon of sabotage, see Eastman, "New Masses for Old," *Modern Monthly,* June, 1934.

4. "Having a free hand on the *Masses* to attack the capitalist system and its beneficiaries loosed energies within me of what I had been unaware. I felt as many a crusader must have felt long ago as he set forth to rescue the Holy Land from the infidels." Art Young, *His Life and Times* (New York, 1939), 277, see also 275; Untermeyer, *op. cit.,* 41–2; *Enjoyment,* 394.

5. Young, *op. cit.,* 273. See also Untermeyer, *op. cit.,* 49; *Enjoyment,* 400, 443. For Eastman's duties, see Untermeyer, *op. cit.,* 44 and *Enjoyment,* 409, also 400.

6. *Enjoyment,* 476. "It cannot, therefore," Eastman went on, "cover the whole range of what has value in current literature and art. It tends to cover the range of what has value without having commercial value." Eastman, "Editorial Policy," *Masses,* December, 1915. For a similar opinion from John Reed, see Hicks, *op. cit.,* 93. See also *Enjoyment,* 74, 540.

7. Untermeyer, *op. cit.,* 46.

8. Quoted in Lewis Coser, *Men of Ideas* (New York, 1965). For Eastman's reminiscences of the meetings, see *Enjoyment*, 399; for Bellows', see Charles Morgan, *George Bellows* (New York, 1965), 169.

9. *Enjoyment*, 548.

10. For criticism of the *Masses'* failure to sustain a completely revolutionary position, see V. F. Calverton, *Liberation of American Literature* (New York, 1932), 451.

11. Eastman, "Clarifying the Light," *Liberator*, June, 1921.

12. *Enjoyment*, 559. See also Walter Rideout, *The Radical Novel in the United States* (Cambridge, 1956), 101.

13. *Love and Revolution*, 18. The *Masses* had, Granville Hicks has written, " 'the seriousness of strong convictions and the gaiety of great hopes.' " Qt. in Coser, *op. cit.*, 125, fn. 4.

14. *Enjoyment*, 414.

15. Mabel Dodge Luhan, *Movers and Shakers* (New York, 1936), 199.

16. Howard Mumford Jones, ed., *Letters of Sherwood Anderson* (Boston, 1953), 275.

17. Hicks, *op. cit.*, 94.

18. Eastman frequently lectured on humor and even wrote a book on the subject: *The Sense of Humor* (New York, 1921).

19. *Enjoyment*, 420.

20. *Ibid.*, 421.

21. *Ibid.*, 475.

22. Daniel Aaron, *Writers on the Left* (New York, 1961), 31. Eastman is referring to Article 2, Section 6, which unequivocally demanded expulsion of party members who favored "political action or advocated sabotage or other methods of violence as a weapon of the working class."

23. Eastman, "Abrakadabra," *Masses*, August, 1913.

24. Eastman, "Knowledge and Revolution," *Masses*, September, 1914; Eastman, "Knowledge and Revolution," *ibid.*, March, 1915.

25. Eastman, "Knowledge and Revolution," *ibid.*, May, 1913. Writing of the Arizona deportation, Eastman estimated Wilson to be "a man with the creed of democracy and the temper of an autocrat. . . . He has failed altogether as a leader or even a defender of democratic life." Eastman, "Revolutionary Progress," *Masses*, October, 1917.

26. Eastman, "Knowledge and Revolution," *Masses*, May, 1913.

27. *Enjoyment*, 449. Eastman, "Class War in Colorado," *ibid.*, June, 1914.

28. Eastman, "The Nice People of Trinidad," *ibid.*, July, 1914.

29. Eastman, "The San Francisco Frameup," *ibid.*, December, 1916. See also Eastman, "Knowledge and Revolution," *ibid.*, October, 1913, and Eastman, "Knowledge and Revolution," *ibid.*, March, 1913.

30. Eastman, "Knowledge and Revolution," *ibid.*, May, 1913. The attack on the Associated Press for withholding the truth about West Virginia's coal strike brought a suit for slander, see Rideout, *op. cit.*, 103, and Young, *op. cit.*, 295.

31. Eastman, "Knowledge and Revolution," *Masses*, February, 1915.

32. Eastman, "Knowledge and Revolution," *ibid.*, October, 1913.

33. Eastman, "Editorial," *ibid.*, September, 1915. See also Eastman, "Our Congress," *Masses*, October, 1917, and *Understanding Germany*, 8–9, 84.

34. Eastman, "Revolutionary Progress," *ibid.*, April, 1917.

35. *The New York Times*, February 2, 1917.

36. Eastman, "Who Wanted War," *ibid.*, June, 1917.

37. Eastman, "Revolutionary Progress," *ibid.*, April, 1917.

38. Young, *op. cit.*, 318.

39. Reed, "Woodrow Wilson," *Masses*, June, 1917.

40. Eastman, "Advertising Democracy," *ibid.*, June, 1917.

41. For an account of wartime censorship, see H. C. Peterson and Gilbert Fite, *Opponents of War* (Madison, 1957), 97; Eastman, "Editorials," *Liberator*, May, 1918; Eastman, "The Post Office Censorship," *Masses*, September, 1917; and Pinchot, Reed and Eastman to Wilson, July 12, 1917, Wilson papers, Library of Congress. For an account of the two *Masses* trials, see Eastman "Bunches of Justice," *Masses*, October, 1917; Dell, "The Story of the Trial," *Liberator*, June, 1918; Untermeyer, *op. cit.*, 68; *Love and Revolution*, 88–122.

42. Aaron, *op. cit.*, 82. See also *Love and Revolution*, 494–5.

43. Freeman, *op. cit.*, 165–6.

44. Rideout, *op. cit.*, 123.

45. Eastman, "The Editor," *Liberator*, March, 1918.

Chapter Six

1. Qt. in Aaron, *op. cit.*, 82.

2. Eastman, "Editorials," *Liberator*, March, 1918.

3. Eastman, "Editorials," *ibid.*, August, 1921.

4. Eastman, "Editorials," *ibid.*, January, 1919.

5. Eastman, "Popularizing the Constitution," *ibid.*, June, 1919.

6. Alexander Berkman and Emma Goldman, in particular, were praised for their willingness to cooperate with Russian authorities. "We bid farewell to him, and to Emma Goldman, and to all those comrades whose love of liberty was too strong for the republic. . . ." Eastman, "Editorials," *ibid.*, February, 1919.

7. Eastman, "Examples of 'Americanism,'" *ibid.*, February, 1920. This article is a sustained attack on American "atrocities of repression." "America is the only place in the world," he declared, "where people

seek office by boasting of their contempt for the legal and constitutional rights of men."

8. Eastman, "Lenin and Wilson," *ibid.*, March, 1919.

9. Eastman, "Editorials," *ibid.*, May, 1919. See also *Love and Revolution*, 151, 153–56.

10. Eastman, "November Seventh, 1918," *ibid.*, December, 1918.

11. *Ibid.*

12. Eastman, "Editorials," *ibid.*, June, 1919. See also Eastman, "A Working-Class Peace," *ibid.*, April, 1918; Eastman, "A Christmas Party," *ibid.*, February, 1922; "The Trial of Eugene Debs," *ibid.*, November, 1918; Eastman, "Greek Drama in Cleveland," *New Leader*, April 4, 1942; *Love and Revolution*, 348, 449; *Enjoyment*, 445, 446.

13. Eastman, "The Trial of Eugene Debs," *Liberator*, November, 1918. See also Eastman, "Greek Drama in Cleveland," *New Leader*, April 4, 1942.

14. *Love and Revolution*, 144, 145.

15. Eastman, "Science on Trial," *Liberator*, December, 1920.

16. Frederick Hoffman, *The Twenties* (New York, 1962 ed.), 394.

17. *Love and Revolution*, 107.

18. Eastman, "For President," *Liberator*, May, 1922.

19. For Eastman's observations of the Socialist and Communist parties and their tactics and characteristics, see Eastman, "The Chicago Convention," *ibid.*, October, 1919; Eastman, "Tactics," *ibid.*, October, 1921; Eastman, "Comment," *ibid.*, January, 1922. See also Theodore Draper, *The Roots of American Communism* (New York, 1957), 222.

20. *Enjoyment*, 424, 446. See also Eastman, *Stalin's Russia* (New York, 1940), 93 and *Love and Revolution*, 165, 49.

21. Eastman, "The Chicago Convention," *Liberator*, October, 1919. See also Eastman, "Editorials," *ibid.*, January, 1919.

22. Eastman, "Statesman of the New Order," *ibid.*, September, 1918.

23. *Ibid.*

24. Eastman, *Since Lenin Died* (New York, 1925), 12.

25. *Marx, Lenin and the Science of Revolution*, 151.

26. Eastman, "Editorials," *Liberator*, April, 1920.

27. Eastman, "Statesman of the New Order," *op. cit.*

28. Eastman, "Class Struggle at Genoa," *ibid.*, July, 1922.

29. Eastman, "Editorials," *ibid.*, April, 1920.

30. *Marx, Lenin and the Science of Revolution*, 174 (ital. added in quotation).

31. Eastman, "Editorials," *Liberator*, April, 1920.

32. Bertrand Russell, "Democracy and Revolution," *ibid.*, May, 1920.

33. Eastman, "Nietzsche, Plato, and Bertrand Russell," *ibid.*, September, 1920.

34. *Ibid.*

Chapter Seven

1. Eastman, "November Seventh, 1918," *Liberator,* December, 1918. See *Love and Revolution,* 241.

2. *Love and Revolution,* 317.

3. *Ibid.*, 316.

4. Edward H. Carr, *The Bolshevik Revolution* (London, 1953), III, *passim.*

5. *Love and Revolution,* 351–6.

6. Edward H. Carr, *The Interregnum* (London, 1954), 116.

7. Eastman, "A Permanent Revolution," *Liberator,* December, 1922. See also, *Love and Revolution,* 318.

8. *Love and Revolution,* 317.

9. *Ibid.*, 347.

10. Eastman, "Moscow's Answer," *Liberator,* July, 1923.

11. *Ibid.*

12. *Love and Revolution,* 360.

13. *Ibid.*, 355.

14. Eastman, "November Seventh, 1918," *Liberator,* December, 1918.

15. *Love and Revolution,* 356. See also, Eastman, "A Permanent Revolution," *Liberator,* December, 1923.

16. *Love and Revolution,* 411. See also, *Stalin's Russia,* 220.

17. Eastman, "Moscow's Answer," *Liberator,* July, 1923.

18. *Love and Revolution,* 213.

19. *Ibid.*, 241.

20. *Ibid.*, 355. See also *Stalin's Russia,* 55.

21. Isaac Deutscher, *The Prophet Unarmed* (London, 1959), 27, 51.

22. *Since Lenin Died,* 12.

23. *Ibid.*, 12–3.

24. *Ibid.*, 15.

25. *Love and Revolution,* 350. See also, Eastman, "The Last Congress of the Bolshevik Party," *New Leader,* Nov. 9, 1964.

26. *Ibid.*, 350.

27. This letter came four days after Trotsky's *New Course* was published, a pamphlet which stated that " 'tradition is not a rigid canon' " and which was the first general attack on the Old Guard. It came amidst the support given Trotsky by the Forty-six (a coalition of revolutionary generals). Stalin's reply to their claim of Trotsky's support

prompted the December 8th letter, with its attack on "bureaucratic degeneration." Deutscher, *op. cit.*, 114.

28. *Love and Revolution*, 409.

29. Lenin, continuing, praised the "exceptional abilities" of Trotsky. Carr, *Interregnum*, 258.

30. *Ibid.*, 263.

31. *Since Lenin Died*, 31

32. *Love and Revolution*, 424.

33. *Ibid.*, 425.

34. *Ibid.*, 443.

35. *Since Lenin Died*, 40.

36. Eastman, "Class Struggle at Genoa," *op. cit.*

37. *Love and Revolution*, 446.

38. Draper, *American Communism and Soviet Russia* (New York, 1960), 545.

39. *Love and Revolution*, 453.

Chapter Eight

1. Eastman, "Knowledge and Revolution," *Masses*, February, 1913.

2. *Since Lenin Died*, 129–30.

3. *Love and Revolution*, 21. See also Eastman, "Knowledge and Revolution," *Masses*, January, 1913.

4. Eastman, "Toward Liberty," *The Masses Review*, October, 1916.

5. *Marx, Lenin and the Science of Revolution*, 122.

6. Qt. in *Enjoyment*, 402.

7. Eastman, *The Literary Mind* (New York, 1931), 6, 7.

8. Eastman, "Editorial," *Liberator*, August, 1920; *Marx, Lenin and the Science of Revolution*, 193, 194; Eastman, "Toward Liberty," *The Masses Review*, October, 1916; *Love and Revolution*, 432.

9. Eastman, "An Editorial," *Liberator*, February, 1920.

10. *Venture*, 226, 227.

11. *Enjoyment*, 480, 419–20, 426–27, 428, 518.

12. *Stalin's Russia*, 162–63 (ital. added).

13. *Enjoyment*, 236. On the impact of Veblen's *Theory of the Leisure Class*, which was "scientific" and which with St. Francis and Tolstoy brought him "several steps toward Marxian socialism," see *ibid.*, 419–20. See also Eastman, "Editorials," *Liberator*, 1921. "Perhaps the greatest book of our day," he wrote at another time, "it combines a new flavor in literature with a new and great truth in science," Eastman, "Rebecca West," *Masses*, January, 1917.

14. *Love and Revolution*, 491.

15. Edmund Wilson, "Max Eastman in '41," *New Republic*, May, 21, 1941.

16. "Toward Liberty, The Method of Progress," *The Masses Review*, September, 1916.

17. Eastman, "Editorials," *Liberator*, March, 1918; Eastman, "The Wisdom of Lenin," *ibid.*, June, 1924; Eastman, "Knowledge and Revolution," *Masses*, April, 1913.

18. *Stalin's Russia*, 197. See also *ibid.*, 203. "It was in examining the existing society and all past societies," Eastman stated, "and trying to find out what forces control them . . . that Marx did his really great work." *Marxism is it Science*, 24. See also *ibid.*, 38.

19. *Marx, Lenin and the Science of Revolution*, 191–92. Eastman qualified this claim by finding that Marx's statement " 'All history . . . was the history of class struggles' . . . [an] obviously preposterous assertion." *Ibid.*, 65. See also *ibid.*, 46.

20. *Ibid.*, 38.

21. *Ibid.*

22. *Ibid.*, 104.

23. *Ibid.*, 92, 105. See also *Stalin's Russia*, 209.

24. *Ibid.*, 93. Elsewhere, he writes, "it is not economic science, but economic metaphysics with some scientific wisdoms wound up in it." *Stalin's Russia*, 208.

25. Eastman, "Philosophy Released," *Masses*, April, 1914.

26. *Writers in Uniform*, 181. Eastman nonetheless recognized the unique merit of Hegel's achievement. *Marxism is it Science*, 38.

27. Eastman, "The Marxian Aesthetic," *Modern Monthly*, April, 1934.

28. *Marxism is it Science*, 20, 33, 267, 270, 53. See also *Stalin's Russia*, 29–30; *Enjoyment*, 453; *Writers in Uniform*, 191. "The pretense of Marxism," Eastman declared, "is to be an objective analysis of history and society, its pretense to the authority of empirical science is a bluff. Marxism is not a valid account of the real world, but a system of ideas to be adopted . . . by those . . . striving to effect a certain change." *Marxism is it Science*, 275. See also Eastman, "Soul of Man Under Communism," *Modern Monthly*, March, 1934.

29. *Marxism is it Science*, 50. See also *Artists in Uniform*, 190; *Marx, Lenin and the Science of Revolution*, 192 (ital. added).

30. *End of Socialism in Russia*, 20. See also *Marx, Lenin and the Science of Revolution*, 103, and *Stalin's Russia*, 199.

31. *Marxism is it Science*, 41.

32. *Ibid.*, 22. See also *Artists in Uniform*, 197. Despite his "arrant declaration of independence from metaphysical conceptions of the universe," Marx never eliminated the notion "that reality is 'dialectic' . . . the very king-pin in the whole soulful-consolatory apparatus." *ibid.*, 186.

33. *Ibid.*, 20. "What is unscientific and untrue in the Marxian system," Eastman stated, is "the reading of the desired result into the limiting conditions, the failure to realize the central role played in all science by the working hypothesis." *Ibid.*, 29.

34. *Marx, Lenin and the Science of Revolution,* 57, 109. See also *Stalin's Russia,* 201; *Artists in Uniform,* 198; and for an attack on Engels, for the same reasons, *Marxism is it Science,* 269.

35. *Stalin's Russia,* 167–68. See also Eastman, "Eastman Replies to Comments on 'Socialism and Human Nature,'" *New Leader,* November 21, 1942, and Eastman, "Can Freedom Survive Under a Planned Economy," *ibid.,* May, 19, 1952.

36. *Marxism is it Science,* 267. "Marx did not draw up any detailed plan of the future society he proposed to build. He merely made a few highly general and wholly dogmatic assertions about how wonderful it would be. Indeed his faith in the benign drift of his material universe was so great that he was for the most part ready to dispense with any plan at all." *Ibid.,* 29.

37. *Marx, Lenin and the Science of Revolution,* 103.

38. On the similarity between Darwin and Marx, see *ibid.,* 67, 68. See also *Stalin's Russia,* 203.

39. *Ibid.,* 113. See also *ibid.,* 116; Eastman, "Lenin the Communist," *Liberator,* June, 1918; Eastman, "Editorials," *ibid.,* April, 1918.

40. *Artists in Uniform,* 209.

41. *Marxist is it Science,* 272. See also *Stalin's Russia,* 261.

Chapter Nine

1. Eastman, "Class Struggle in Genoa," *Liberator,* July, 1922.

2. *Since Lenin Died,* 103, 118.

3. *Love and Revolution,* 250, 125, 126. See also *Enjoyment,* 125, 286; *Marxism is it Science,* 272. The hypothesis, he says elsewhere, must include a "method for proceeding toward our end." Eastman, "Toward Liberty—The Method of Progress," *The Masses Review,* September, 1916.

4. Eastman, "Toward Liberty—The Method of Progress," *The Masses Review,* September, 1916.

5. *Enjoyment,* 285.

6. Eastman, "Concerning an Idealism," *Masses,* July, 1913.

7. Eastman, "Rupert Hughes and the Constabulary," *Masses,* February, 1915.

8. Eastman, "Churchly Rockefeller," *ibid.,* June, 1916. Eastman continued: "He was not willing to give back any of the money, or any of the liberty, he had taken out of those towns. He was not willing to *talk about* such matters with his serfs. He would not allow them to form unions, but he will *give* them churches." *Ibid.*

9. E.g., Eastman, "The Betrayed," *ibid.*, January, 1917.

10. *Enjoyment*, 580.

11. Eastman, "The Religion of Patriotism," *Masses,* July, 1917. See also *Stalin's Russia*, 129.

12. *Marxism is it Science*, 35.

13. *Enjoyment*, 285.

14. *Ibid.*

15. Qt. in May, *op. cit.*, 303, and Aaron, *op. cit.*, 9.

16. *Marx, Lenin and the Science of Revolution*, 121, 113–14. See also *Marxism is it Science*, 169. He insists 'that thought is in origin an instrumental function," and "we must beware . . . of all philosophies strictly so-called." *Ibid.*, 171.

17. *Marxism is it Science*, 169, 170, 172. See also *Love and Revolution*, 125.

18. Eastman, "Knowledge and Revolution," *Masses,* February, 1913.

19. *Marx, Lenin and the Science of Revolution*, 19. "Thought," he declared, "is tentative action; it is action in the process of formation. It is adjustment. . . ." *ibid.*, 14.

20. Eastman, "Lincoln was no Pragmatist," *New Leader*, September 23, 1947.

21. Eastman, "A Debate on Pragmatism," *ibid.*, February 10, 1958.

22. These dates were characteristic of the polemics of the 1930's. Eastman accused Hook of borrowing his ideas, and Hook replied that "not only is Eastman unable to do justice to the thought of Marx, he cannot be trusted to give an elementary honest account of any man with whom he disagrees." *Modern Monthly*, September, 1933. Upon Calverton's request, the two men signed a truce; but the battle flared up again in September, 1934. In an open letter to Steffens about *Artists in Uniform*, Hook conceded that Eastman "may have invented a few details," but that his account of the "intellectual pogrom was essentially true." *Ibid.*, September, 1934. Eastman interpreted this letter as a slur, insisting that every statement had been double checked, Eastman to Calverton, September 25, 1934, Calverton papers, New York Public Library.

23. Eastman, *Great Companions I Have Known* (New York, 1959), 293.

24. *Marx, Lenin and the Science of Revolution*, 16. See also *Stalin's Russia*, 178. Marxism, he insisted, "failed to allow man any biological character at all." Eastman, "Eastman replies to Comments on 'Socialism and Human Nature,'" *New Leader*, November 21, 1942.

25. Hoffman, *op. cit.*, 42.

26. Frederick Hoffman, *Freudianism and the Literary Mind* (Baton Rouge, 1957), 72–3.

27. E.g., *Marx, Lenin and the Science of Revolution*, 18.

28. Eastman errs in stating that he went there "a few months after Freud" visited Clark University. *Enjoyment*, 248. See also *ibid.*, 240, 273.

29. She went to Brill for help in "bringing her 'libido' down, as he put it, *von oben nach unten.*" *Ibid.*, 356, 244. See also *ibid.*, 491–92. Hoffman claims that Jellife was more the Jungian analyst than a Freudian. Hoffman, *Freudianism*, 57.

30. Eastman, "Exploring the Soul and Healing the Body," *Everybody's Magazine*, XXXII (1915); "Mr. -er-er-oh! What's His Name," *op. cit.*, XXXIII (1915).

31. Eastman, "Exploring the Soul," *op. cit.*, 746; Eastman, "Mr.-er-er-oh!", *op. cit.*, 96.

32. Freeman, *op. cit.*, 117.

33. Malcolm Cowley had advised: "Instead of striving and racking our minds, we should let ourselves go, abandon wife and job and family, follow our mood wherever it may lead us." Cowley, *After the Genteel Tradition* (Gloucester, 1959), 216. Eastman, endorsing this view, was determined to " 'live a wild life,' a life that would 'bring the wolf and lion and panther to the door' "; and he regretted being unable to go to "the upper reaches of the Amazon any more," that he "was too burned with intellect. . . ." *Enjoyment*, 237. Feminists hailed Freud since the lay interpretation of his teachings was consonant with the liberating direction of their movement. Hoffman, *Freudianism*, 55. And so did liberal intellectuals: Lippmann, in *Preface to Politics* (1914), urged his readers to abandon artificial restrictions on desires and seek to understand our inner natures. If Eastman had any doubts about Brill and the "new science," the fact of his mother's willingness to seek help enabled him to overcome them. For she retained an enormous hold over him; and, he reminisced with pride, "her mind's everlasting thirst for experience" sent her to Brill. *Enjoyment*, 344.

34. *Marx, Lenin, and the Science of Revolution*, 17.

35. *Ibid.*, 80–1.

36. *The Literary Mind*, 7.

37. *Venture*, 147.

38. Eastman, "Knowledge and Revolution," *Masses*, October, 1913.

39. *Enjoyment of Laughter*, 249.

40. *Marx, Lenin, and the Science of Revolution*, 81.

41. *Venture*, 213.

42. *Marx, Lenin and the Science of Revolution*, 83, 85, 113.

43. Eastman, "Max Eastman Poses New 'Human' Problems for Socialist Thinkers in Second Reply to Critics," *New Leader*, November 28, 1942. In this article, Eastman also compares Freud and Marx, and criticizes the latter as well as Reinhold Niebuhr for "reading psycho-

logical concept into Marxism." See also *Marx, Lenin and the Science of Revolution*, 123.

44. E.g., *The Literary Mind*, 25.
45. *The Sense of Humor*, 40.
46. *Venture*, 178.
47. E.g., *The Literary Mind*, 192, 193.
48. *Marx, Lenin and the Science of Revolution*, 177–8.
49. *The Literary Mind*, 196, 197.
50. *Ibid.*, 288–89.

Chapter Ten

1. *Enjoyment*, 281.
2. *The Literary Mind*, vii, viii.
3. *Ibid.*, 133.
4. *Ibid.*, 212, 213, 89.
5. *Ibid.*, 123, 145.
6. *Ibid.*, 130–31.
7. *Ibid.*, 128, 129, 256.
8. *Venture*, 42.
9. *Ibid.*, 393.
10. *The Literary Mind*, 84.
11. *Ibid.*, 169–70, 90, 91.
12. *Ibid.*, 158, 149–50.
13. E.g., Freeman, *op. cit.*, 166–68.
14. While not stressing the novelist, he noted a similar tendency to "renounce, or at least to relax, the claim to be a sage, a critic of life." *The Literary Mind*, 229. See also *ibid.*, 254.
15. *Ibid.*, 50, 53.
16. *Ibid.*, 258, 259, 15–16.
17. *Ibid.*, 266.
18. *Ibid.*, 16.
19. *Ibid.*, 50, 43, 36, 30, 266, 121–22.
20. *Ibid.*, 113.
21. *Ibid.*, 237. "To imagine that this excellent invention [the novel] will disappear from the earth before civilized man disappears, seems to me the most outlandish of all dismal dreams about the future of literature." *Ibid.*, 227–28.
22. *Ibid.*, 292–93. See also *ibid.*, 316–7, 297, 301; and 303 for further equivocal comments about *Science and Poetry*. See also *ibid.*, 305, 308–9, 312, 313.
23. Eastman, "A Letter to Romain Rolland," *Liberator*, December, 1919. "The disagreement between us is certainly complete," Rolland replied; "so complete that I will not attempt to discuss it."

24. Eastman, "Editorials," *ibid.*, August, 1921.

25. *Love and Revolution*, 238.

26. "A Reviewer's Notebook," *The Freeman*, June 29, 1921.

27. For further salvos in this literary war, see Eastman, "Clarifying the Light," *Liberator*, June, 1921; "A Reviewer's Notebook," *op. cit.*, May 12, June 20, 1921; Eastman, "Inspiration or Leadership," *op. cit.*, August, 1921; "A Reviewer's Notebook," *op. cit.*, August 31, 1921; Brooks, *Sketches in Criticism* (New York, 1932), 279–290.

28. Brooks, *Sketches in Criticism*, 282.

29. *Ibid.*, 290.

30. *Ibid.*, 279–81.

Chapter Eleven

1. Wilson, *op. cit.*

2. Eastman, "What is the Matter with Magazine Art," *Masses*, January, 1915. See also *Love and Revolution*, 238.

3. *Artists in Uniform*, 33, 34.

4. *Ibid.*, 33.

5. *Ibid.*, 124. He noted, for example, the Symbolists, Imagists, Acmeists, Moscow Parnassians, Father Damiens, neo-Classicists, Constructivists, proletarian poets, peasant poets, Futurists. See also M. Slonin, *Soviet Russian Literature* (New York, 1964), 53. See also *Artists in Uniform*, 42–43.

6. Vera Alexandrovna, *A History of Soviet Literature, 1917–1962* (New York, 1963), 20.

7. *Artists in Uniform*, 76. Eastman enthusiastically praised their revolutionary service, *ibid.*, 75. See also *ibid.*, 127, 97, 151.

8. *Ibid.*, 152. See also Slonin *op. cit.*, 46.

9. *Ibid.*, 153.

10. E.g., Slonin, *op. cit.*, *passim*; Alexandrovna, *op. cit.*, *passim*.

11. *Artists in Uniform*, 167.

12. Quoted in *ibid.*, 214.

13. *Ibid.*, 76.

14. Eastman, "What is the Matter With Magazine Art," *op. cit.*

15. *Artists in Uniform*, 34.

16. *Marx, Lenin and the Science of Revolution*, 186.

17. *Ibid.*, 184, 185–6. Elsewhere, he wrote, creative work, has to be very free and irresponsible. It cannot submit to the control of a party." *Love and Revolution*, 238. See also *Artists in Uniform*, 76, 215, and *The Literary Mind*, 126.

18. *Artists in Uniform*, 56.

19. Slonin, *op. cit.*, 80, 81.

20. *Artists in Uniform*, 85.

21. *Ibid.*, 158–9.

22. *Ibid.*, 101, 102.

23. *Ibid.*, 95, 97, 99.

24. *Ibid.*, 108.

25. Eastman, "Artists in Uniform," *Modern Monthly*, August, 1933, 397–404.

26. *Artists in Uniform*, 13.

27. Ernest J. Simmons, "The Organization Writer," in Max Haywood & Leopold Labedz, *Literature and Revolution in Soviet Russia, 1917–1962* (London, 1963), 77.

28. *Artists in Uniform*, 3.

29. *Ibid.*, 39–40.

30. *Ibid.*, 216. Eastman was rarely more involved, more abusive, more motivated. His language, in this extended polemic, is blunt and corrosive. E.g., *ibid.*, 119–120. At stake was his lifelong belief in "an independent vision of the world," and his need to approach life affirmatively, *ibid.*, 150, 206.

Chapter Twelve

1. *Stalin's Russia*, 10. See also *Understanding Germany*, 123.

2. *Enjoyment*, 4; *Love and Revolution*, 241.

3. *Love and Revolution*, 242.

4. *Venture*, 99, 147.

5. Eastman, "Present Trends in Russia," speech before the American Foreign Policy Association (New York, [March 29] 1930), 16.

6. *Ibid.*, 22.

7. Eastman, "New Masses for Old," *Modern Monthly*, VIII (June, 1934), 295.

8. Eastman, "Bunk about Bohemia," *Modern Monthly*, VIII (May, 1934), 202–203.

9. Eastman, *Last Stand of Dialectical Materialism* (New York, 1934), 36.

10. *Marxism is it Science*, 341.

11. Hook, [Letter] "To the Editor," *Modern Monthly*, VII (September, 1933), 510.

12. *Marxism is it Science*, 300, 301, 313.

13. *Artists in Uniform*, 13; *Love and Revolution*, 452.

14. Alfred Kazin, *Starting Out in the Thirties* (Boston, 1962), 70.

15. *Since Lenin Died*, 59.

16. Deutscher, *op. cit.*, 436.

17. *The End of Socialism in Russia*, 18.

18. *Ibid.*, 14, 16, 24–25, 34, 39, 17, 4–5, 10.

19. *Ibid.*, 22–23, 34.

20. *Stalin's Russia*, 52, 55, 67, 75, 278, 76, 77.

21. *Ibid.*, 181, 269, 27–28.

22. *Marxism is it Science*, 269, 267, 268, 270. See also *Stalin's Russia*, 163, 190, 8. (Ital. added)

23. *Stalin's Russia*, 9, 12, 134, 153.

24. *Ibid.*, 123, 187, 235, 281.

25. *Ibid.*, 126.

26. *Ibid.*, 161–62, 149. See also *End of Socialism in Russia*, 3.

27. *Ibid.*, 58, 77, 68–9. For further speculation on their motives, see *ibid.*, 134–35. See also *End of Socialism in Russia*, 46, 44.

28. *Ibid.*, 71. See also *Love and Revolution*, 638 and *End of Socialism in Russia*, 22. Steffens, "an objective and penetrating as well as a brilliant reporter" (*Enjoyment*, 430), had grown progressively more enthusiastic about Bolshevik Russia as Eastman's own enthusiasm waned. He attacked Eastman, in a review of *Artists*, and identified with young communist activists "out in the field." Eastman, in rebuttal, accused him of having become a Stalinist tool.

29. *Ibid.*, 268, 138, 240, 251–52, 140, 142, 138. See also Frank Warren, *Liberals and Communism* (Bloomington, 1966), 213.

30. *Love and Revolution*, 626.

31. For an explanation of Russian chauvinism, see *Stalin's Russia*, 99. See also *ibid.*, 60–61, 25, and *End of Socialism in Russia*, 12–13.

Chapter Thirteen

1. *Stalin's Russia*, 24, 29–30, 60, 152, 226. See also *End of Socialism in Russia*, 11, 12; *Marxism is it Science*, 215; Eastman, "Mark Twain's Elmira," *Harpers* CLXXVI (May, 1938), 347.

2. He did endorse the Swedish experiment in social democracy. *Stalin's Russia*, 252.

3. Richard Crossman, ed., *The God That Failed* (New York, 1950), 10.

4. Steffens to *New Republic*, August 1, 1934, in Ella Winter & Granville Hicks, eds., *The Letters of Lincoln Steffens* (New York, 1938), II, 988.

5. *Stalin's Russia*, 157.

6. *Love and Revolution*, 638.

7. *Ibid.*, 643.

8. Eastman, "Eastman Replies to Comments on 'Socialism and Human Nature,'" *New Leader*, November 21, 1942. In 1942, Lenin's name was now coupled with Marx's as "amateur mystics"; and he was found guilty of ignoring the question—"How is this new-fangled contraption [a socialist society] going to fit in with the natural tendencies of the animals it is made for?" Eastman, "Socialism and Human Nature," *ibid.*, January 24, 1942.

10. Eastman, "Can Freedom Survive Under a Planned Economy?" *ibid.*, May 19, 1952.

11. Eastman, "The Notion of Democratic Socialism," *ibid.*, January 27, 1945.

12. Eastman, "The Notion of Democratic Socialism," *ibid.*, February 10, 1945. See also "Socialism and Human Nature," *op. cit.*

13. Eastman, "Let's Face the Facts About Russia," *Reader's Digest* XLII (July, 1943), 1–14; "Stalin's American Power," *American Mercury*, LIII (December, 1941), 671–80; "Our Quarrel with Russia Is Moral Rather than Political," *Saturday Evening Post*, CCXXII (November 5, 1949), 12.

14. Eastman, "Let's Face the Facts About Russia, *op. cit.*, 9.

15. Eastman, "Political Reality and the Atom Bomb," *New Leader*, November 17, 1945.

16. Eastman, "Help Russia But Keep Your Head," *ibid.*, June 13, 1942.

17. *Ibid.*

18. Eastman, "In My Opinion," *ibid.*, November 10, 1945.

19. Eastman, "Political Reality and the Atom Bomb," *op. cit.*

20. Eastman, "The Purge of the Children," *ibid.*, December 27, 1947.

21. Eastman, "The Contemporary World Mess," *ibid.*, December 4, 1944.

22. E.g., Eastman, "In My Opinion," *ibid.*, December 30, 1944.

23. Eastman, "Our Quarrel with Communism is Moral Rather than Political," *Saturday Evening Post*, November 5, 1949, 12.

24. Eastman, "The Contemporary World Mess," *op. cit.*, see also Eastman, "The Notion of Democratic Socialism," *ibid.*, January 27, 1945, and Eastman, "A Case of Campaign Oratory," *ibid.*, November 25, 1944.

25. Eastman, "The Contemporary World Mess," *op. cit.*

26. *Ibid.*, see also Eastman, "Help Russia But Keep Your Head," *op. cit.*

27. Eastman, "Can Freedom Survive Under a Planned Economy," *op. cit.*

28. Eastman, "Help Russia But Keep Your Head," *op. cit.*

29. Eastman, "Why Must We Outlaw the Communist Party?" *Reader's Digest*, September, 1950.

30. *Ibid.*

31. Eastman, "Misrepresentation," *New Leader*, December 5, 1955.

32. Eastman, *Enjoyment of Poetry*, 107.

33. *Ibid.*, 128.

34. Edmund Wilson, *Classics and Commercials* (New York, 1950), 58.

35. *Ibid.*

Selected Bibliography

PRIMARY SOURCES

I. Books

Journalism Versus Art. New York: Alfred A. Knopf, 1916.
Understanding Germany. New York: Kennerley, 1916.
Colors of Life. New York: Alfred A. Knopf, 1918.
The Sense of Humor. New York: Charles Scribner's Sons, 1921.
Leon Trotsky, Portrait of a Youth. New York: Greenberg, 1925.
Since Lenin Died. New York: Boni & Liveright, 1925.
Marx, Lenin and the Science of Revolution. London: George Allen & Unwin, Ltd., 1926.
Venture. New York: Albert & Charles Boni, 1927.
The Literary Mind. New York: Charles Scribner's Sons, 1932.
Art and the Life of Action. New York: Alfred A. Knopf, 1934.
Artists in Uniform. New York: Alfred A. Knopf, 1934.
The End of Socialism in Russia. Boston: Little, Brown & Co., 1937.
Marxism is it Science. New York: W. W. Norton & Co., 1940.
Stalin's Russia and the Crisis in Socialism. New York: W. W. Norton & Co., 1940.
Great Companions. New York: Farrar, Straus & Co., 1942.
Heroes I Have Known. New York: Simon and Schuster, 1942.
The Enjoyment of Laughter. New York: Simon & Schuster, 1948.
The Enjoyment of Living. New York: Harper and Brothers, 1948.
Reflections on the Failure of Socialism. New York: Devin Adair, 1955.
Love and Revolution. New York: Random House, 1965.

II. Other Writings

PAMPHLETS:
Present Trends in Russia. New York, 1930.
A Letter to Americans. New York, 1941.

ARTICLES:
The major sources of articles by Eastman were the *Masses*, II-VII (1912–1917), and *Liberator*, I-VI (1918–1922). During the years of

service on these two monthlies, he wrote countless editorials and articles. In addition, there were the following articles:

"Excommunication and Exorcism," *Modern Monthly*, VII (May, 1933), 210–13.

"A Master Magician," *Modern Monthly*, VII (June, 1933), 290–93.

"Man in History," *Modern Monthly*, VII (July, 1933), 348–51.

"Letter," *Modern Monthly*, VII (August, 1933), 447–48.

"Bunk About Bohemia," *Modern Monthly*, VIII (May, 1934), 200–05.

"New Masses for Old," *Modern Monthly*, VIII, (June, 1934), 292–300.

"Artists in Straight Jackets," *Modern Monthly*, VIII (August, 1934, 445–47.

"Discrimination About Russia," *Modern Monthly*, VIII (Sept., 1934), 473–77.

"Russia and the Socialist Ideal," *Harper's*, CLXXVI (March, 1938), 374–85.

"Communist Constitution," *Nation*, CXLVI (June 4, 1938), 655.

"Character and Fate of Leon Trotsky," *Foreign Affairs*, XIX (Jan., 1941).

"Limits of Free Speech," *American Mercury*, LIII (October, 1941), 444–47.

"John Dewey," *Atlantic Monthly*, CLXVII (December 1941), 671–80.

"Stalin's American Power," *American Mercury*, LII (December, 1941), 671–80.

"Socialism and Human Nature," *New Leader* (January 24, 1942), 5–6.

"Socialism and Human Nature (2)," *New Leader* (January 31, 1942), 5, 7.

"Eugene Debs Trial," *New Leader* (March 28, 1942), 5, 7.

"Eugene Debs Trial," *New Leader* (Apr. 4, 1942), 4, 7.

"Proletarian Novelists Old and New," *American Mercury*, LIV (April, 1942), 456–500.

"How Decadent Are We," *American Mercury*, LIV (April, 1942), 456–500.

"Walt Whitman, Poet of Democracy," *Reader's Digest*, XLII (June, 1943), 29–33.

"Let's Face the Facts About Russia," *Reader's Digest*, XLIII (July, 1943), 1–4.

"Gamblers With Liberty," *American Mercury*, LIX (July, 1944), 42–49.

"Notions of Democratic Socialism," *New Leader* (January 27, February 3, February 10, 1945), 5–6.

"Political Reality and the Atom Bomb," *New Leader* (December 17, 1945), 7.

"The Fate of the World is at Stake in China," *Reader's Digest*, XLVI (April, 1946), 59–63.

"Robert Burns, Poet of the People," *Reader's Digest*, XLVIII (June, 1946), 59–63.

"Behind Soviet Foreign Policy," *American Mercury*, LXIII (September, 1946), 261–69.

"Our Quarrel with Communism is Moral Rather than Political," *Saturday Evening Post*, CCXXII (November 5, 1949), 12.

"Footnote to Churchill," *New Leader* (May 13, 1950), 8.

"Why Must We Outlaw the Communist Party?" *Reader's Digest*, LVII (September, 1950), 42–44.

"Can Truman be Educated?" *American Mercury*, LXXIII (December, 1950), 726–32.

"The Greeks had a Man for it," *American Mercury*, LXXIII (September, 1951), 93–99.

"Buckley Versus Yale," *American Mercury*, LXXIII (December, 1951), 22–26.

"Letter to the Editor," *New Leader* (April 28, 1952), 26–28.

"Can Freedom Survive in a Planned Economy?", *New Leader*, (May 19, 1952), 16–19.

"Freedom Means Balanced Conflict," *New Leader*, (December 29, 1952), 16–19.

"John Dewey, American Philosopher," *Saturday Review*, XXXVI (January 17, 1953), 23–24.

"The Kremlin, Grim Symbol," *Reader's Digest*, LXIII (December, 1953), 105–8.

"Within Vortex," *Saturday Review*, XXXVIII (June 18, 1955), 22–23.

"One Man Turning Point in History," *Reader's Digest*, LXXIV (June, 1959), 204–208.

"Autobiographical Blues," *Saturday Review*, XLIV (April 22, 1961), 6.

"Is This the Truth About Sacco and Vanzetti?" *National Review*, XI (October 21, 1961), 261–264.

"My Flight to the Front Page," *Saturday Review*, CXLIV (October 14, 1961).

"Am I a Conservative?" *National Review*, XVI (January 28, 1964), 37–38.

SECONDARY SOURCES

AARON, DANIEL. *Writers on the Left.* New York: Harcourt, Brace & World, 1961. The best commentary on the radical literary scene, with ample coverage given to Eastman, and his days on the *Masses* and the *Liberator*. The story of Eastman's quarrels with Gold, Minor, *et al.* are clearly and authoritatively described.

BROOKS, VAN WYCK. *America's Coming of Age.* New York: B. W. Huebsch, 1915. Major influence on literary radicals, Brooks' study comments adversely on the literary attitudes and criticism of East-man.

CARR, E. H. *The Bolshevik Revolution* (1917–1923). London: Mac-millan, 1950. Some of the chapters in this multi-volume work are extremely useful for the background material they provide.

COWLEY, MALCOLM. *Exile's Return*. New York: Viking Press, 1951. Cowley's luminous classic is also useful primarily for the back-ground it provides, for the atmosphere in which the emigres lived and to which the returnees came, for the graceful descriptions of their activities and aspirations.

CROSSMAN, RICHARD, ed. *The God That Failed*. New York: Harper & Row, 1959. Searing, path-finding collection of portraits. These vignettes of and by men who became disillusioned with Commu-nism, by extrapolations, may provide insight into Eastman's mo-tives.

DELL, FLOYD. *Intellectual Vagabondage*. New York: George H. Doran Co., 1926. Saturated in the atmosphere of the age and reflecting Dell's wry and insightful mind, this book deals with the age and personalities that Eastman encountered when he first entered the Village.

DEUTSCHER, ISAAC. *The Prophet Unarmed*, New York: Oxford Univer-sity Press, 1959. One of three volumes by the author which to-gether form the definitive study of Trotsky's fall from power. Once again, it is essential background reading—for an under-standing of Eastman's early hero and the Russian scene of 1920–1924.

DRAPER, THEODORE. *The Roots of American Communism*. New York: Viking Press, 1957. Essential reading for anyone interested in the immediate postwar origins of the Communist Party and Commu-nist Labor Party. It is extremely useful as background, since it gives a detailed account of Socialist Party struggles and of the schismatic character of American radicalism.

EGBERT, DONALD & PERSONS, STOWE, eds. *Socialism and American Life*. Princeton: Princeton University Press, 1952. Daniel Bell's essay, "The Background and Development of Marxian Socialism in the United States" is of fundamental importance, again as the *mise-en-scene* for Eastman in 1919–1922. It complements Draper's, and Howe and Coser's volumes on the subject.

FREEMAN, JOSEPH. *An American Testament*. New York: Farrar & Rine-hart, 1936. Personal document of considerable importance, since Freeman knew Eastman and most of the Village's radicals, and comments extensively on the *Masses*, its contributors, viewpoints, aspirations.

HICKS, GRANVILLE. *John Reed, the Making of a Revolutionary*. New

York: Macmillan, 1936. This biography of Eastman's close friend and contributing editor on the *Masses* and *Liberator* is fascinating and instructive—for Reed, the archetypal Revolutionary hero, was greatly admired by his colleague. Moreover, it fills in, in considerable detail, the picture of life among New York's radical cognoscenti, 1914–1919.

HOFFMAN, FREDERICK J., *Freudianism and the Literary Mind*. Baton Rouge: Louisiana State University Press, 1945. Exhaustive account of the impact of Freudian thought upon American men of letters; and, given Eastman's interest in psychoanalysis, important for this reason.

————. *The Twenties*. New York: Viking Press, 1949. Comprehensive, admirable synthesis of the decade. It is important for what it says about the decade rather than for its comments on Eastman and the magazines he edited.

LASCH, CHRISTOPHER. *The New Radicalism*. New York: Alfred A. Knopf, 1965. A book of brilliant *aperçus* that, in its discussion of Bourne, Mabel Dodge Luhan, Sidney Hook, *et al.*, tells us, at least obliquely, a good deal about Eastman's personality and motivation.

LLOYD, STANTON W., "Max Eastman: An Intellectual Portrait." A Harvard honors essay (ca. 1965) that shows some signs of haste and uncertainty, but is astonishingly good for an undergraduate paper. It has some useful insights about the formative influences upon Eastman, and the intellectual and emotional properties that helped shape him.

LUHAN, MABEL DODGE. *Movers and Shakers*. New York: Harcourt, Brace & World, 1936. A work that is usually chatty and filled with gossip, it nonetheless provides some valuable suggestions and a sense of what life was like in pre-war New York, particularly in its intellectual community.

MAY, HENRY. *The End of American Innocence*. New York: Alfred A. Knopf, 1959. The definitive account of pre-war America, 1912–1917, it provides a fresh and lively view of these critical years. Eastman has his place; so, too, do most of the major revolutionary poets and political radicals whom he admired and who were his acququaintances.

PARRY, ALBERT. *Garrets and Pretenders*. New York: Covici & Friede, 1933. Interesting account of Bohemian life in New York in the first two decades of the century.

ROEBUCK, C. M. "Since Eastman Lied," *Worker's Monthly*, IV (June, 1925) 369–372.

RIDEOUT, WALTER. *The Proletarian Novel in the United States*. Cambridge: Harvard University Press, 1956. Essential reading (to-

gether with Aaron's study) of the radical novel in the period
under consideration. It is a useful compendium of left-wing letters
—and more, since it tells something about the scene within
which this literature was placed.

WOLFE, BERTRAND D. "Eastman Revises Marx and Corrects Lenin,"
    Communist, VI (November 1927), 304–12.

———. "American Discusses Opposition," *Communist*, VII (January
    1928), 49–55.

Index

(Max Eastman's works are listed under his name)